LOVE, LOSS, AND LONGING

Also from Dalbir Singh
Performing Back: Post-Colonial Canadian Plays

LOVE
LOSS
LONG
ING

AND

SOUTH
ASIAN
CANADIAN
PLAYS

edited by Dalbir Singh

PLAYWRIGHTS CANADA PRESS
Toronto

LIBRARY AND ARCHIVES CANADA CATALOGUING IN PUBLICATION
    Love, loss, and longing : South Asian Canadian plays / edited by Dalbir Singh.

A collection of six plays written by South Asian Canadian theatre artists.
Includes bibliographical references.
ISBN 978-1-77091-348-6 (pbk.)

    1. Canadian drama (English)--South Asian Canadian authors.
2. Canadian drama (English)--21st century. I. Singh, Dalbir, 1979-, editor

PS8315.1.L68 2015   812'.6080895071   C2015-902452-8

We acknowledge the financial support of the Canada Council for the Arts, the Ontario Arts Council (OAC), the Ontario Media Development Corporation, and the Government of Canada through the Canada Book Fund for our publishing activities. Nous remercions l'appui financier du Conseil des Arts du Canada, le Conseil arts de l'Ontario (CAO), La Société de développement de l'industrie des médias de l'Ontario, et le Gouvernement du Canada par l'entremise du Fonds du livre du Canada pour nos activités d'édition.

Canada Council for the Arts   Conseil des arts du Canada

ONTARIO ARTS COUNCIL
CONSEIL DES ARTS DE L'ONTARIO
an Ontario government agency
un organisme du gouvernement de l'Ontario

Canada

Ontario
Ontario Media Development Corporation

This book is dedicated to my family: Mom (Gian Kaur), Dad (Ravinder Singh), Wendy, Bobby, Tina, and Ariya.

CONTENTS

INTRODUCTION
Dalbir Singh

I was elated when I was first approached to edit the first-ever collection devoted exclusively to the topic of South Asian Canadian plays. However, it was a daunting task; how do I choose what to include and what not to include? This volume certainly doesn't attempt to represent all of South Asia and doesn't intend to. Several volumes of plays devoted to the subject would still come to represent only a small fraction of the many voices that inhabit South Asia and its diaspora. This collection, however, does reflect a wide array of perspectives that are reflected through a variety of genres. I believe that the plays in this anthology speak to each other in interesting and complex ways, each telling stories rooted in themes that are universal in scope yet are specific in detail and context. Introductions accompany each play and are written by prominent members of the Canadian theatre industry who have served and supported the development of the writer.

All of the plays are from the past decade—a fruitful period for South Asian Canadian artists compared to years prior. While I was growing up, theatre created by South Asian Canadian artists was scarce and virtually non-existent or was relegated to predominantly Hindi- or Punjabi-language dramas performed in suburban school gymnasiums and community centres. The Desh Pardesh festival (a lively progressive arts initiative founded by a collective of Indo-Canadian artists) flourished well into the 1990s, but the main focus certainly wasn't on theatre creation. Unfortunately, none of these early productions were adequately archived, so there is a lack of material that has remained.

Rahul Varma, (whose most well-regarded play *Bhopal* is featured in this anthology) was one of the first Indo-Canadian artists to craft English-language work that challenged the status quo by focusing on issues such as immigration, racism, global terrorism, and corporate malfeasance. His founding of Teesri Duniya Theatre in Montreal and the magazine *alt.theatre: cultural diversity and the stage* helped promote not only the productions of his and other South Asian artists' plays but of many minoritized writers' works as well.

Bhopal was the first production I attended (in 2004 at Toronto's Theatre Centre, directed by Guillermo Verdecchia) that featured a mostly South Asian cast, which was unheard of for that time. Written by an Indo-Canadian and focusing on issues that still reverberate to this day, *Bhopal* is a play that examines what is widely believed to be the world's worst industrial disaster, resulting in an estimated 16,000 deaths in Bhopal, India. The play depicts the tragedy from multiple viewpoints, including families affected by nerve gas (as a result of a gas leak from a Union Carbide Corporation's pesticide plant), doctors, and government officials. It serves as a reminder of corporate ineptitude and exploitation and how human suffering becomes quantified in terms of a loss of profits. This play was important in many ways, but it was especially notable for paving the way for other Indo-Canadian artists to pursue theatre and write their own stories.

A Brimful of Asha couldn't be more dissimilar to *Bhopal*. Written and performed by real-life mother and son, Asha and Ravi Jain, the piece has run to sold-out audiences across the country. I've seen a few productions of the play, and every time there has been a standing ovation with audience members utterly enthralled by the witty repartee between the pair. It's a genuinely engaging tale about a mother who is desperate to get her adult son married off. Her painstaking efforts to arrange a marriage for him are beset by numerous obstacles—not least of which is Ravi's hesitancy. *A Brimful of Asha* is humorous, but the fact that it's based on real events, situations, and conversations between the two gives it an authentic air of intergenerational conflict. Ravi Jain is the artistic director of Why Not Theatre and has produced, directed, and acted in many of the company's notable productions including *Iceland*, *I'm So Close*, and *Spent*. His residencies at influential theatres like Tarragon, the Theatre Centre, and the Young Centre for the Performing Arts provide a glimpse into how so many leading figures in the theatre industry cherish his work and recognize his talent. *A Brimful of Asha* is one such example of the formidable skills of both Ravi and Asha Jain (in her theatrical debut) as both writers and performers.

Pyaasa, *Bombay Black*, and *CRASH* have all won the Dora Mavor Moore Award for Outstanding New Play. *Pyaasa* by Anusree Roy, a monodrama featuring several characters all played by the playwright herself, is set in Kolkata, India. The play was a resounding hit in Toronto and brought Roy not only critical acclaim but a devoted fan base as well. Her subsequent plays like *Brothel #9* have further cemented her status as one of the leading playwrights in this country, having received eight Dora Awards, a nomination for the Governor General's Literary Award, and the Carol Bolt Award for Playwriting amongst many other honours. *Pyaasa* instantly struck a chord with me. It dealt with a contentious issue in the South Asian community that many choose to ignore. By examining the caste system and its destructive hierarchy through a group of characters from different caste affiliations, it posits the notion that caste is inherently performative—something to be adorned in order to delineate one's superiority over others. Roy expresses this in a myriad of ways, by embodying each character's joys, frustrations, and tragedies, as well as portraying their complex relationships with one another. It was truly astonishing to witness Roy perform these roles with such ferocity, stamina, and humour.

Anosh Irani is a playwright, but he also happens to be the sole novelist in the group of writers who have contributed to this anthology. His novels, like his plays, focus on the interplay between gender, politics, and locale. Most of his work is set in India, like the aptly titled multi-award-winning play, *Bombay Black*, which is included in this anthology. There's a haunting quality to Irani's work, as his texts are laden with images derived from impoverished settings. He's written about the citizens that comprise the underbelly of Mumbai society, from homeless youth to brothel patrons. *Bombay Black*'s action takes place within such a brothel, examining the relationship between a young female dancer and a patron who also happens to be blind.

Several works collected in this book have been significantly rewritten or changed from their originally published state, and they are appearing in their revised form for the first time in these pages. *Bombay Black* is perhaps the most revised of these pieces, showcasing a plot device that is completely from its original production and thus completely changing the trajectory of the play. It'll be interesting for those who have seen the play to now read it in this new incarnation. Regardless of the revisions, the play continues to evoke a surreal and hypnotic take on relationships and the kinds of power dynamics that shape the views of a chaotic and often hostile world.

The first time I met Pamela Mala Sinha, it was to discuss the inclusion of her brilliant one-woman show, *CRASH*, in this anthology. It was a wonderful opportunity to meet such a warm-spirited writer and artist and to engage in intellectually stimulating conversations regarding the state of Canadian theatre today. *CRASH* is perhaps the most amenable play in regard to casting in this anthology. Sinha has expressed the notion that she'd be open to the idea of the next production of the piece employing a non-Indo-Canadian actor; to have the character be portrayed by other ethnicities. The play, therefore, operates similarly to Sinha's second play, *Happy Place* (premiering in Soulpepper's 2015 season). The casting of her characters is open to diversification and isn't pigeonholed into a certain way of thinking or representing a particular community. *CRASH* portrays in chilling detail a young woman's past traumas that become awakened through the loss of a loved one. The play not only garnered a Dora Award for Outstanding New Play (in a year that included other strong contenders like Ins Choi's hit show *Kim's Convenience*) but she landed the Dora for Best Actress as well—in a brave and mesmerizing performance. Pamela has received many accolades for her work by such noted figures as J. Kelly Nestruck (*Globe and Mail* theatre critic), Ann-Marie MacDonald, Sarah Polley, and Judith Thompson, and I have no doubt that she will be receiving similar praise for years to come.

Anita Majumdar's *Boys With Cars* is part of her Fish Eyes Trilogy that examines, through three young women, their relationships to dance, fellow dancers, life in high school, and yes, boys. The play centres on Naz, who longs to leave her hometown of Port Moody, British Columbia, in order to attend university.

However, complications arise before her dream can be realized. Majumdar's plays are often characterized by feminist-oriented political relevance, breathtaking choreography, and a balance between dramatic and comedic tensions. The unfortunate aspect of reading a play versus seeing it in production is that it negates the opportunity to witness Majumdar's skills as a classically trained dancer. However, the writer's notes regarding the many dances evoke a sense of their purpose and how they're imagined. Her skills as a comedian are showcased not only physically in performance but are reflected in the written text through the ironies laden throughout the play critiquing Bollywood conventions and employing those critiques via her own unique perspective. Her plays read as a pastiche of multiple genres, conventions, attitudes, ideas, and physicalities and are acutely attuned to Indo-Canadian youth and their constant struggles of belonging and maintaining some sense of identity.

I am so incredibly honoured to be able to present Anita Majumdar, Rahul Varma, Anosh Irani, Pamela Mala Sinha, Anusree Roy, and Asha and Ravi Jain together in this anthology. This book not only brings together a collection of important and beautifully written work from a group of diverse writers from the South Asian Canadian community but I firmly believe that it's also a collection of some of the strongest plays produced in the past ten years by Canadian playwrights, regardless of national origin. Furthermore, it's important to note that many of the included writers are in the middle of their careers, thus indicating that we're in the throes of a thriving cultural renaissance happening within the South Asian theatre community. One can see this in the many other Indo-Canadian playwrights currently creating intelligent, humorous, and poignant work such as Anand Rajaram, Sunil Kuruvilla, Nisha Ahuja, Sheila James, Tanya Pillay, Bilal Baig, Jiv Parasram, Rana Bose, Doris Rajan, Raoul Bhaneja, Radha Menon, Uma Parameswaran, Bill Bhaneja, Serena Parmar, and many more. My hope is that this book will help spur the public's interest in this community of artists and supports their work by not only reading their brilliant plays but by attending their shows as well.

PYAASA
Anusree Roy

This play is dedicated to Ma, Baba, and Didi,
for surviving 147-8th Street

To Thom and Dave,
thank you for being my brothers and co-creators

ACKNOWLEDGEMENTS

My sincere thank you to Andy McKim, Hugh Neilson, and everyone at Theatre
Passe Muraille; Annie Gibson, Blake Sproule, and everyone at Playwrights
Canada Press; my family in India; Non; Peter Lewis; Aaron Armstrong;
Barbara Lorainne Laing; Cathy Stasko; Dawn Nearing; Erika Batdorf; Gregory
Danakas; Iris Turcott; Judith Thompson; Marie Dame; Paige Moore; Rachel
Katz; Suzy Yim; Tammy Fox; Yvette Nolan; Colin Rose; and Layne Coleman.
Amma and Laxman Da—thank you for the inspiration.

I first met Anusree Roy when she performed a short solo piece titled *breath-lessness* for a York University playwriting project in 2006. It was a class project based on an assignment to meet and then write about Layne Coleman. It was a short piece, but it was packed with a political, spiritual, and emotional power that I would later recognize as a trademark of Anusree's work. I stayed in touch and in the first season that I programmed as the new artistic director of Theatre Passe Muraille, I was excited to select *Pyaasa* for production.

Pyaasa is set in colonial Bengal, India, and focuses on the untouchable sect of Hindu society. It is the story of an eleven-year-old girl named Chaya and her journey from childhood to adulthood; a journey that occurs in just ten days. As the daughter of a toilet cleaner, Chaya learns at a young age the realities of an untouchable's life and is forced to confront the consequences and struggles of her caste.

Anusree's writing is moving and insightful. On the surface *Pyaasa* seems a play solely about a foreign culture in a foreign land, but it is simultaneously a play that reflects life today in Canada. At the heart of her story, she is addressing powerful and uncomfortable realities that she herself discovered in her own life in Toronto, having moved to Canada with her family fifteen years ago. Adapting to a new culture turned out to be a challenging learning experience, and what she learned from that experience profoundly informed her first professional play. *Pyaasa*, at its core, is about the dehumanizing effect of privilege, in any form.

In India her family was from the upper caste so she experienced a privileged life. Speaking about the challenges she faced when her family moved to Canada, Anusree says "it was a very difficult time because I had a very comfortable lifestyle in India . . . [but] in the first month of being here the suitcase which contained all our money, passports, and landing papers got stolen. We were left with nothing but the $36 in our bank account. We had to build from the ground up. My father had to struggle tremendously, all of us had to get jobs. It went from a have situation to a have not."

Being forced to learn what it was like to live in a less privileged situation gave her a new perspective on the life she had left behind in India. It forced her to re-evaluate her behaviour towards others who were less privileged and she reflected in particular on her relations with one person from her family home in India. In Anusree's words, "I was raised in a household where our 'toilet cleaner' came in every week to do his job while we pretended not to watch him, but ensured that his shadow did not fall on us since that would supposedly demean our caste. Writing this play was an emotional journey for me, forcing me to confront both personal and social issues while dealing with subject matter that is tremendously sensitive. While recognizing my social location in the system I would hope that this play gives a voice to the unheard and creates a dialogue about an issue that is still prevalent in India today."

The power of *Pyaasa* rests in the fact that Anusree was able to place the spotlight on herself and dig into her own experiences of having privilege. As a writer she became so vulnerable that she was able to dive into the complexity of this situation from both sides. This play is all the more astonishing in knowing that it is a young writer's first play. It holds such powerful insights. Anusree tells this story with economy, yet creates a vivid cast of characters, who live within a fully realized world, where the dramatic stakes are extremely high. *Pyaasa* is a perfectly crafted gem of a play that will stand up to the test of time.

—Andy McKim

This play is a solo play, written and intended for a single actor to play all roles. The play should be performed without an interval, with a running time of approximately forty minutes.

Pyaasa was first produced by Theatre Jones Roy at Theatre Passe Muraille, Toronto, between September 25 and 30, 2007, with the following company:

Playwright / performer: Anusree Roy
Director / dramaturg: Thomas Morgan Jones
Lighting designer / stage manager: David DeGrow
Costume painter: Evan Ayotte
Technician: Ryan McDougall
Poster design: Aimee Nishtoba

CHARACTERS

Chaya: Eleven years old. She is bright, filled with energy, and has tremendous determination. She is hopeful for the future.

Meera: Mid-forties. She is very shrewd, very strict with her daughter, Chaya, and fully understands how to use her social disadvantage to her advantage. She is plagued with lower-back pain.

Kamala: Mid-forties. She is confident, incredibly manipulative, and enjoys holding power over the lower castes.

Mr. Bikash: Mid-fifties. He is a rich, educated, and stern man. He loathes the untouchables.

SETTING

Pyaasa is set in present day Bengal, India.

SCENE ONE: MR. BIKASH'S HOME

Lights gradually come up on stage. MEERA *is sitting crouched on the floor. She watches* KAMALA *come from stage right as she starts speaking in Bengali.*

MEERA: Oh didi! Kamon aacho didi? Mone hocche koto din tomake dhekhi na didi . . . saree ta ki bhalo lagche tomake! Notun shari naki? Na didi, aami kicchu dhori ne. Chup kore boshe aachie . . . dhako balti-o-okhane aache. Na didi chui ne.[1]

She gets up.

No didi. You didn't give soap no, so I didn't put. Bishash koro didi . . . Kothai dile shaban bolo?[2] I wait here every day didi, until you come, turn the tap on, and then I go in. When have I ever touched anything in this house? I would rather die, jump off a bridge, be killed by a bus, set fire to my own tent, didi, before I would touch anything. No didi, I didn't touch it. I swear on my child.

MEERA *touches* KAMALA's *hand on the word "child."*

---

1   Oh sister! How are you, sister? Feels like I haven't seen you in so long, sister . . . your saree looks amazing! Is it new? No sister, I haven't touched anything. I have been sitting here real quiet . . . look, the bucket is right there. No sister I didn't touch it.

2   Believe me, sister . . . When did you give me soap?

KAMALA: What are you doing . . . ki korcho ta ki?[3] Uff. Now your shadow fall on me, now I have to go take another shower. When will you people learn? You people come from somewhere and then chew my head. There is little food for your daughter, underneath the sink, take it before you leave.

MEERA: Thank you so much didi. You are so kind. Jano, didi, tomake ki jige-sha korbo bhabchilam . . . [4] Is your boy still running the tea stall?

KAMALA: Ha kano?[5] Why you want to know?

MEERA: Na, didi . . . bhabchilam,[6] if you can please talk to him. Ahh ha, didi, oeirokom kore dhekhcho kano?[7] Chaya is getting old, no, and she has no job. Today she has no job, tomorrow she will have no food to eat, and the next day she will be eating from the garbage. The next thing you know some street vendors will be coming and cutting off her hand and she will be sitting there, beside the streets, with a little begging bowl; begging, begging, begging, no-body is even listening to her, nobody is even giving her one *paisa* didi. The next thing you know, there will be some flies buzzing around some wound in her eye and then she will be losing one eye didi. No didi, that I cannot take. She cannot be losing one eye when she will already be having no hand. So, if she can come and clean all the teacups in your son's tea stall, that would be good, no? Whatever your son can pay . . .

KAMALA: Ummmm . . . *Moree na.* Ahh ha.[8] Tea stall! You have some guts to you, na? Coming here and asking me to give your Chaya a job? *Aacha,*[9] Meera, tell me something; why you are forgetting that you are untouchable caste? Now your shadow fall on me, now I have to go to the Holy River to wash myself!

---

3 What are you doing?

4 You know what I was thinking of asking you . . .

5 Yes, why?

6 No, sister . . . I was thinking

7 Ahh ha, sister, why are you looking at me like that?

8 An Indian expression of disgust.

9 Okay.

Ungrateful. I give her food to eat, is that not enough? The more we give your caste the more you want. Do you know what would happen if Sir Ji found out that I give you all their leftover food . . . ? All you do is talk talk talk . . . you are lucky that I let you even talk to me. All the untouchables in your *basti* are scared to even look at me. I am the head servant of this house . . . not an untouchable like you.

What hand cut off? There will be no hand cut off . . . you have not changed one bit since I have known you. Hand cut off. Kotha theke je tumi eai gulpo gulo pao na ta aami aar ki bolbo.[10]

MEERA: Na, didi.[11] I didn't mean it that way didi. How long you have known me didi? Why you are saying things like that? Okay okay . . . your son does not even have to pay Chaya for the first two months; she will just sit there and clean. Tell him to give her some tea some time. She is loving tea, didi. Actually, come to think of it, she has never even tried tea, so that would be good beverage, no? Incentive to go to work. See didi, I save your son some money didi. I am always thinking of you didi. Shob shomai tomar kotha chinta korchie.[12]

KAMALA: Ummm . . . koto jano chinta . . . chini na jano aami tomake.[13] Okay. Okay. Now get back to your sweeping.

Eaai,[14] my husband brought fresh cow dung from the dump; you come to my house tonight and make those cow-dung cakes . . . I told you about this a week ago . . . he needs fresh cow-dung cakes to sell in the market next week. You come and I will give you some stale roti I save for your daughter.

And don't just come prancing around inside the house, wait outside, I will bring it to you.

---

10 Not sure where you get all these stories from.

11 No, sister.

12 I am constantly thinking for you.

13 Ummm . . . so many thoughts . . . as if I don't know you.

14 An Indian expression of calling someone without proper respect.

MEERA: Oh didi, yes then? So didi, yes then? I will send Chaya to work tomorrow morning didi. Tell your son she is a very good girl, will not touch anything. Nothing at all . . . all they have to do is bring the teacups to her, and she will wash them very well. God will bless didi!

MMMMM. Look at her, thinks she is *maharani*.[15] Wait till Sir Ji comes and then she will know . . . servant like me. Joto shob. Neeje ke je ki mone kore na shae aami aare ki bolbo?[16]

MEERA makes one swift turn and walks upstage right and transforms into CHAYA, *who is eating the leftovers from a bowl in her hand. She gradually makes her way to downstage centre.*

SCENE TWO: MEERA'S HOME

CHAYA: Ummm ummm. Ma, Ma, Ma, I liking it very much. Ammar khhob bhalo lagche.[17] Can I have some more? *Jano,* Ma, there is something different in it today.

MEERA: And what is there to be different Chaya? Every day you drink boiled rice water. Now hurry up, your father will be back from the police station soon. I don't want him to see you standing around doing nothing.

(indicating the nearby bucket) And . . . look at THAT bucket. It is filled with water already.

MEERA looks up at the tent and finds a hole in it. She walks up to the spot.

God knows when they will fix this bridge. Every day they say, today today today, and nothing is ever done. I don't think that they think people living underneath this bridge are even alive. Chaya, be a doll and go dump the

---

15 The queen.

16 Nonsense. What does she think of herself?

17 I really like it.

bucket out . . . my back is hurting from sitting and making all those cow-dung cakes. Uff.

MEERA walks towards stage left and transforms into CHAYA, who walks towards the bucket placed stage right. She takes the bucket filled with water and disposes of it off stage right. Laughter/giggling can be heard off stage. CHAYA comes back in with the empty bucket and places it stage right. She realizes she has misplaced the bucket and corrects its placement. She runs towards her mother, hesitates, and then speaks.

CHAYA: Ma, Ma, Ma, today morning when I went by English school the Nun Sisters were handing out free times-table books. I took two, Ma . . . they are not that hard. They only go up to about five . . .

Pause.

Hih?[18] Kano Ma kano. Na na na . . . Ma, please. Aami chai na kaj korte. Kano?[19] You told me that I could go to school when I was ten; I'm eleven now.

She walks, forming a semicircle from upstage left to upstage right, and stands upstage right.

But this is not fair. Why? Didn't Kamala Aunty say that she would give you all her son's old books if you made cow-dung cakes for her? Then? You always do that for her . . . why doesn't she give you books?

CHAYA walks to centre stage.

You know what I forgot to say?

She sits.

Yesterday morning when I was coming back after picking up empty cans the Murialla man said that his daughter just passed class eight from an English

---

18 What?

19 I don't want to work. Why?

school and and and he said that he would give me all her old books. So when I go to class eight, you don't have to buy me books; I will have them already.

She gradually moves to stage left while seated.

See see see, Ma. Isn't that a good thing? You want me to make tea, Ma? What if I burn myself . . . ? Then nobody will be wanting to marry me and I have to sit at home all day.

CHAYA *physically transforms into* MEERA *and gets up with great effort, walks stage left, and speaks to* CHAYA, *who is sitting centre stage.*

MEERA: Chaya, ekdom chup koro. Ekdom mook bondo koro.[20] All this education will be getting you nowhere.

You think somebody will be wanting to marry you? Then they will come and tell me that you have too much education and you will be sitting at home for the rest of your life. Just like Shampa's daughter. It is all Shampa's fault, who told her to put her daughter in English school. Now look at her; she is fourteen, fatherless, and not a single person wants to marry her. Plus, Kamala said that her son thinks that you will work very hard and he will give you tea some time. See, tea; you have never been having tea before. Now you can go tell all your friends that you have been having tea before they do. Muk gomra korle cholbe bol.[21] Don't make that face; see how hard your father has to work cleaning the toilets in the police station? Chaya, don't look at me like that. Chaya, don't make that face!

MEERA *physically transforms into* CHAYA *and walks towards stage left on a sharp angle, turning around to face* MEERA.

CHAYA: I don't want to go. It's not my fault that they think that they can't touch us so all we have to do is sit there. I should have been born into Mr. Bikash's house; his daughter gets to touch everything because they are higher caste than us. Don't touch this . . . don't touch that . . . don't do this, don't do that, ahhhh.

---

20   Keep quiet. Keep your mouth absolutely shut.

21   There is no point in making that face.

She crosses her arms and faces the audience. Beat. She feels MEERA *touch her left arm.*

Fiiinnnneeee. When do I have to start?

MEERA: Five thirty tomorrow morning, I will wake you up. We can both get dressed together and then you can help me cook. Then, after work, we can go to the community well to get some water.

SCENE THREE: COMMUNITY WATER LINE

MEERA *smiles, picks up the bucket, and looks at* CHAYA. *She turns and physically transforms into* CHAYA. *They both walk upstage. They are now standing in line to get water at the community well. The line keeps moving through this scene.*

CHAYA: *(walking)* Na, Ma . . . That was wrong. I'm going to try again, okay?

She takes position in line.

Two times one is two; two times two is four; two times three is six; two times four is NINE; two times five is . . . Uff ho Ma, you're not catching my mistake. When I said nine that was wrong . . .

CHAYA *physically transforms into* MEERA *and takes one step forward.*

MEERA: Move with the line no, Chaya.

MEERA *notices her friend Shampa at a distance and waves.*

Ohh *aarre aarre*²² Shampa. Ki khobor . . . koto din tomar shate dhaka hoy na. Shob khobor thik aache? Bhalo?²³ How is your daughter doing? Any news

---

22 An Indian expression to draw attention.

23 Anything new? I haven't seen you in so long. How is everything? Well?

on the marriage proposal? Na, na. Meyer shate ashechie[24] to get some water from the well. I should have come last night, look at this lineup. Every day it is getting longer and longer. Guaranteed those basti people are coming and stealing our water. Theirs is not fixed, no! No, it is still not fixed . . . all the basti people have been lining up in the government office for so long. Aarre, move the line no, man . . . a little bit faster . . . I have to go home and wash utensils.

MEERA *moves forward in line and indicates* CHAYA *to keep moving.*

So as I say, I hear every month government inspector comes, looks at it, and goes away. Nothing is ever done. I am sure they come to our well to steal our water. Thieves!

MEERA *moves forward in line and indicates* CHAYA *to keep moving.*

Aacha, do you know anything about the bridge being fixed? Ki mushkil bo-loto,[25] there is water all over my tent plastic.

Yes, we are still living there . . . last year my husband was going to build us a mud house, but it is so expensive, no? Also, my sister built one. The tin door cost her so much money . . . but this monsoon season, the entire thing collapse due to rain. She cried so much. AND THIS LINE IS NOT EVEN MOVING! All I want is a good tent plastic. But all government will give us is torn blue plastic? They might as well give us paper from now; we can only take newspaper and put on our roof and it will leak anyway. You only tell me, what is the difference between torn blue plastic and newspaper? The next thing you know, they will be coming and living underneath our tent with us and eating our food . . . which, come to think of it, will be a good thing. They need to see how we live and what we never eat!

She laughs.

Can you imagine . . . if they came and we gave them boiled rice water?

---

24   With my daughter here.

25   This is so much trouble.

MEERA chuckles.

Ha? Yes, my husband? He is doing very well. Yes, he is becoming permanent now. They all love him very much. No, same pay as last time; every year they say they will give him more money. But this year it is for sure happening. I am having good feeling about it . . . and when it does, we will build a house with a tin door.

CHAYA: Ma, *chalo na.*[26]

Annoyed by the interruption, MEERA gives CHAYA a sharp look and turns back to realize Shampa has left.

MEERA: Okay okay Shampa. I will see you later. Bye bye.

She turns to look at CHAYA.

Chaya, when I am talking, don't talk in the middle. She must have felt insulted by you. And this line is not even moving!

She notices Kamala's son downstage left.

LOOK. Kamala's son. Chaya, don't look at him like that. He is higher caste than us, so don't even have any ideas. Now you are looking at him, the next thing you know he is touching your face, and the next thing you know he is buying you bangles, and the next thing you know you are having his babies! You are working for him now. Move eye, move eye.

CHAYA: Na Ma, I am not even looking at him. Can I try my tables again?

MEERA: Tables, tables, tables, how much will your tables help you when you're sitting there washing all those teacups?

MEERA suddenly races towards downstage left to speak to Kamala's son.

---

26 Ma, let's go.

Aaaaiiieee . . . Na na na na na na na we have been waiting in line. Jao pechone jao.[27] Go to the back of the line. We have been waiting in line far longer than you. And which basti you are from? No! We are from the bridge basti and this is our tap . . . you have to have your own tap; you cannot come here and steal our water. Now you are stealing our water, the next thing you say that the pump is yours and the next thing you say is that you will be coming and living underneath the bridge with us, the next thing you say that you want our food and our daughters too! I know your kind very well. What you think, we have no brain? We understand all. So, don't come here and do your *chalaki*.[28] Go along. Go! My husband works at the police station; you give me problem and he will send police after you!

Kamala's son spits on her face. She turns her face sharply downstage right. She touches her face with her right hand to remove the spit.

Aamar mukheo thutu fello![29] He spit on me! Come on, come move the line.

She storms off to join the line again. She takes position in line as CHAYA.

CHAYA: *(looking upstage left)* Ma. Why do you go to argue with them?

MEERA: They will turn the tap off in the next two hours and some people need it more than he does. But don't worry Chaya, one day my shadow will fall on him, and then he will know.

---

27   Go to the back.

28   Chalaki is a Bengali word that means, in this context, "to pull a fast one."

29   You spit on my face!

SCENE FOUR: TEA STALL

MEERA physically transforms into CHAYA. *She walks downstage centre and sits. She takes tea glasses from the floor and wipes them (glasses should be mimed). On the second and third glass she spits and then wipes them, laughing hysterically. She suddenly notices Kamala's son stage right and stands up, looking down at the floor.*

CHAYA: Ha . . . hello. See, these teacups are almost clean and I have one more hour to go.

Pause.

No I cannot look at you . . .

She turns left on the spot.

No. My ma said that I cannot look at anyone that is higher caste than us. So . . . umm . . . I cannot look.

CHAYA *quickly walks downstage left and stands.*

No no no no no no please don't make me look. My ma said that if I look at you, then you will go tell that we people look. Then my father will lose his job; he is a toilet cleaner in a lot of the police stations in this area, and then my mother will lose her job. She is a toilet cleaner in a lot of the houses . . . so, I cannot look. Yes . . . but.

In a sharp move she covers her eyes with her palms. Slowly she turns to face Kamala's son with her eyes still covered.

Nooooooo, I will get in trouble. My ma said that I have to come here and clean all the teacups so I can get some tea; she doesn't have enough money for me for lunch . . . yes . . . but.

Gradually CHAYA *uncovers her face and turns her head stage right, and then her body turns stage right (still on spot). She cups her hand and takes biscuits from Kamala's son in an "untouchable" manner. She smiles and looks at the food. She feels him watching her eat. She turns and starts to gobble her food. She picks up the last piece and looks at it. She physically transforms into* MR. BIKASH, *who is also looking at the piece of food. She walks downstage centre and throws the food away.*

SCENE FIVE: MR. BIKASH'S HOME

MR. BIKASH: Kamala? Kamala.

He turns and snaps.

Stand here. Have you been giving the toilet cleaner food?

Pause.

Answer me?

Pause.

Do not make me repeat the question.

KAMALA: Na na, Sir Ji. I didn't do anything wrong. That toilet cleaner Meera said that if I didn't give her some food she would take her dirty hands and put it all over your house. So I got scared, Sir Ji, and gave her some food. But don't worry, nothing fresh. All the uneaten from your plate I gave her.

MR. BIKASH: Where does she live?

KAMALA: Underneath the bridge they have a tent. She lives there.

MR. BIKASH: Go tell her that she is no longer to work for me. I don't need her anymore. Bloody ungrateful bloodsucking untouchables. Dogs should eat them all! I give her place to work and she is stealing my food.

Now go! What are you waiting here for?

KAMALA: Na na, Sir Ji. She is very poor, Sir Ji.

MR. BIKASH: Kamala, tell me one thing. Do you like your job here?

KAMALA: Yes, Sir Ji. No problem, I will go tell her that she is no longer to work for you.

SCENE SIX: OUTSIDE MEERA'S HOME

KAMALA physically transforms into CHAYA, *who is skipping and then suddenly stops when she reaches stage left. She notices* KAMALA.

CHAYA: Oh, hello. Yes. Yes, I know you. My ma and you work at the same house, right? I work at your son's tea stall. Did you know that? Yesterday, he gave me a tea biscuit and . . .

She listens.

What? Why? Did I do something wrong? But Ma said that she can't lose her job; then we will have to drink boiled rice water all the time. No . . . please tell them not to fire her! What did she do?

She realizes that KAMALA *has left. Beat. She thinks for a moment and then enters her house running.*

Ma Ma Ma Ma Ma, guess what I just found out . . . okay. So hear this. From now on I will work full time . . . like, like how you say? Like permanent, in the tea stall. And and and . . . he said that he would give me two tea biscuits . . . See, see, Ma, isn't that a good thing? If I went to school, I would probably not even do well and who needs school when I can learn how to make tea and cook. I can help you now. I promise, Ma, I will not even think of school anymore. All my times tables, I will not even say them anymore, Ma; I will not even bother you anymore, Ma, because I know that it is a waste of my time. And, when he starts to pay me, I can run the family. I can buy food and you won't even have to make cow-dung cakes for Kamala Aunty. You can just sit at home and rest.

Beat. She contemplates her next words, and then speaks.

Okay, in other news, I just met Kamala Aunty outside. She said that you don't have to go to your job anymore because they don't want you anymore.

She didn't say why.

But don't worry, Ma. I will work from now. So you can sit at home and rest. See see, Ma . . . isn't that a good thing?

MEERA: Chaya, ekdom muk bondo Koro.[30] "I can run the family"! How old are you? Go wash your face and bring a bucket. The tent plastic is leaking again. Put it right there. There is little boiled rice water in the pot; drink it. Put some salt in it to bring the flavour.

   MEERA watches CHAYA walk to and sit downstage right.

Has crying ever changed anything? Look at me!

   Pause.

No. Then swallow your tears; I don't want to see them anymore.

SCENE SEVEN: RIGHT OUTSIDE MEERA'S HOME

   MEERA physically transforms into CHAYA. CHAYA turns to check if anyone is watching. She picks up the bucket and sits with it, placing it stage centre. She takes out a kajal container hidden in the folds of her saree and applies the eye makeup. She undoes her braid. She checks her makeup and hair in the reflection of the water in the bucket. During this process she constantly looks back to check if anyone is watching. She dips her hand in the water and drinks. She looks up and speaks to God.

CHAYA: The tea-stall boy gave it to me . . . don't tell Ma. He is higher caste than us. She will break my bones with a bat.

   She hears MEERA call her from offstage.

---

30   Close your mouth.

Ha, aaschie.[31]

Aaschie. Aaschie.

She picks up the bucket and walks two steps back. She places the bucket down and pays salutation to God.

Aaschie.

She says "aaschie" as she keeps walking backwards. She places the bucket upstage and is now in the tea stall. She accepts tea.

SCENE EIGHT: TEA STALL

CHAYA *speaks nervously as she holds her tea glass. She is speaking to Kamala's son.*

CHAYA: Did you know that this is my first cup of tea? Ever. Nooo, I have never been having tea before. And now you are so sweet to making me tea. It is sweet tea, right?

She takes a sip.

Oh . . . it's so hot . . . but I liking it very much. My ma says that all rich people drink tea at four o'clock in the evening . . . I know it is not four o'clock in the evening, but I feel like a rich people.

Did you know that my ma thinks that I am at my friend's house . . . yes, Durga; she works here. My ma doesn't know I am working here this late . . . it's ten o'clock . . . she will get very angry.

Surprised, she feels the tea-stall boy trying to touch her. She walks two steps forward.

Here, my tea is done.

---

31   Yes, coming.

No, please don't touch me again. I have to go now.

CHAYA *feels his touch again and takes two steps forward.*

Ma aamake boleche tomar shate beshi kotha na bolte. Aami tomar jonno kaj korte aachis. Ha, I shotti bolchi.[32] Ma tells me this all the time. I only come to work here. You told me if I work till ten you will give me two tea biscuits. Well you should give them to me now.

Shocked, she turns to face the tea-stall boy stage right.

What? Why? I have to keep working here. You cannot fire me like that.

She hurries downstage.

No . . . please don't touch me again.

No, my mother will get very angry.

I don't want any more tea . . . I am leaving now.

She is raped by the tea-stall boy. This segment is executed only through CHAYA's *breath and gesture.* NO *rape screams.*

Lighting note: The rape should take place in a tight box of light created by a top light.

Sharp inhale—her hand opens to indicate the teacup dropping.

Inhale from mouth—chin on left shoulder. Exhale.

Inhale—chin on chest right. Exhale.

Inhale—right hand on left breast. Exhale.

Inhale—left hand on inner right thigh. Exhale.

Inhale. Both hands on chest, looking upstage left.

---

32 Ma told me not to talk to you. I only come to work for you. Yes, I am telling you the truth.

She is now at the police station being interrogated.

The interrogator stands downstage left to create the police officer.

No nooo.

She looks upstage right.

I was having tea. No. I didn't steal it. He made it for me and gave me tea.

It's not my . . .

She looks downstage left.

Sorry.

She looks upstage right.

He wanted to touch my face.

She looks downstage left.

I told him it was wrong though.

She looks upstage right.

Sorry.

No, he didn't listen.

Ten o'clock.

He told me if I worked till ten he would give me two tea biscuits, and I wanted my ma to have two tea biscuits.

It's really not my fault. I told him to leave me alone. He didn't listen and I . . .

She looks upstage left and then looks down. Pause.

Here.

She touches her lips.

Here.

> *She touches her neck.*

Here.

> *She touches her left breast and her inner right thigh.*

> CHAYA *inhales deeply.*

I didn't do anything. I didn't.

He forced me . . .

> *She looks upstage left.*

Why will you not help?

> *She looks downstage right.*

Sorry, but this is my life. My father works here; why will you not help?

> *Long pause. A moment's beat. She is now outside the police station.*

Honour. Honour honour.

School school school.

No no no no no no no no no no no no no.

> *As she says her "nos" she starts walking and transforms into* MEERA, *who has just entered* MR. BIKASH'S *house.*

MEERA: NO NO NO NO NO.

Kamala!

Kamala? Come down here right now.

> *Pause.*

I have been working here for years after years scrubbing this very floor and cleaning that toilet!

Pause.

I am never disrespecting you; I touch nothing! Always smiling. Always, always, always. Smiling I talk to you, smiling I come to your house to make YOUR cow-dung cakes, and smiling I let your son not pay my daughter! And this is what he does?

Rascal.

Long pause. MEERA takes a deep breath. She removes her aachal (the part of her saree that goes over her chest) with her right hand and stands facing the audience. She takes the aachal and wipes each wall of MR. BIKASH's house while laughing hysterically. By doing this she has now soiled MR. BIKASH's house with her untouchable hands.

SCENE NINE: MEERA'S HOME

MEERA enters her house and notices CHAYA sitting on the floor crying. She pauses and remembers a story.

MEERA: When your father saw you for the very first time he held you. The shadow of the moonlight was falling on your face. And he named you Chaya. Shadow. We both loved that name very much, because you were the only one. I think it is a good thing. Believe it or not, it's a good thing.

She takes a step closer to CHAYA.

Chaya, you are lucky that this man has agreed to marry you. These days it is very hard to find a husband, and that too, to find a husband for somebody that is used, is even harder.

She takes a step closer to CHAYA. Pause.

I know that he is very old but he will know what to do to make you happy. Plus, they are not asking for a lot of dowry Chaya . . . only three goats, one cow and some sarees. We can do that . . . we will manage that somehow. You will be happy. I am telling you. The best thing we can do for you is to get you married . . . but you have to make sure you have a son Chaya. That will take care of everything. Life is not easy, Chaya . . . but you have to believe in it.

MEERA *takes out a container of vermilion from the folds of her saree and sits beside* CHAYA.

Today when this red vermilion will be touching your forehead you will be married . . . and you will be happy. I know that. This is for you Chaya.

MEERA *slowly transforms into* CHAYA. *She watches her mother leave and mouths the word "Ma." Gradually she removes the lid of the container and places it stage left. She takes the red vermilion with her right hand and puts it on her forehead with her eyes closed. Her hand works its way down from her head to her neck. She makes two soft crying sounds and looks up at God.*

The end.

BOMBAY BLACK
Anosh Irani

ACKNOWLEDGEMENTS

The playwright is extremely grateful to the Canada Council for the Arts for its generous support.

Two moments come to mind when I think back on the experience of working with Anosh Irani on *Bombay Black*. I met Anosh through Factory Theatre's CrossCurrents Festival when we programmed his play *The Matka King* for a workshop. I directed a public reading of the script and loved investigating the vivid world Anosh created. Some months later I asked him if he was contemplating ideas for new plays, as I was interested in exploring a possible commission with my own company, Nightswimming.

Anosh said he had an image of a blind man falling in love with a dancer as she performed, even though he couldn't see her dance. I was intrigued; what was it that entranced the man? The sound of her feet? Her scent? The context of the dance? What? We are so seduced by the visual world, that it was hard for me to imagine the equation at work in this strange romance. Anosh wasn't sure yet either, though as we talked he slowly teased out that one central image, learning just a bit more about the man and the dancer. I was convinced there was a play to be built around that image, and around the question of what made that love blossom. Nightswimming commissioned Anosh to write the play.

Then . . . nothing. When we signed the commission, Anosh said he needed to think about the characters, the situation, and the image for a year, and that he wouldn't write anything until he'd taken the time to think through the story. So we waited. And, true to his word, about sixteen months later, a fully formed first draft arrived, in which Anosh had answered those questions, made sense of that initial image of blind man and dancer, added a wild mother to the recipe, and invented the raw, magical, awful, and wondrous set of stories that brought them all together.

Anosh's faith in his instincts, in the images that lodge in his mind, in his process of finding the story, was a tremendous lesson in giving a writer the time and space to make a world.

After the first production of *Bombay Black*, which garnered four Dora Mavor Moore Awards, including Outstanding New Play, Cahoots Theatre Company pursued a tour for the following year. Meanwhile, Anosh watched the creation of a Hindi production of the script in Bombay and concluded that one element of the story that developed as he wrote the play—the fact that the dancer too goes blind—could be reconsidered. So as we headed back into rehearsal, Anosh provided us with a new version of the play (the one in this volume, not published until now) with substantial changes for all of us to adapt to. Again, Anosh's faith in his instincts, in the peculiar magic of his imagination to see what is there and what is only thought to be there, guided him to this powerful and fabulous version of his story. Where *Bombay Black* takes the spectator is often unpleasant and even cruel, but its beautiful dance, razor-sharp language, precise character delineation, fantastical images, and rich, provocative thinking about the nature of ritual, family, and tradition ensure that our journey contains as many pleasures as it does challenges. Anosh's instincts led him to a final image that challenged us as we made the production, and rewarded the audience for their faith in his story. Anosh finds his way, just as people do, convinced that the unknown ahead of us must be faced.

—Brian Quirt

Bombay Black was commissioned and developed by Nightswimming Theatre and produced by Cahoots Theatre Projects. It was workshopped and given a public reading at the On the Verge Festival 2005 at the National Arts Centre, Ottawa. The play premiered in January 2006 at the Theatre Centre, Toronto, with the following cast and creative team:

Padma: Deena Aziz
Apsara: Anita Majumdar
Kamal: Sanjay Talwar

Director: Brian Quirt
Assistant director: Andrea Romaldi
Set design: Camellia Koo
Lighting design: Rebecca Picherack
Composer/sound design: Suba Sankaran
Choreographer: Nova Bhattacharya
Production manager: Stephen Lalande
Technical director: Greg Poulin
Design assistant: Jung-Hye Kim
Scenic artists: Camellia Koo and Jung-Hye Kim
Stage manager: Isaac Thomas

The play was subsequently revised and toured to Mississauga's Living Arts Centre (February 8–10, 2008) and Vancouver's Arts Club Theatre as part of their subscription season (February 21–March 15, 2008).

Bombay Black was translated into Hindi by Saurabh Shukla and staged in Bombay at the National Centre for the Performing Arts and the Prithvi Theatre, and in New Delhi at the India Habitat Centre in 2007. It was directed by Anahita Uberoi and produced by Shiamak Davar.

CHARACTERS

Apsara: A dancer in her twenties.
Padma: Apsara's mother. In her forties.
Kamal: A blind man in his thirties.

SETTING

The play is set in an apartment in Bombay overlooking the Arabian Sea.
The time is the present.

ACT ONE

1.

Evening. The stage is dark.

The sound of a woman's anklets beating against the floor in the darkness.

This is APSARA.

Only she can be seen.

She performs the "Dance of Empowerment."

The music and the dance should have a modern sensibility. The dance APSARA performs borrows from the courtesans of ancient India as well as present-day Bombay bar girls.

The idea is that she is sucking away the energy of the man she is performing for, all the while pretending that she is serving him. The dance progressively becomes more and more seductive.

After a minute of dance, a voice:

PADMA: Make eye contact with the man. Then lower your eyes from time to time as though you cannot bear the strength of his gaze. This will make him feel powerful. Go slower when you reveal your thighs. Make the man wait. Punish him. That's the true purpose of dance, my dear—to turn men into vegetables.

APSARA stops dancing.

Lights.

PADMA is revealed.

What's wrong? Why did you stop? I thought you liked vegetables.

Pause.

I've been meaning to ask you: Isn't it time you learnt some new moves? It's quite charming, your little dance, but . . . I need you to swivel your hips more. Dance more like a *tart* and less like an *artist*. Yes, that's it. Be more tartish. And make sure you oil your hair every night. It needs more shine.

APSARA: It's too much work.

PADMA: Being a tart is hard work. Requires dedication and commitment. That's the problem with you young people. You don't take anything seriously. Now get some rest. You have an appointment at nine.

APSARA: Who is it tonight?

PADMA: A new client.

APSARA: From where?

PADMA: He's from the suburbs—Malad or Mulund, one of those—I can't remember. Anyway, I spoke to him over the phone. He has no reference so I'm charging him three thousand rupees—not bad for an hour of dance, hah? Now. Let's go for a walk.

APSARA: No.

PADMA: Fifteen minutes. That's all. The sun's about to set. Whenever I watch the sun go down, I always ask myself, "What if the sun doesn't show up tomorrow?" Such a massive universe, one wrong turn and the sun is lost. That's why I always thank the sun each day. To make it feel appreciated.

APSARA: You need to make some friends, Mother.

PADMA: I have friends. The butcher's my friend. What's his name . . .

APSARA: The butcher cannot be counted as a friend.

PADMA: But I bought a knife from him. What's his name . . . Hanif Bhai, that's it. We had a friendly exchange once. "What nice meat you have," I said, and he replied, "It's all in the knife, Madam. The way you cut meat is important." I have friends.

APSARA: You can't go for a walk with the butcher.

PADMA: That's why I'm asking you to go with me.

APSARA: I don't want to.

PADMA: Fine. Then I won't go either. There will be no one to thank the sun. If the sun doesn't rise tomorrow, it will be your fault. The whole world will be plunged into darkness because you are a selfish little bitch.

Pause.

Is it such a task for you to spend time with your dying mother?

APSARA: I wasn't aware you were dying.

PADMA: I might, I might. Anything can happen. Heart attacks come when you least expect them. They're like surprise tests.

APSARA: You're a beacon of hope today, Mother.

PADMA: By the way, I had a new costume made for you. It reveals your stomach more. Every man that comes in here wants to lick your stomach and thighs. So we must open the door a little more. Not a lot, just a little.

APSARA: How thoughtful of you.

PADMA: More meat, more heat.

Pause.

Apsara, what's the matter with you today? You're not your usual unintelligent self. You look like you're actually contemplating something. Even during the dance, you were distracted.

APSARA: It's nothing.

PADMA: Tell me. You know how soothing I can be.

APSARA: It's just that I can smell country liquor. You know, the kind father used to drink. I smell country liquor made out of orange peels and leather. It's been years since I've got that smell.

PADMA: It's probably the sea. It's called the Arabian Sea because it smells like a camel.

APSARA: It's not the sea. My father smells nothing like the sea. You know that. It's that thick, heavy smell . . .

PADMA: First of all, your father's probably dead. No one in the village knows where he is and it's been years since anyone's seen him. But if he's alive, we're in a city of eighteen million people. He'll never find us.

APSARA: What if he does?

PADMA: I won't let him near you. I promise.

Pause.

Now let's go—the sun is waiting.

2.

Night.

PADMA *is preparing the apartment for the customer's arrival. She fluffs the cushions on the swing, dims the lights to set a mood.*

There is a knock on the door.

PADMA *opens the door.*

It is KAMAL. *He is unseen.*

KAMAL: Is this apartment 4-A? Ocean Heights?

PADMA: Yes.

KAMAL: I spoke to you over the phone.

PADMA: You're late.

KAMAL: I'm sorry. It's just that . . .

PADMA: Why are you panting? We're only on the fourth floor.

KAMAL: Yes, but there's no lift . . . and the stairs are very steep.

PADMA: Come in.

KAMAL *walks in.*

His manner of walking suggests that he is blind.

Are you blind?

KAMAL: Yes.

There is a long silence.

I apologize.

PADMA: Would you like me to help you?

KAMAL: Yes, please.

He offers her his hand.

But she does not take it.

PADMA: Keep walking straight for four feet. Then turn left about one foot. There's a swing. Sit on it.

He finds the swing.

Don't you people normally use a cane?

He sits.

KAMAL: I lost my cane. The footpath is dug up just outside your building. I think I might have tripped over some wires.

PADMA: Yes, yes. Telephone wires. Those phone company dogs are always digging. So many cross connections because of that. The other day I was on the line with a client and this little girl enters the conversation—she was trying to call her mathematics teacher. So I said to her, "Listen, little one, there's no use studying. Only your *body* will be of use." She started yelling for her mother. I quickly put the phone down. Some children are just not ready for the truth. Anyway—you were saying?

KAMAL: Er . . . nothing. I wasn't saying anything.

PADMA: You lost your cane.

KAMAL: Yes. I lost my cane because I tripped over telephone wires. That's why I'm late.

PADMA: Did you fall?

KAMAL: No.

PADMA: Were you robbed?

KAMAL: I'm fine.

PADMA: Good. Then I'll take the money first.

He reaches into his pocket and hands her a wad of money.

KAMAL: No need to count. Fresh from the bank.

PADMA: Before we begin, let me explain the rules to you.

KAMAL: You make it sound like a jail.

PADMA: Apsara must be safe.

KAMAL: Apsara. Beautiful name.

PADMA: Bombay's Celestial Nymph.

KAMAL: That's not what her name means.

PADMA: I *know* what her name means.

KAMAL: Apsara. Water that moves. A literal translation.

PADMA: As I said, you need to know the rules. First and foremost: This is not a brothel.

KAMAL: I'm aware of that.

PADMA: That's what they all say. So allow me to get it through your thick skull. In a way it's good that you are blind. You people are acute listeners. This is *not* a brothel. There will be no touching. At all. She will not touch you. You will not touch her. Is that clear?

KAMAL: No problem.

PADMA: If at any point you do touch her, your hands will be broken with an iron rod. There are one-way mirrors. So I can see you, but you can't see me. A concept you're more than familiar with.

KAMAL: Understood.

PADMA: Any questions?

KAMAL: No.

PADMA: I have one.

KAMAL: Go ahead.

PADMA: What pleasure does a blind man get from dance?

KAMAL: None whatsoever.

PADMA: Then why do this?

KAMAL: Tax writeoff.

PADMA: You look suspicious. Do you work for the police?

KAMAL: No, Madam.

PADMA: If you do, you're wasting your time. The ACP is our client. He loves Apsara.

KAMAL: The assistant commissioner of police is your client?

PADMA: He loves to watch her dance. He requests the same bloody song each time he comes. He's an odd fellow. Doesn't smoke, doesn't drink . . . sips orange juice as Apsara dances. But he's a kind man. He said if I'm ever in any trouble, I should call him. So whatever department you're from, you're wasting your time.

KAMAL: I work for no one.

PADMA: What do you do for a living?

KAMAL: I sell books.

PADMA: You sell books. And you can afford to pay three thousand rupees.

KAMAL: I sell *lots* of books.

PADMA: I'll have to check you.

KAMAL: What for?

PADMA: I don't know. A knife, maybe. Stand up.

He does.

She frisks him.

No ID? Where's your wallet?

KAMAL: I don't carry one.

PADMA: What's your name?

KAMAL: I don't pay three thousand rupees to reveal my name.

PADMA: So you're married.

KAMAL: For many years.

PADMA: Don't worry. We don't blackmail. Our reputation is very good.

KAMAL: That's why I'm here.

PADMA: Now I did not mention this over the phone, but we offer cocaine as well. We charge extra for that.

KAMAL: No thank you.

PADMA: I can assure you the quality is perfect. Movie stars come here especially for that.

KAMAL shakes his head.

Perhaps something low grade then, to match your personality? May I suggest some Bombay Black?

KAMAL: Bombay Black. What's that?

PADMA: A local drug made from hashish and shoe polish.

KAMAL: Sounds delicious. But no.

PADMA: One last question then. Are you vegetarian or non-vegetarian?

KAMAL: What difference?

PADMA: If you want to eat. Maybe your wife's a bad cook.

KAMAL: I'm vegetarian.

PADMA: A blind vegetarian. You poor man.

She walks away.

KAMAL: Madam.

PADMA: Yes?

KAMAL: Put the lights off. I want complete darkness.

PADMA: What for?

KAMAL: When I meet a woman for the first time, I want her to see me the same way I see her.

PADMA puts the lights out and exits.

APSARA enters.

We hear her anklets in the dark.

KAMAL stands in the centre of the room.

He walks towards the door in the darkness.

We hear the door open and close.

APSARA turns the lights on.

KAMAL is gone.

3.

APSARA is seated on the swing.

PADMA opens the door to the room very slowly.

She is surprised to find that APSARA is alone.

PADMA: Is he in the bathroom?

APSARA: No.

PADMA: Where is he then?

APSARA: I have no idea.

PADMA: What happened?

APSARA: Nothing happened. He just left. He walked out the moment I entered the room.

PADMA: You did not dance for him?

APSARA: I entered. The lights were off. Then I heard him walk towards the door. By the time I put the lights on, he had gone.

PADMA: That's strange. Perhaps you made him sad.

APSARA: How?

PADMA: You have that gift. Maybe his wife was a dancer, and she died in a car accident while he was driving—that explains his loss of sight—and he feels guilty, tremendously guilty, but at the same time he wants to be with her again, and since he's blind all he needs to do is be in the presence of a dancer, and the rest is in his mind—you become someone else, his wife, a lady named Sharmila or Shabana or something.

APSARA: That's quite a story.

PADMA: When your own story is a piece of shit, you tell someone else's.

APSARA: Why not re-dream your own story instead?

PADMA: How futile that would be. Like an artist trying to paint the same picture twice.

APSARA: In any case, I hope that's not the blind man's story.

PADMA: Don't feel sorry for him.

APSARA: He's the first blind person I've met.

PADMA: He's not a person. He's a man. At the end of the day, he's a man. His blindness does not make him compassionate. Or valiant. Or worthy of love.

APSARA gets up.

Where are you going?

APSARA: To my room. Your optimism is infectious.

PADMA's cellphone rings. It is tucked in the folds of her saree. She picks up. She listens.

PADMA: Yes . . . okay then . . . nine tomorrow.

(to APSARA) It's the blind vegetarian. He wants to see you again.

APSARA: What for? Is he just going to throw away his money again?

PADMA: Oh don't be so harsh on yourself. He's not *throwing* it away. You provide a valuable service, my dear. All these men who come here have wives who are ugly old bags who, if they tried to dance, would have the effect of an enema. So hold your head up. Be proud. You are of *some* worth. Not a lot. Just a little.

4.

Morning.

APSARA is asleep on the ground.

The sun shines on APSARA's face.

There is the crackling sound of a fire.

The chanting of prayers.

APSARA is extremely uneasy.

PADMA enters carrying a shopping bag.

She wakes her daughter up.

PADMA: Apsara . . . Apsara . . .

APSARA sits up. She is disoriented.

Did you spend the whole night on the floor? I've told you not to sleep on the floor. You'll catch a cold.

APSARA: I had that dream again. I'm walking round a fire, there's smoke in my eyes, and I'm crying.

PADMA: Stop having that dream. Dream about something positive. Your father is walking down an empty road. Suddenly a car races towards him. Its brakes have failed. There is the look of terror on your father's face. But he manages to step out of harm's way in the nick of time. He looks skywards and thanks God for saving him.

Pause.

Then a truck appears out of nowhere and flattens the bastard. *That's* the kind of dream that is soothing.

APSARA: This time my dream was different. I was crying out to you. That's never happened before.

PADMA: I'm going to the market. Do you want anything?

APSARA: Why was I crying out to you?

PADMA: Apsara, please. I've just had my tea. Don't ask me morose questions just after my morning tea. It's about the only time I can barely manage to stay neutral. Now make yourself some breakfast. Don't starve while I'm gone.

PADMA exits.

A few seconds later there is a knock on the door.

APSARA opens the door.

You?

It is KAMAL.

KAMAL: May I come in?

APSARA: What are you doing here?

KAMAL: It's nine o'clock. I had called last night and fixed an appointment at nine.

APSARA: That's nine at night.

KAMAL: Morning and night look the same through my eyes.

APSARA: I can't dance for you in the morning.

KAMAL: I don't want you to dance.

He starts walking towards the swing.

(*imitating PADMA*) "Keep walking straight for four feet. Then turn left about one foot. There's a swing. Sit on it." Your mother is absolutely charming.

APSARA: You can't just come in like that.

He sits on the swing.

KAMAL: I haven't eaten a thing all night.

APSARA: I'm sorry, but you'll have to leave.

KAMAL: I spent the night outside your house.

APSARA: What for?

KAMAL: Not right outside your door. I wouldn't do that. I slept by the sea-wall. I live in the suburbs and I had to be here first thing in the morning. It's wonderful to wake up by the sea, especially here. The voices of beggars, stray dogs, pigeons, some roadside radio playing old Hindi songs.

APSARA: If you spent the night outside, where did you call from last night? It would be hard for you to find a public telephone around here.

KAMAL: Oh, I called from your neighbour's apartment. I told your neighbours that my car had broken down and I needed to call my mechanic. I dialed your number and said, "Hello, it's the blind man. I'd like to make an appointment at nine." Then after your mother hung up I said, "Can you please ask some-one to pick me up outside Ocean Heights? The engine has stalled. Again."

APSARA: The blind don't drive, you know.

KAMAL: Your neighbours didn't seem to mind. They're a nice old couple.

APSARA: Look—what do you want?

KAMAL: Eggs would be nice.

APSARA: A cup of tea. My mother just made some. That's all you get. Then you'll have to come back tonight.

KAMAL: Five spoons of sugar, please.

APSARA: Five? You want diabetes?

KAMAL: Oh God, no. Diabetes leads to blindness.

APSARA: I'll get your tea.

She exits.

He talks to her loudly.

KAMAL: I love this area, you know. Apollo Bunder, isn't it? Wonder where the name is from. Anyway, like I said, I just love it here. I was talking to this little beggar last night by the seawall. Her name was Mangal. I always thought it was a man's name. Anyway, I asked her to describe the area for me; you know, since I can't see. She said, "I can see boats on the water. There are little boats and big boats but just now since it is night they are all silent, and I can see a lighthouse and the light is on, otherwise the boats will bang, and I can see men selling boiled eggs and bananas, and I am getting hungry, so that will be five rupees." Can you imagine? So I said, "No money, sorry. I spent it all on this dancer in that building opposite whose horrible mother charges three thousand rupees!" So she said, "Three thousand rupees for dance? Are you mad?"

Pause.

I must be, no?

APSARA returns with a cup of tea.

She hands him the cup.

He drinks.

It's lukewarm. Chai should be hot. But it'll do.

Pause.

I have something important to tell you. But I wanted to wait until your mother was out of the house.

APSARA: What is it?

KAMAL: I will reveal something to you that will change your life. But first we must get to know each other.

APSARA: Why would I agree?

KAMAL: Because you love me.

APSARA: Really.

KAMAL: You're worried about my health. I like that in a woman. You put less than five spoons of sugar in my tea. Good for you.

APSARA: Look, we can continue this tonight.

KAMAL: Then I must get going. Your neighbours' house. To thank them for their generosity last night.

He gets up.

Don't tell your mother I came here.

APSARA: Why not?

KAMAL: I don't trust her.

APSARA: And why is that?

KAMAL: Because in all these years, she hasn't told you a thing about me.

KAMAL exits.

APSARA *watches him closely as he leaves.*

5.

PADMA has just returned from the market.

PADMA: It looks like you haven't moved at all since I left. Did you eat anything?

APSARA: No. What did you bring from the market?

PADMA: Cauliflower, cabbage, lettuce. And some fresh meat for the eagles.

APSARA: You have to stop feeding the eagles. Every time our building council has a meeting, they complain about you tossing chunks of meat out of the window.

PADMA: I don't *toss* chunks of meat out of the window. That's uncivilized. I wait for the eagles to collect them from my hand. Now that's a good breed of bird. The general of all birds. They see red and they swoop.

Pause.

Whose cup of tea is that?

APSARA: Mine.

PADMA: In all these years, you haven't touched a drop of tea.

APSARA: You drive me to drink, Mother.

PADMA: Don't be smart, Apsara. Someone was here.

APSARA: The blind man.

PADMA: At this time? What did he want?

APSARA: He wanted to talk to me. He knocked immediately after you left. I thought it was you.

PADMA: What did he want?

APSARA: I'm not sure. He's crazy.

PADMA: Tell me exactly what he said.

APSARA: He said he'll be back at nine.

PADMA: What else?

APSARA: Nothing. He just sat in silence, drank his tea, and left.

PADMA: He wants something.

APSARA: What makes you say that? Maybe he just came for a dance.

PADMA: Apsara, you're a good dancer. But you're not *that* good. Perhaps this blind man can see something we can't.

APSARA: Like what?

PADMA: A blind spot.

6.

Night.

KAMAL is seated on the swing.

He is alone in the room.

APSARA enters.

APSARA: I see you have a new cane.

KAMAL: It's not mine. The old man gave it to me. He told me he has no use for it anymore. He's full of mischief, that old bandit. He offered me tea this morning, hot tea, unlike the lukewarm tea you gave me. Anyway, just before I put the cup to my lips, I heard something fall into my teacup and his wife shouted, "Stop putting your dentures in the blind man's cup."

APSARA: And you prefer their tea to mine.

KAMAL: Dentures are harmless. Teeth without jaws. No malice.

APSARA: Have you got the money?

KAMAL: Ah, the money. Yes . . . the money. Is your mother around?

APSARA: She's in bed.

KAMAL: But it's only nine.

APSARA: She's not sleeping. She's just lying down.

KAMAL: Are we disturbing her?

APSARA: We had this place soundproofed.

KAMAL: Has she ever broken anyone's hands with an iron rod?

APSARA: Once. A man came here and tried cocaine. It was his first time. After that he was like a bull. He started touching me. She came in with an iron rod and broke both his wrists. Any more questions?

KAMAL: As I explained to you this morning, we have to get to know each other.

APSARA: As long as you pay.

KAMAL: Payment is a problem. I can't afford to pay you. I'm quite poor.

APSARA: No money, no conversation.

KAMAL: But I'm a bookseller.

APSARA: Then stop coming here. Do bookseller things.

KAMAL: I'm not even a bookstore owner. I work on commission.

APSARA: No money, no conversation.

KAMAL: But these are my life savings.

APSARA: You expect me to believe you're spending your life savings on dance?

KAMAL: They're called life savings for a reason. You spend them on things that will save your life.

APSARA: How am I going to save your life?

KAMAL: We'll need all the money we have for our life together when you leave this place. So please don't make me pay you.

APSARA: You have quite an imagination.

KAMAL: Fine. Here's three thousand more.

But KAMAL does not move.

APSARA: Where is it?

KAMAL: Oh, you noticed.

He blows her a kiss.

The currency of love.

APSARA: What a nightmare.

KAMAL: Love is full of nightmares, my dear. I learnt that as a child.

APSARA: How touching.

KAMAL: Love is a big fat flower. Petal by petal it unfolds. Then it gets thinner and sicker, sicker and thinner, until it is just a stalk. Sharp enough to poke someone in the eyes with.

APSARA: Is that what happened to you? Did someone poke you in the eyes and cause you to lose your sight?

KAMAL: What beast would do such a thing?

APSARA: One of your customers, perhaps. After reading the rubbish you tried to sell him.

KAMAL: That's funny. It's funny that someone who should be wracked with guilt is so . . . so frivolous about my blindness.

APSARA: Guilt? Why would I be wracked with guilt?

His tone changes.

KAMAL: Because *you're* the reason I'm blind.

APSARA: What?

KAMAL: You took my sight away.

APSARA: Have you lost your mind?

KAMAL: I was ten when it happened. In the village of Vajra.

APSARA: Vajra? But that's where . . .

KAMAL: You're from. Your mother's name is Padma. Your father's name is Vishnu. He's a priest.

APSARA: Look—who are you?

KAMAL: I am ten years old. You are three. You're walking around a fire. There's smoke in your eyes. You're crying out for your mother.

APSARA: How do you know that?

KAMAL: I was there.

APSARA: That's a dream I've had since I was little.

KAMAL: A dream? So you've converted our life into a dream. That's okay with me. The crackling of wood can be heard even in dreams. It starts slowly at first . . . faint . . . as though it isn't really there . . .

The sound of a fire.

Slowly, whatever KAMAL describes comes to life before them.

You're three years old and you're dressed in yellow. You're circling around the fire and its smoke is making your eyes water. But there are also tears. The sound of the priest chanting. You're scared and so am I. I'm scared, and as we circle the fire I look at you, a sorry three-year-old girl, crying for her mother, begging her to take you away. And I'm ashamed of myself. Even though it's not my fault, I feel responsible for making you scared. And all those people. Those stupid, stupid villagers with grins on their faces as though we were in a circus, you and me, two little monkeys getting married. That's what it felt like. We were monkeys forced to walk round a fire by our parents. And then I did it. I touched you. I held your hand out of pity because you were more scared than I. And the moment I did that, a blinding flash of light . . .

A blinding flash of light on stage.

. . . like a rod of lightning had pierced my eyes, as though my pupils had committed some horrible crime and needed to be punished. And then it was I who was screaming for my mother. I should have run into the flames, Apsara. I'm sorry that I ran the other way, into the crowd. Into that dumb, sweaty, brain-fucked crowd.

Pause.

So let me ask you now: Do you know who I am?

She is nervous. She gets up.

He senses this.

Don't try to leave.

He moves towards her.

You took my sight. Now I want it back.

She tries to move away from him, but he senses where she is.

He is like a predator now waiting to pounce on her.

She is extremely still, aware that he can sense the slightest movement.

Your touch made me blind all those years ago. If I touch you again, I will see. That's why I'm here. I want you to hold my hand, Apsara. Give me my sight back.

He extends his arm to her.

She does not take it.

Don't make me force you.

She makes a run for it.

He grabs her.

APSARA: I don't remember any of this. I swear.

KAMAL: There's only one thing you need to remember. My name is Kamal. I, my dear, am your husband.

7.

APSARA *is seated, clearly disturbed by what has just transpired.*

PADMA *enters.*

PADMA: What did he want? What did you find out about the blind man?

APSARA: When was the first time I dreamt about the fire?

PADMA: What difference?

APSARA: Just tell me.

PADMA: You must have been four or five.

APSARA: Are you sure?

PADMA: I remember it clearly. You came crying to me in the middle of the night. You said that you dreamt you were around a fire and there was smoke in your eyes.

APSARA: Then what happened?

PADMA: Nothing. I held you in my arms and put you back to sleep.

APSARA: Is that all you did?

PADMA: I whispered in your ear, "It's only a dream. Go to sleep. It's only a dream."

APSARA: Who is Kamal?

No response from PADMA.

Tell me about Kamal.

PADMA: I don't know any Kamal. What's wrong with you?

APSARA: I'm terrified, Mother.

PADMA: Of what?

APSARA: My husband.

PADMA: What? But there is no . . .

PADMA reaches to comfort APSARA.

APSARA recoils the moment PADMA touches her.

8.

Later. The same night.

There is a knock on the door.

The knocking continues.

APSARA *slowly finds her way to the door in the darkness. But she does not open it.*

KAMAL: Apsara, it's Kamal. Open the door.

Pause.

I want to know if you're okay. Let me in.

APSARA: I want you to leave.

KAMAL: If that's what you want, then I will walk away this instant. But understand that every single day I live in one colour—black. A colour you are responsible for. I've had to learn everything all over again. How to walk. How many steps to take to go to the toilet. Each and every sound haunts me. To this day, I feel there are snakes at my feet. In the village, on my way to school, the children would shout, "Snake, snake," and I'd freeze in terror, until I heard their laughter.

APSARA: What do you want from me? Are you here for revenge?

She opens the door.

KAMAL: No. I don't want revenge.

APSARA: Then why are you here?

He enters.

KAMAL: Love. A mad love. A love so strong we could uproot trees with it.

She walks away from him and sits on the swing.

APSARA: I don't love you.

KAMAL: Not now, maybe. But in a day or two, who knows? In a day or two we could be lovers. You are an Apsara. And I am a lotus. We are bound together.

APSARA: What are you talking about?

KAMAL: The name Kamal means lotus.

APSARA: I know that.

KAMAL: The very first Apsara lived in a lake with a single lotus. The two were inseparable.

APSARA: I am not a celestial nymph in heaven. And you are not a flower. We are in Bombay and there's shit on the road and it costs only a few hundred rupees to have someone murdered.

KAMAL: That might be true, but let us not forget what the name means. "The Good Bay." That's what the Portuguese called this city. So good things can happen here too, if you believe. Let us believe that I am indeed a lotus. The only time the lotus withered was when the Apsara left the lake on a mission.

APSARA: And what mission would that be?

KAMAL: Do you not know the story of the first Apsara?

APSARA: I don't like stories.

KAMAL: Centuries ago, when heaven existed, it had many gods. There was Brahma the Creator, Shiva the Destroyer, Krishna the Lover . . .

APSARA: Were there no goddesses?

KAMAL: Not yet. So at the end of the day, when these male gods were done creating mountains, rivers, and gardens, when they were done designing planets and answering people's prayers, they sat in heaven's court and someone suggested, "How about some dance?" All the gods loved the suggestion, so they created this beautiful woman. The world's first Apsara. She danced for them and all the gods were mesmerized.

APSARA: They became like vegetables. Each and every god wanted Apsara to himself.

KAMAL: So you do know the story.

APSARA: No, but I know men.

KAMAL: The gods started using their powers against each other. Shiva released cobras from his matted hair and choked Brahma's throat. Krishna transformed his flute into a spear and hurled it at Shiva. Suddenly the gods realized what they were doing.

APSARA: Fighting over a woman. A mere dancer. The shame of it.

KAMAL: They were so enraged that they banished Apsara to a lake. The lake contained a single lotus. The Apsara and the lotus fell in love. But that love was not enough. The Apsara left the lake to seek revenge on the gods. The moment she left, the lotus started to wither.

APSARA: Did she get her revenge?

KAMAL: She secretly went to each god and professed her love. She danced for the god, sucked up all his energy, and killed him. Until there were no gods left.

APSARA: So what's the moral?

KAMAL: I find questions more interesting than morals.

APSARA: What's the question?

KAMAL: On whom does *this* Apsara want to take revenge?

APSARA: No one. Mythology is the poor man's diet.

KAMAL: The rich can afford to be realistic.

Pause.

A lotus cannot survive without an Apsara. That's why I'm here. I need you so that I may live. Come with me, my Apsara.

APSARA: I'm not going anywhere.

KAMAL: Can you hear that?

APSARA: Hear what?

KAMAL: The spinning of wheels. It's a horse carriage. All the lovers of Bombay go for rides on them.

APSARA: I don't like lovers.

KAMAL: Listen.

APSARA: I can't hear a thing.

KAMAL: The blind pluck things out of thin air. That's how we live. Darkness is a blank slate. Draw what you want on it. Listen. Listen to that carriage.

The sound of the carriage.

Hear its wheels spinning, grinding against the uneven road. It's coming closer. Now smell the *beedi* that the old man smokes as he rides his carriage. There is also the fragrance of flowers that are on the floor of the carriage. Take it all in. Now feel the horses. Touch the sweat on their backs. See their skin shining under the street lights. Can you see them? They're black. The horses are pure black. Smell them. Smell the shit they leave on the road below. Don't be afraid to smell the shit. The carriage is very close. Are you ready? We'll jump on the count of three.

The sound of the carriage gets louder.

One, two, three.

He sits on the swing. It becomes the carriage.

Sorry, excuse us. The old man looks a bit concerned. Ignore him. Look at the Gateway of India instead.

APSARA *is silent.*

Describe it to me.

APSARA: It's brownish yellow. It has four turrets and a central dome.

KAMAL: What else? Describe the scene to me.

APSARA *is silent.*

What do you see?

APSARA: Photographers.

KAMAL: Photographers?

APSARA: Yes, amateur photographers who take photos of the tourists beside the gateway for a few rupees.

KAMAL: What else?

APSARA: There's a *chaiwala* with a small kerosene stove selling tea in paper cups. There are stray dogs playing, there are workers asleep on the ground, and there's a security guard keeping people away from the gateway.

KAMAL: Now we're standing right under the dome. I can feel the heat of lights all over my body. Do you notice anything unusual about the gateway?

APSARA: No, nothing unusual.

KAMAL: The Gateway of India is now moving off the ground and sliding into the water. Quietly. Like a stranger sneaking into someone else's pool. It's floating on water, Apsara, and no one's on it but us. We will let it take us far out to sea. Now everyone from the Taj Mahal Hotel behind us is looking in astonishment. All those foreigners who stay at the Taj are calling their loved ones in London, New York, and Paris, "Bombay is demented. Buildings float on water." And their relatives abroad are replying, "Stop smoking that Bombay Black! It's all that Bombay Black!"

Pause.

We must be careful we don't collide into any ships. We just passed the *Vikrant.* Now we're approaching the *Sea Princess.* Now we're past the huge ships. We're so deep into the Arabian Sea even the fish don't wander here. So here we are, you and I, not a soul around, only the sound of the waves and the whisper of the wind to keep us company. Let's talk.

They stand in the middle of the Arabian Sea.

They listen to the wind and the waves.

APSARA: It's not possible. It's just not possible.

KAMAL: What?

APSARA: That one person can blind another by mere touch.

KAMAL: The universe is a complete bastard.

They sit in silence in the middle of the Arabian Sea.

So tell me, is it just you and your mother? Or does someone else live with you?

APSARA: Just us.

KAMAL: What about your father?

APSARA: We don't know where he is.

KAMAL: How long has it been since you saw him?

APSARA: Ten years. Why are you asking me about my father?

KAMAL: Because he's dying.

APSARA: What?

KAMAL: Your father doesn't have much time left.

APSARA: You know him?

KAMAL: He was the priest at our wedding. In order to find you, I had to start with him. I promised him that if I ever found you, I'd tell him. He wants to see you.

Silence.

He's dying. He wants to see you before he dies.

APSARA: What illness does he have?

KAMAL: He hasn't been to a doctor. He doesn't believe in them.

APSARA: Does he know where we are?

KAMAL: I haven't told him.

APSARA: Are you sure?

KAMAL: Yes, I'm sure. Why don't you want him to know?

APSARA: Where is he? The last we heard he had left the village.

KAMAL: He's in Bombay. Do you want to see him?

APSARA: No.

Pause.

No.

KAMAL: But the man's dying.

APSARA: Look—what the hell do you want from me?

KAMAL: I don't believe my sight has been lost forever. I think it's been banished to make way for something greater.

APSARA: Like what?

KAMAL: I don't know. All I know is that there's all this water around us. We're in the middle of the Arabian Sea. Step into the water with me. An Apsara belongs in the water with the lotus.

He steps into the water.

She does not. He senses this.

I don't know how this is going to turn out. Come with me. Right now, all I have to offer is the water.

9.

APSARA is alone in the room.

She is packing her suitcase.

PADMA enters.

PADMA: What are you doing?

APSARA doesn't answer.

Apsara, what are you doing?

APSARA: You need to pack. Pack your things.

PADMA: What for?

APSARA: We must leave. We must leave Bombay. We must leave before he finds us.

PADMA: Who?

APSARA: My father. Kamal met my father.

PADMA *stands still.*

PADMA: Are you sure?

APSARA: In order to find me Kamal started with him.

PADMA: He's alive . . . the bastard's alive . . .

APSARA: He's dying.

PADMA: Of what?

APSARA: I don't know. Kamal said he's very sick.

Pause.

My father wants to see me. We must leave at once.

PADMA: He wants to see you.

APSARA: We must move to another city.

PADMA: We can't keep running from him.

APSARA: We have to.

PADMA: What if you were to see him again?

APSARA: I can't.

PADMA: But suppose you *have* to.

APSARA: Why would I have to?

PADMA: Let him find us.

APSARA: What?

PADMA: It might be your purpose.

APSARA: My purpose? What the hell are you talking about?

PADMA: Let me rephrase it. What if it's your *function*—leading your father here. To *me*.

APSARA: To you?

PADMA: You know, when you use a piece of meat.

Pause.

There was this hunter once. And he was tired and hungry and wounded. A hyena had wounded him and now he was alone in the forest . . . tired and hungry . . . and if he did not eat, he'd die . . . so he cut off a piece of his own flesh, from his thigh, and left it on the ground and hid. The hyena came for that flesh and it was too distracted to see the hunter . . . and so the hunter got his chance—he killed the hyena.

APSARA: What are you saying?

PADMA: I'm saying that I'm tired and hungry . . . and . . .

APSARA moves away.

APSARA: You're out of your mind.

PADMA: And it's a beautiful, magical feeling.

APSARA: But what about me?

PADMA: What about you?

APSARA: I never want to see him again. You promised.

PADMA: You'll have to.

PADMA caresses APSARA.

Apsara, in order to survive, I will sacrifice my own flesh.

APSARA walks away from her.

Where are you going? I need you more than ever, my dear.

APSARA: What is wrong with you?

PADMA: Nothing. I'm finally telling you the truth.

APSARA: I'm leaving.

PADMA: Oh really? Here, let me help you.

She opens the door for APSARA.

APSARA *walks towards the door. Then stops. She is unable to leave.*

You can't even go out for a walk by yourself. You're terrified of being on your own. You need me, Apsara. You can't survive in this world on your own. You need me. Just as I need you.

PADMA *moves towards* APSARA.

There was a hunter.

She moves closer.

There was a hyena.

PADMA *pushes* APSARA. APSARA *falls to the floor.*

There was a piece of flesh.

End of Act One.

ACT TWO

1.

APSARA and PADMA on stage.

APSARA: Why didn't you tell me I was married to Kamal?

PADMA: What good would it have done?

APSARA: Whose idea was it?

PADMA: Idea? It's been going on for hundreds of years. To protect the girl child from being raped by sultans and warlords and whatnot, parents married off their infants when they were in their cradles. So don't worry—historically, you were well past the marriageable age. Kamal's family asked for you because your father was the most respected priest in the village. And Kamal's family owned land. The alliance made sense.

APSARA: Made sense? I was three.

PADMA: We had found a good match. There were two baby girls in the village who were drowned in tubs of milk simply because they were girls. But we kept you. So be grateful.

APSARA: What exactly happened that day?

PADMA: The moment Kamal touched you he went blind.

APSARA: How?

PADMA: Who knows? Perhaps it's nature's way of proving that it's more powerful than man. You were doomed right from the start, Apsara. A boy went blind the moment he touched you. The villagers wanted your blood. They started shouting that you were cursed, that you were a dangerous child. So your father announced there and then that if you were to devote your life to the temple as a dancer, it would appease the gods and it would prevent anyone else from getting hurt. That was the only way to calm the villagers down, those hungry, bloodsucking fools.

APSARA: And you let Father take me away?

PADMA: I objected. I refused to let you go. He said that if we offered you to the temple, the gods would offer us a boon. I would be granted a son. He was the head priest of the village, a learned man. I believed him.

APSARA: You sacrificed one child so you could have another.

PADMA: The universe plays us. We are pawns. We always sacrifice ourselves for something greater.

APSARA: A son is greater.

PADMA: A son will always be greater. It was a matter of face. How could I stand before my family and say, "My only contribution to this world is a *girl*"?

APSARA: But the son never came. That brother of mine was never born. What happened, Mother? Did you not appease the gods enough?

PADMA: Don't worry about the gods for now. Just make sure you appease *me*. Ask Kamal to bring your father here.

APSARA: I can't.

PADMA: Don't make this difficult.

APSARA: I won't do it.

PADMA: I see. Stay here. I'll be right back.

APSARA: Where are you going?

PADMA: To get some meat.

She exits and returns with a large chunk of red meat.

She puts it under APSARA's nose.

Smell this.

She thrusts it into APSARA's hand.

Squash it. Feel it between your fingers. Soon, your father will feel like that. Soft and dead.

APSARA tries to break away from her grip. But PADMA is strong.

She takes APSARA to the window.

APSARA: Where are you taking me?

PADMA: To feed the eagles. It's a little early for them, but we'll wait. Now I'm asking you again: Will you make Kamal bring your father to me?

APSARA: No.

PADMA: I see an eagle. It's far away, but it's coming.

APSARA: I don't like this. Please.

PADMA: Look at it. Those powerful wings. Now that's a *man*. If only I could have those wings over me for just one night. What a man an eagle is. A protector. A god. It's spotted us. Perhaps you'd like to lose your sight, just like your husband?

APSARA: Mother, please . . .

PADMA: Will you bring your father to me?

APSARA: He's dying. Let him go.

PADMA: He shall die by *my* hand. You will help me.

APSARA: I can't see him again. Please.

PADMA: Listen. Listen to that sound.

The frenzied sound of eagles, frighteningly loud and close.

PADMA presses the meat against APSARA's face.

Will you help me?

APSARA: I will . . .

She lets go of APSARA.

PADMA: *(to eagles)* Come, my children. Come to Padma.

2.

Afternoon.

KAMAL and APSARA are together.

They sit in silence for a while.

KAMAL: There are two kinds of silences. The first is a peaceful one. But the silence I hear right now, the silence that comes from you, is a loud, screaming silence.

APSARA does not respond.

You should have stepped into the water with me.

APSARA: What difference does it make?

KAMAL: We belong in the water. Together.

APSARA: Stories don't decide where I belong. I do.

KAMAL: By rejecting the water, you have chosen something else.

APSARA: What's that?

KAMAL: Revenge. The Apsara told the lotus that she could not truly love until she had taken revenge. The lotus begged her to stay, but the Apsara did not listen. When the Apsara returned to the lake after vanquishing the gods she looked for the lotus. She was crushed to find the lotus withered and dead on the surface of the water. She spent the rest of her days staring at her reflection in the water until she grew old, until she could no longer tell the difference between the ripples in the water and the lines on her face. Had she chosen water, things would have turned out differently.

APSARA: What would have happened?

KAMAL: We'll find out only if you join me.

APSARA: I don't understand you. How can you live in a story after spending so many years without sight?

KAMAL: If a snake bites you, what will you do? Will you spend your time chasing the snake, or ensuring that the poison does not paralyze you?

APSARA: Once the poison enters your bloodstream it stays there forever.

KAMAL: Why don't you want to see your father?

APSARA: Why do you care?

KAMAL: We must know everything about each other. That's the only way for us to find a way to . . . to *solve* this.

APSARA: Tell me to dance.

KAMAL: What for?

APSARA: Just tell me to dance.

KAMAL: Dance.

APSARA: No, not like that. Command me. Command me to dance for you.

KAMAL: Dance for me, Apsara.

They are in the temple.

She dances.

At first, the dance is innocent. It is the dance of a girl.

APSARA: Now let the force of your words turn a child into a woman.

KAMAL: Dance for me.

APSARA: Say it as if every bit of flesh in your body is reaching for me.

KAMAL: Dance.

The dance becomes seductive.

APSARA: Yes, Father. You are the most respected priest in the village. I am seven years old. Maybe eight.

She moves towards KAMAL.

She holds him, lies on the floor, lowering him as well.

She makes him lie on top of her.

She spreads her legs.

KAMAL tries to get off her.

APSARA holds him by the hair and prevents him from getting off her.

You said we must know everything about each other.

She pulls his mouth close to hers.

She is trembling; her voice quivers.

I ask my father what he is doing. He tells me not to worry. He tells me to close my eyes. I am seven years old. Maybe eight. I look at my father's face and his eyes are closed. He starts making sounds. His mouth smells of country liquor. So I turn my face away from him and stare at the white floor of the temple . . . and I feel my father's amulet against my cheek, the cold steel of his amulet . . . as he rocks back and forth . . . back and forth . . . and whispers into my ear, "I love you, Apsara . . . I love you . . . "

. . . And my father opens his eyes . . . he is pleased with me . . . he is full of sweat and he strokes my head, "You are the only thing I can ever love, Apsara . . . you are the only thing I love . . . "

KAMAL *finally breaks away.*

KAMAL: I'm sorry . . . I . . . I had no idea.

APSARA: Will you help me kill him?

KAMAL: What?

APSARA: I want you to help me kill him.

KAMAL: I'm not a murderer. The lotus had no part in the revenge.

APSARA: That's why the two didn't last. What if the lotus had helped the Apsara to seek revenge? Maybe the lotus would have survived. You won't have to lay a finger on him.

KAMAL: I won't allow you to kill.

APSARA: My mother will do it.

KAMAL: You speak of this as though you are killing a goat or chicken.

APSARA: So you think he deserves to live.

KAMAL: No, I . . . what good will it do?

APSARA: All you need to do is lead him to us. Tell him I want to see him. Tell him I live alone. That my mother and I are separated.

KAMAL: I won't lead a man to his death.

APSARA: You said you loved me.

KAMAL: But this is madness.

APSARA: You said it was a mad love.

KAMAL: This is not a game.

APSARA: Of course it is. "Close your eyes, Apsara. Don't tell mother otherwise I will kill her." Trust me. It's a game. Will you do it?

Pause.

You prefer to tend to the poison. I prefer to kill the snake.

He walks away.

Where are you going?

KAMAL: I . . . I don't know.

APSARA: Sit down. We're not done yet.

KAMAL: We're done. All these years I've been obsessed with finding you. I wanted to find the woman who blinded me. I wanted to find my wife. There's a part of me that does not believe my sight is lost. I came here expecting to find *something* when I touched you.

APSARA: No, that's not why you're here. You are here so you can bring me my father.

3.

PADMA and APSARA on the swing.

PADMA: Did he agree?

APSARA: No.

PADMA: Why not?

APSARA: He's too soft.

PADMA: Then make him hard.

APSARA: This is *your* little fantasy, Mother.

PADMA: My dear daughter. This is about killing the man who raped you at the age of eight.

APSARA: Seven. Not eight. If you're going to kill him, get the facts straight.

PADMA: When your father called us whores and suddenly banished us from the village, he was right about one of us.

APSARA: You could have fought him.

PADMA: I did. But he accused me of selling you for money. Everyone believed him. My own family spat on me. The entire village spat on us. Do you not remember? Or did you think their spit was nourishing rain? Perhaps you deserve to be spat on.

APSARA: Yes. All those days when I shivered under his body, as he kept whispering that he would kill *you* if I told a soul . . . yes, I deserve to be spat on.

PADMA: You were a beautiful, horrible child. I saw how he looked at you. I saw the way his eyes moved.

APSARA: You knew. You knew he wanted me and you created a little paradise for him.

PADMA: What wife does not look the other way? What wife can bear to see that the man she loves, the man she gave her heart to, is happier with a . . . with a child! It's what women do. We're taught to look the other way.

APSARA: It was your idea to send me to the temple.

PADMA: I told you. It was your father's. After the wedding, the villagers saw you as a threat. As something demonic.

APSARA: I understand.

PADMA: What do you understand?

APSARA: I was his universe. I understand how you feel, Mother. It's one thing to be abused. But to be humiliated and completely unloved . . . perhaps that's more painful.

APSARA smiles.

Yes, that is more painful . . .

PADMA: Tell me, in all these years, have I ever forced you to live with me?

APSARA stays silent.

Answer my question.

APSARA: No.

PADMA: Have I ever stopped you from leaving?

APSARA: No.

PADMA: Then why do you choose to live with me?

APSARA: I need you to put food in my mouth.

PADMA: On the contrary; I need you. Dance is your gift. Not mine. You could go and dance in any one of Bombay's bars. Bar girls make lots of money. Tell me the real reason you continue to stay by my side.

APSARA: That *is* the real reason.

PADMA: No, my dear. The truth is you are terrified of leaving, of being on your own. Even when we go to the market, you hang on to my saree like a little child. You live in my shadow because it makes you feel warm. You hope that by staying with me, someday we can put the past behind us and we'll have a normal mother-daughter relationship. You know, we'll have our quarrels, but we'll also chit-chat, watch movies, go for walks. But more than anything, you are looking for me to tell you that the pain you feel will go away. You want some *solution* to that pain. Now I'm giving it to you.

Picture this, my love: Your father will come to meet his beloved. The two of you will sit on this swing and talk. There will come a point when he will rest his head on your shoulders and you will comfort him, breathe into his ear like you did when he was on top of you. You will stroke his back, his smooth lizard's back, and you will think of the time you lay under him, trembling, your head turned to the side like a corpse, and that is when I will walk up to him, tap him on the back, look him in the eye, and . . .

PADMA moves towards the exit.

APSARA: Where are you going?

PADMA: To fetch Kamal.

APSARA: He won't do it. He's not a killer.

PADMA: Everyone's a killer. It's just a matter of incentive.

4.

PADMA enters the room.

This time she helps KAMAL walk.

KAMAL: You're helping me find my way this time.

PADMA: You scratch my back . . . or I'll scratch your eyes out.

KAMAL: There's not much you can do to me that life hasn't already.

PADMA: It's dangerous to think that way, my friend.

KAMAL: I am not your friend.

PADMA: Have a seat.

KAMAL: I'll stand.

PADMA: I'll keep it simple then. There is something I want from you.

KAMAL: I know.

PADMA: There is something you want from me.

KAMAL: I want nothing from you.

PADMA: You want Apsara.

KAMAL: Apsara is not yours.

PADMA: The problem with you is that you rely too much on sound. The most important things are unspoken.

KAMAL: Enlighten me.

PADMA: Hate makes for much stronger glue than love. Apsara and I are connected with a beautiful common hatred. A bond that will last a lifetime.

KAMAL: She can choose to leave you.

PADMA: It's been ten years since she saw her father. But he is by her side every second. It's the same with me. You can take her with you. But you will never have her. Only I can give her to you.

KAMAL: I'm listening.

PADMA: Bring my husband to me. And you shall have Apsara. After all, she does love you.

KAMAL: She said that?

PADMA: Not at all. But in all these years, she's never spoken to a man. Even the smell of a man makes her ill. She is at ease with you and it frightens her. She is afraid that you are a man who might be *good* for her. All she needs is for me to tell her that she can love. That she can *be* loved.

KAMAL: And you will do that?

PADMA: If you bring my husband to me.

KAMAL: There's no guarantee that she will go with me. She might still choose to stay with you.

PADMA: Not if I don't give her that choice.

KAMAL: What do you mean?

PADMA: I have no use for Apsara once my husband is gone. The only reason I kept her was because I knew he would come back for her. Once he is gone, I will go too.

KAMAL: What will you do?

PADMA: I don't know. I'll go back to my village. Watch children fly kites. Grow vegetables. And then one day, as I'm plucking my beloved tomatoes and carrots, I'll slice my throat. Or maybe I won't. In a way, my future is in your hands. Can you bring yourself to kill a child-fucker in order to gain Apsara?

KAMAL: I think I can.

PADMA: Don't think.

KAMAL: I can. I will.

PADMA: Then I shall give you your wife back.

KAMAL: I'd like to speak to her before I leave.

PADMA: I'm not done yet. I'd like to know about my husband. I need to form a fresh picture of him in my mind. It's been ten years. Would you mind answering a few questions?

KAMAL: Go ahead.

PADMA: What does he sound like? Is his voice still rough and raspy?

KAMAL: You don't need to test me. His voice is smooth.

PADMA: Ah, yes, smooth as ever.

KAMAL: Except when he coughs.

PADMA: Is he dying of TB?

KAMAL: He wouldn't say.

PADMA: What else?

KAMAL: What would you like to know?

PADMA: Does he live alone?

KAMAL: No, he has a servant.

PADMA: Man or woman?

KAMAL: An old woman.

PADMA: I see. Did he mention Apsara to you?

KAMAL: Yes. I told him I was looking for her. He said he didn't know where she was. He said that if I ever found her I should let him know.

PADMA: What else did he say about her?

KAMAL: That he would like to see her before he dies.

PADMA: Did he say why?

KAMAL: He wants to be at peace. He said she is the only thing he ever loved.

PADMA: Is that what he said?

KAMAL: Yes.

PADMA: Tell me his exact words.

KAMAL: I just did.

PADMA: Word for word. Say it.

KAMAL: "Apsara is the only thing I ever loved." That's what he said.

PADMA: Again.

KAMAL: "Apsara is the only thing I ever loved."

PADMA: Again.

KAMAL: "Apsara is the only thing I ever loved."

PADMA: One last time.

She exits.

KAMAL: "Apsara is the only thing I ever loved."

APSARA enters.

Apsara?

APSARA: Yes.

KAMAL: Before I fetch your father, I want you to be sure.

APSARA: What did my mother tell you to make you agree?

KAMAL: I just want you to be sure that you want him dead. Think hard. This is not something we can ever come back from.

APSARA: When I remember the first time I saw his cock, I want him dead. When I think of my mother and the fact that she knew what he was doing to me, I want *her* dead. The rest of the time I feel numb. It's like trying to decide if I should raise my right hand or my left hand to scratch an itch. Does it matter?

KAMAL: Is the itch really there?

APSARA: It's there. The itch is there.

KAMAL: I want you to take a good look at yourself.

APSARA: I know what I look like. I have mirrors.

KAMAL: A mirror is the last thing we should look at ourselves in. A reflection is a *likeness* of the self. It means we only see the things about ourselves that we like. We must use our hands. The lines on your hands correspond to the lines on your face. When you move your hands against your face, the lines fit in. The parts that don't are the parts that are wrong with you. Why is it that whenever we are in grief or shock, we put our face in our hands? Because new lines have appeared and we are trying to make sense of them. But the lines that *fit* will lead you to what's good for you. Trust me. Hold your face in your hands.

Slowly she does.

Now glide your palms across your face. Very slowly. Your hands will fit in. As though the lines are grooves.

She tries but nothing happens.

APSARA: I don't feel anything.

KAMAL: You're going too fast. Think of your face as a vault. And you have to listen to the clicks to get the combination.

She does. Her hand clicks in.

Do you feel anything?

APSARA: Yes.

KAMAL: Now pick a line on your face. Pick a line that fits really well into your hand. Can you find one?

APSARA: Yes.

KAMAL: Now pull it, gently, like you are pulling an eyelash that just keeps on getting longer and longer. Follow it. Let it lead you.

APSARA: I'm moving very fast. As though my brain is travelling at great speed along a thin railway track.

KAMAL: Follow it to the end of the line.

APSARA: I've stopped.

KAMAL: Where are you?

APSARA: I'm by a lake. It's very sunny. I know this place. I used to sit there alone when I was little. My mother used to meet me there. She used to bring me food because I was never allowed into the village. I used to sit there and imagine myself dancing on the water's surface. It's been ten years since I last saw the lake. I'm moving again. Slower this time. There's a row of coconut trees and a well.

KAMAL: Look around you.

APSARA: There's a small group of thatched houses. An old man is selling bananas from his small shop. The bananas hang like yellow garlands in front of him.

KAMAL: What else?

APSARA: I'm walking with my father. We stop outside the banana shop and I buy bananas from the old man. That's me; I'm three years old. I see a young boy appear from behind the banana shop. He's looking at me . . . but I don't know who he is. He's looking at me very closely.

KAMAL: Is he dressed in blue?

APSARA: Yes. How did you know that?

KAMAL: That boy is me. That was the first time I saw you. I was taking a look at my future bride.

APSARA: You're crying.

KAMAL: I was scared. I was ten years old and all I knew was kite flying. All I knew was how to run in the rain, and when the rain got too heavy I would use a large banana leaf to shield myself. My whole body fit under a banana leaf—that's how small I was, and I was being forced to get married. I kept looking at you and wondered what it all meant. But then I saw that you were tinier than I was.

    Pause.

Take a good look at that girl. Is that a girl who can kill?

    Pause.

Is that a girl who can kill?

APSARA: I'm no longer that girl.

KAMAL: Come with me. We can start a new life. Darkness is a blank slate. Draw what you want on it.

APSARA: I want to draw blood.

    Pause.

KAMAL: Then I shall deliver your father to you. But before I go, I need to know something. Do I frighten you?

APSARA: All men frighten me.

KAMAL: What I mean is: Are you afraid that I might be good for you?

She does not answer.

That's all I needed to know.

He leaves.

5.

APSARA is sitting on the swing.

PADMA: You will tell him I am dead. I died three years ago. Tell him I killed myself. That I ate rat poison. Yes, tell him that. For a while, I'll hide and watch. I'll listen to him whisper into your ear. I've never seen him do it. I want to see what it's like. When fathers and daughters are lovers, how do they speak to each other? I want to feel the electricity in the air. I want to taste the poison in the room. Then, once I've had my fill . . .

She produces a butcher knife.

. . . I will plunge this knife into his stomach. Let the knife remain there for a while. I'll watch him convulse. I'll look into his eyes, I'll comfort him. I'll place his head in my lap. Let him die in his wife's lap like a bleeding vegetable, as every husband should.

She places the knife in APSARA's hands.

Feel that. Feel its thickness. It's length.

APSARA: Where did you get this?

PADMA: I told you the butcher was a friend of mine. Feel that blade. It's enough to make you believe in love again.

APSARA: What if Kamal doesn't come?

PADMA: That's not an option.

PADMA takes the knife back.

APSARA: But it's been three days since he left.

PADMA: He'll be here.

APSARA: But let's just say that he doesn't show up.

PADMA: The eagles will be devastated.

APSARA: The eagles?

PADMA: Why do you think I've been feeding them meat all these years? I'm going to cut your father up into little pieces and feed him to the eagles. In this city, the undertaker comes flying right to your window and you don't even need a coffin. Isn't Bombay beautiful?

Pause.

I envy you, Apsara. You're a lucky girl. Your rage can be channelled to your father because of something that was done to *you*. My rage is empty. I'm angry about what he did to someone else.

APSARA: It's not my fault, Mother. It never was.

PADMA: I don't know. At times, I feel you're right. I want to wake up just one morning, just one single morning, and feel no rage. I want to look at the sea and feel like I belong to it. That it moves for me, at least one small ripple exists for me. But how can I be at peace when I don't know whom to blame?

APSARA: It burns you, doesn't it? You can't understand why I don't want my father dead.

PADMA: What I love about you, dear child, is that you cannot decide who you want dead *more*. Me or him.

APSARA: What did you tell him?

PADMA: Who?

APSARA: Kamal. What did you say to change his mind?

PADMA: Nothing.

APSARA: I want to know.

PADMA: It might change the way you feel about him.

APSARA: I don't feel anything for him.

PADMA: Then why do you need to know?

APSARA: Tell me what you said.

PADMA: Money. If he brings your father to me, he gets lots of money.

APSARA: I don't believe you.

PADMA: He's a poor bookseller. Money is more useful to him than a wife.

APSARA: Kamal doesn't think that way.

PADMA: You're right. Forget about it. Perhaps I made the whole thing up. You're right. Kamal's not like that at all. But this blade is getting cold. It needs warm flesh. I want your father, Apsara. If I don't get your father . . . I hope you haven't hatched a little plan with Kamal. I don't like being double-crossed.

APSARA: He'll be here.

PADMA: And how can you be sure? Perhaps he will knock on the door this very moment? Hah?

There is a knock on the door.

They both acknowledge the absurdity of the knock.

A knock again.

APSARA: That's him.

PADMA: *(to eagles)* The feast is about to begin.

She exits.

KAMAL enters.

He is alone.

He holds an earthen pot in his hands.

KAMAL: Apsara? I've come alone.

APSARA: You're not alone. He's here.

KAMAL: I've come alone.

APSARA: But the scent of him is so strong.

KAMAL: I've brought his ashes. Your father passed away two days ago.

APSARA is unable to move. She just stands still.

Apsara?

PADMA enters.

PADMA: What is it? Why are you holding that pot?

(to APSARA) Why is he holding a pot?

KAMAL: It's not a pot. It's an urn.

PADMA: Why are you holding an urn?

KAMAL: I went back to get him. He got up from his bed with great difficulty. I helped him get dressed. We started walking towards the door to come here when he collapsed in my arms. After a few minutes he stopped breathing.

PADMA: No.

KAMAL: I had him cremated that very night.

PADMA: But . . . you promised to bring him here. You promised. Why did you cremate him? We could have done something with the body. Why didn't you bring his body here? You're lying to me.

KAMAL: I'm not lying.

He places the urn on the ground.

This is your husband.

PADMA slowly moves towards it.

She looks into the urn.

She does not touch it.

PADMA: That's not him.

KAMAL: It's him.

PADMA: You couldn't go through with it. I knew it.

KAMAL reaches into his pocket and takes out an amulet.

KAMAL: Perhaps you will recognize this. His amulet.

He hands it to PADMA.

He exits.

PADMA: He never took this off. Even when he had a bath . . . he never took this off . . .

PADMA looks at the ashes again.

She sits cross-legged on the ground, the urn in front of her.

But he had a lizard's back. Very smooth. And his lips were quite thin, almost like a woman's. And his breath . . . it was full of country liquor . . .

She smells the ashes.

This doesn't smell like him . . .

She kneels and finally puts her hand in.

He used to sweat a lot. This is dry, so dry . . .

She picks up some ash.

Is this what your skin felt like when you were old? Is this . . . is this you . . . tell me if it's you . . . come on . . . touch me . . . say something . . . please touch me . . . here . . .

She rubs the ash on her arms, slowly.

Feel me . . . please . . .

She slowly starts smearing the ashes all over her face.

Is this you? Feel me, please . . . touch me. Is this you . . . tell me this is you . . .

6.

PADMA and APSARA are seated.

PADMA still has ash all over her.

PADMA: Years and years of treachery in a pot. That's love. A woman can love a man. But a man cannot love back. When a man says, "I love you," he means, "I will cause you so much pain that your heart will eat itself." You give a man all you have. At the end of the day he will scorn you because he has cunt hair stuck between his teeth.

Pause.

I don't think you should see Kamal anymore.

APSARA: Why not?

PADMA: Because you care about him.

APSARA: I don't.

PADMA: No matter where you look, you will see your father. When you kiss Kamal, you will taste your father's tongue. His hands will be your father's. His voice will turn into your father's. I don't think you should see Kamal anymore.

APSARA: I feel responsible for what's happened to him.

PADMA: But it's impossible for him to love you.

APSARA: And why is that?

PADMA: Because you're not a woman. You're a piece of meat shaped by your father. At a time when most children were singing songs, playing in the village fields, you were turning rotten. You have nothing to offer.

APSARA: You're scared, aren't you?

PADMA: Of what?

APSARA: You're scared that I may leave this place. Leave *you.*

PADMA: Why would I be scared?

APSARA: Because now that father's dead, you have nothing to live for. But you'll still live long—*very* long—but it will be a life without revenge, without a daughter upon whom you can unload your spleen. You're scared, Mother; I know it.

PADMA: I'm not scared. You never meant anything to me.

APSARA: Then hold me. Hold me, Mother.

PADMA does not respond. So APSARA holds PADMA. PADMA moves away.

Why can't you hold your own child?

PADMA: Because you remind me of your father.

APSARA: No. I remind you that I am yours. You love me.

PADMA: I don't.

APSARA: Then prove it. Hold me close. You shouldn't feel a thing.

PADMA reluctantly holds APSARA.

You're trembling, Mother.

PADMA is unable to speak.

I forgive you. I forgive you, Mother.

PADMA cannot go on. She tries to break away. APSARA holds on and does not let go.

Finally, she stands. PADMA is still seated.

She looks down at PADMA.

I forgive you.

7.

APSARA is seated on the swing.

KAMAL enters.

KAMAL: I've come to say goodbye.

APSARA: I see.

KAMAL: I think you should say goodbye too.

APSARA: Goodbye.

KAMAL: Not to me. Say goodbye to this place. To your mother.

She does not answer.

We can help each other. Make each other happy.

The shadow of PADMA looms in the background.

APSARA: You should leave.

KAMAL: I'm not leaving without you.

APSARA: I can still feel my father's ashes lingering in the air. They're falling against my face. Maybe he'll never leave. I want you to leave, Kamal.

KAMAL: In the past, when you saw a man—his face, his eyes, his hair, his chest—you saw your father. And it repulsed you, it made you angry. Every man looked the same through your eyes. But with me you have found a man who is *not* your father. I know you care about me.

APSARA: But can I trust you?

KAMAL: For that you'll have to close your eyes. And look through the eyes of the blind. Take my face in your hands. If the lines fit, I'm good for you. Look at me. That's all I ask.

He holds her hands. Puts them to his face. Then lets go.

Do the lines fit, Apsara? Tell me the lines fit . . .

APSARA: The Apsara chooses revenge.

KAMAL: No . . .

APSARA: But this time, she will need the lotus's help.

KAMAL: I don't understand . . .

APSARA: The lines fit, Kamal . . . the lines fit. My revenge is to leave this place.

PADMA's shadow disappears.

Are you ready to leave?

KAMAL: Yes.

She holds KAMAL's hand.

She whistles loudly.

A horse carriage gallops at tremendous speed.

APSARA: On the count of three. One, two, three!

They jump.

There is a strong wind against their faces as the carriage races.

The sound of the wind and the carriage is very strong.

KAMAL speaks above it, jubilant.

KAMAL: So you do trust me.

APSARA: I might learn to.

KAMAL: There's one more thing we need to do.

APSARA: What's that?

KAMAL: We need to fall in love.

The carriage rocks heavily as it gathers even more speed.

APSARA: It might take a few years. A few hundred, perhaps.

KAMAL: On land, yes. Everyone knows it's impossible to fall in love on land. Ask this old man. Even he will agree. Old man, can a man and woman fall in love on land? See? Even he turns his head to the sky and laughs.

APSARA: So what do you propose?

KAMAL: An Apsara and a lotus belong in the water. That's where we first met thousands of years ago. To fall in love, we must fall into the sea. Are you in the mood to do something dangerous?

APSARA: Yes!

KAMAL: Old man, I want you to take this carriage and dive into the sea. Oh come on, old man, help us. Throw away that cigarette and do something daring. We're about to fall in love. Shower some flowers on us, old man! Lovers need flowers! I demand some flowers!

The horses rear up.

The carriage races at incredible speed.

A burst of flowers from the sky. They revel in the shower of flowers.

Take those horses over the seawall! Make us fly, old man! Make us fly!

The carriage jumps over the seawall.

Silence. They are in the air, high up in the air. Only the sound of the wind.

We're in the sky now, Apsara. We're so high we could pluck the moon and shove it up your mother's arse. This is wonderful. The whole of Bombay will see us tonight. People in the Taj Mahal Hotel will call up London, Paris, and New York and say, "I see flying horses. The whole of Bombay has gone mad."

APSARA: What will we do, Kamal?

KAMAL: Can I take a look at you?

KAMAL gently touches her face.

APSARA: A woman blinds a man by mere touch. And then they want to fall in love. How can such a thing be possible?

KAMAL: I don't know.

The sound of birds flying.

APSARA: Perhaps they know.

KAMAL: Who?

APSARA: The birds. Perhaps the birds might know how such a thing can happen.

KAMAL: The birds don't know.

APSARA: What makes you say that?

KAMAL: They're in the air all the time.

APSARA: The fish. The fish must know.

KAMAL: The fish think water is air, and its surface, sky.

APSARA: The trees, then. It is said that trees are wise.

KAMAL: Trees know a lot. But have travelled so little.

APSARA: What about the wind?

KAMAL: Would the wind be so restless if it knew?

APSARA: The moon then. Surely the moon must know.

KAMAL: The moon, you say? But the moon has no light of its own.

APSARA: The grass knew. But someone cut it.

KAMAL: If the stars knew, they wouldn't shine.

APSARA: And if God knew . . .

KAMAL: . . . would he compose this symphony of idiots?

Pause.

I can see that it's going to be very easy.

APSARA: What is?

KAMAL: Falling in love with you. Then having you crush my heart to bits.

APSARA: Ever so gently I will step on your red thumping heart and all that love will ooze like blood, and my mouth will water because that's what I was born to do.

End of play.

BHOPAL
Rahul Varma

To my father, Dr. Daya Ram Varma (August 23, 1929–March 22, 2015), who conducted research on the survivors of the Bhopal disaster. His untiring commitment to victims was the motivating force behind the character of Dr. Sonya Labonté.

ACKNOWLEDGEMENTS

My thanks to India's pre-eminent theatre artist, Dr. Habib Tanvir, who conducted the very first workshop of this play on the basis of a one-page synopsis I showed him during his visit to Montreal in 1997. His workshop taught me how to approach this play. In 2002 he translated *Bhopal* into Hindi as *Zahreeli Hawa*. The productions in Bhopal and other cities in India under Habib Tanvir's direction is a dream come true. Dr. Tanvir's association with this play is a matter of great honour for me.

To directors Tapan Bose and Suhasini Mulay for their documentary *Bhopal: Beyond Genocide*, which exposed me to the heart-wrenching image of Zarina, a baby girl born after the accident.

To Satinath Sarangi, Rashida Bie, and Champa Devi, dedicated and tenacious activists who introduced me to many of the survivors of Bhopal.

To Mrs. Krishna Varma, my mother, who is an example of resilience.

To Paul Lefebvre, for his insightful dramaturgy and for the translation of *Bhopal* into French.

To Jack Langedijk, under whose direction *Bhopal* premiered in Montreal in 2001. His contribution to the play went beyond that of a director and production dramaturg.

To Guillermo Verdecchia, who sharpened my way of seeing this play. To dramaturgs Ann Van Burik, Peter Hinton, and Brian Quirt for their valuable thoughts. And to my friend Sally Han, who represents a turning point in my playwriting pursuit.

To Kathryn Cleveland, who played a much bigger role in the premiere production in Montreal than what the title of stage manager suggests. And to Tracy Martin for designing an eye-catching poster for the play.

To Ken McDonough, my friend, for editing my work with deep understanding of all I write. To Ted Little, Laurel Sprengelmeyer, Anisa Cameron, and Carlo Proto, whose mere presence is a source of confidence.

To my wife, Dipti, and my daughter, Aliya—their role cannot be described in a one-line acknowledgement. To my late stepbrother Sanjay, who was a committed environmentalist. To Ila, Sonia, Sarah. To my brother Prem Saroj, and to all my nieces and nephews, who keep my attachment to India alive.

I also gratefully acknowledge the Canada Council for the Arts, the Conseil des arts et des lettres du Québec, and Conseil des arts de Communauté Urbaine de Montréal for their financial support.

Thirty years ago, highly toxic methyl isocyanate (used in the manufacture of the insecticide Sevin) leaked from a Union Carbide factory in Bhopal, India, killing thousands of people while they slept, and poisoning hundreds of thousands more in what is now acknowledged as the worst industrial accident in history. The repercussions of this "accident" can still be felt. Over twenty thousand people have died to date and an estimated one hundred and fifty thousand people continue to suffer from the long-term effects of gas exposure: reduced vision and cancer, as well as respiratory, neurological, and gynecological disorders. Children of survivors are born deformed and endure severe menstrual disorders.

The Union Carbide site (at the centre of this populous city) has never been properly cleaned up. Chemical waste continues to poison people living near the abandoned factory. Testing conducted by Greenpeace in 1999 found cancer-, brain-damage-, and birth-defect-causing chemicals in the soil and groundwater in and around the factory site, at levels up to fifty times higher than US Environmental Protection Agency safety limits. Mercury levels were twenty thousand to six million times higher than levels accepted by the World Health Organization. A 2002 study by the Fact-Finding Mission on Bhopal found traces of lead and mercury in the breast milk of nursing women.

Shortly after the Bhopal disaster, *The Wall Street Journal* argued " . . . it is worthwhile to remember that the Union Carbide insecticide plant and the people surrounding it were there for compelling reasons. India's agriculture had been thriving, bringing a better life to millions of rural people, and partly

because of the use of modern agricultural technology that includes applica-
tions of insect killers . . . "

To what degree were these claims accurate or defensible?

Union Carbide and other companies that produced fertilizers, herbicides,
and pesticides were part of a massive effort during the 1970s and '80s known
as the Green Revolution. This term described a movement that aimed to increase food yields through the use of new strains of food crops, irrigation,
fertilizers, pesticides, and mechanization. The Green Revolution promised
to harness the power of science, technology, and industrial development to
tackle hunger in the developing or Majority World. Unfortunately, the prom-
ises of the Green Revolution were never realized.

The challenges to corporate attempts to control the basic building blocks of
life are critical. But the fight is an uphill one because the stakes and spoils are
enormous, perhaps unprecedented. Atal Bihari Vajpayee, the former prime
minister of India, has proclaimed that "biotechnology is a frontier area of science with a high promise for the welfare of humanity. [. . .] I am confident
that fruits of biotechnology would be harnessed for the benefit of millions of
poor people as we move into the next millennium."

Of course, science and developing technology offer great possibilities for
humanity. The problem lies in the responsible application and control of
those technologies. This problem is at the heart of Rahul Varma's play. He is
expert at revealing the web of interests—competing, colliding, intermittent,
colluding, opportunistic, overt, covert, conscious, and unconscious—that un-
derscore arguments and proposals about wealth and economic development.
His play is a powerful memorial and a tocsin. We would do well to listen, to
remember, to remain vigilant, and to resist.

—Guillermo Verdecchia
excerpted from the foreword of the 2004 publication of *Bhopal*

Bhopal was developed as part of Cahoots Theatre Projects's Lift Off program; Teesri Duniya Theatre's intercultural play-development program, Fireworks; and The Banff Centre's Playwrights Colony in 2000.

Bhopal was first produced in Montreal by Teesri Duniya Theatre at the Arts Interculturels from November 15 to December 9, 2001, with the following cast and creative team:

Dr. Sonya Labonté: Rachell Glait
Izzat Bai: Micheline Dahlander
Mr. Devraj Sarthi: Shomee Chakrabartty
Minister Jaganlal Bhandari: Ivan Smith
Madiha Akram: Millie Tresierra
Pascale Sauvé: Nikija Malialin
Mr. Warren Anderson: Frank Fontaine
Storyteller: Shalini Lal
Chorus: Andrea Cochrane, Cortney Lohnes, Young Choi, Dipti Gupta, and Aliya Varma

Director: Jack Langedijk
Stage manager: Kathryn Cleveland
Set design: Sheida Shojai
Lighting design: Andrew Calamatas
Music: Scott Murray and Brian Vockeroth
Poster design: Tracy Martin

The play was subsequently produced by Cahoots Theatre Projects at the Theatre Centre, Toronto, in 2003, directed by Guillermo Verdecchia; by Illinois State University's Crossroads Project in 2011, directed by Mark Baer; by Masquerade Youth Theatre, Chennai, India, in 2011, directed by Dushyanth Gunashekar; by Dramanon Hyderabad, India, in 2012, directed by R.K. Shenoy; by Bond Street Theatre and Epic Actors Workshop in New Jersey, Kolkata, Mumbai, and Nepal in 2012; by Natya Bharti, Washington, in 2013, directed by Joanne Sherman; by Shunya Theatre, Houston, Texas, in 2014, directed by Diane K. Webb; by the Bay Area Drama Company, California, in 2014, directed by Ravi Bhatnagar; and by Teesri Duniya Theatre at the Segal Centre for Performing Arts, Montreal, in 2014, directed by Liz Valdez.

The play was translated into Hindi as *Zahreeli Hawa* by Habib Tanvir and produced by Naya Theatre in India from 2002 to 2004, directed by Habib Tanvir. The play was also translated into French by Paul Lefebvre and was produced by Théâtre Sortie de Secours at Théâtre Periscope in Quebec City in 2005 and at Espace Libre in Montreal in 2006. *Bhopal* was most recently translated into Punjabi as *Khamosh Chiragan Di Daastan*, and produced by Manch Rangmanch, India, in 2013, translated and directed by Kewal Dhaliwal.

SPECIAL CREDIT

The song "Ek Zahreeli Hawa" was written by Dr. Habib Tanvir especially for this play.

"Aise kihis bhagwan" is a tribal song from the state of Madhya Pradesh, which Dr. Tanvir found in his book archives.

CHARACTERS

Dr. Sonya Labonté: A Canadian doctor and an activist who works with slum-dwellers in Bhopal, India. She is the head of a Canadian NGO based in Bhopal.

Izzat Bai: A young mother who lives in a Bhopal slum.

Devraj Sarthi: Head of the Indian subsidiary of an American multinational called Karbide International. The company produces a pesticide called Karbide Thunder. He is an Indian national who was trained in the US and has returned to head Karbide in India.

Jaganlal Bhandari: Chief Minister of the state in which Bhopal exists.

Madiha Akram: An employee at Karbide International. She is the personal assistant and lover of Mr. Sarthi.

Pascal Sauvé: Canadian Deputy Minister on a special assignment in India.

Warren Anderson: President and the supreme head of the parent company Karbide International.

Chorus: Consisting of men, women, and children.

NOTE ABOUT THE CHORUS

The chorus plays a wide range of roles, such as police officers, photographers, ministers' aids, office workers, crowds, patients, and doctors' assistants. I have restricted the chorus to non-speaking roles and have underwritten its actions. The size of the chorus is flexible. The Montreal production had a five-member chorus, while the Indian production had over twenty members.

The play starts with a song. A dancer performs the "Ek Zahreeli Hawa"
(poisoned gas) dance.

SONG: Gaib say chalnay lagee jub
Ek Zahreeli Hawa
Dil kay phapholo say bhari
Kis kis kay nalo say bhari
Khamosh cheekho say bhari
Yeay kahan say utha rahi haiaisi dardili hawa
Gaib say chalnay lagee jub
Ek Zahreeli Hawa.

Ek mauzay lahoo aa rahee hai
Maut ki jaisi boo aa rahi hai
Kubooku suboosu aa rahi hai
Apni bayrangi maien bhi hai ek zara peeli hawa
Gaib say chalnay lagee jub ek Zahreeli Hawa

SCENE 1

A slum. IZZAT's hut. The police are taking SONYA away. A crowd follows them saying, "Police, police." DEVRAJ enters and stands at the entrance to IZZAT's hut. Slum dwellers start to converge at some distance, watching DEVRAJ. DEVRAJ knocks at IZZAT's door. IZZAT charges out of the hut.

IZZAT: Who is it?

IZZAT is shocked upon seeing DEVRAJ. She turns to the crowd.

Get the hell out of here, you no-good rascals. What are you doing here? Uh?

The crowd disperses.

(to DEVRAJ) Oh forgive me, *sahib*; I thought some police *wallah* . . . bloody father of law. Not a moment of peace from them . . . You forgive me, *sahib*?

DEVRAJ: Why do you seek forgiveness?

IZZAT: *Sahib*, I'm a poor woman, rotting in this slum. What do I know about law and order?

DEVRAJ: You don't need to worry.

IZZAT: How can I not worry, *sahib*? Who knows when one of them shows up, orders me to get lost, and flattens my hut . . .

DEVRAJ: That goat of yours . . . the one that died?

IZZAT: Yes, *sahib*. I'm not lying. My child lived on her milk. My own—my own chest, *sahib*—dried up long ago. I swear, *sahib*, my goat died. Do you want to check?

DEVRAJ: I believe you.

He gives her some money.

Here, keep this.

IZZAT: *Maherbani, sahib,* may God give you happiness, may you live a long life.

DEVRAJ: Let's go inside.

IZZAT: *Hai bhagawan.* My hut is uninhabitable for your comfort, *malik.* What can I offer you? My food may be too strong for your stomach. My water is undrinkable, for your standard. *(laughs)* Even I cannot digest my food, *malik*; how will you?

DEVRAJ: I need to talk to you. Let's go in.

They step inside the hut.

IZZAT: *Sahib,* I'll run to the tea stall. A *tarak chai* or *masala*?

DEVRAJ: Don't bother.

IZZAT: I'm a poor woman, *sahib,* but I can't let you leave without sweetening your mouth, *sahib* . . . Won't be long. Just from across the street . . .

DEVRAJ: Just stay. I don't have much time.

The feeble sound of a baby is heard from a wooden basket. IZZAT *picks up the basket.*

What's that?

IZZAT: My Zarina! My little daughter.

DEVRAJ *looks inside.*

DEVRAJ: Oh God! What has happened to her?

IZZAT: Don't let her fool you, *sahib.* She's a tough little monkey. God willing, she'll make me smile one day.

DEVRAJ: Did you bring her to a doctor?

IZZAT: Dr. Sonya Labonté, *sahib*; lady doctor Sonya!

DEVRAJ: Oh really! She's a good doctor . . .

IZZAT: But she doesn't know what Zarina has.

DEVRAJ: Well, does she know what you have?

IZZAT: Me, *sahib*?

DEVRAJ: You have poverty. Does the lady doctor Sonya know this?

IZZAT: What?

DEVRAJ: If you weren't poor, Zarina wouldn't be sick.

IZZAT: What are you saying, *sahib*?

DEVRAJ: Your little Zarina—she wasn't born sick, was she?

IZZAT: She, *sahib*? She was so sweet; her skin so smooth, so shiny, she looked like an angel at birth. Now she's always sick.

DEVRAJ: Of course. I don't know how you survive surrounded by filth.

IZZAT: Cleaning up filth costs money, *sahib*. Where's the money?

DEVRAJ: It's the filth that's the mother of all diseases. Among animals and among children! Someone told me there are other babies sick like Zarina. And they go to see this lady doctor, Dr. Sonya?

IZZAT: Yes, yes. I know them. I bring her patients.

DEVRAJ: Are they getting better?

IZZAT: Well . . . Veena, her baby . . . no! Budhiya . . . no, no, no, they don't get better.

DEVRAJ: Do you know Dr. Hans Weil?

IZZAT: No, *sahib*.

DEVRAJ: He lives behind the factory.

IZZAT: The yellow house?

DEVRAJ: That one. The yellow house! He is a tall man.

IZZAT: Pink skin. Thick cigar. I know who it is.

DEVRAJ hands her a card.

DEVRAJ: Give him this. Take Zarina to him.

IZZAT: Yes.

DEVRAJ: And if anybody's animal dies, let me know. I will compensate.

IZZAT: Shanta's goat died yesterday, and Kachari's pig passed away last week. You give me the money, *sahib*, and I will give it to them.

DEVRAJ: Thank you, but I'd prefer to give them the money myself.

IZZAT: *Theek hai, sahib.*

DEVRAJ: You give me the names of the mothers who visit this Dr. Sonya for their sick children.

IZZAT picks up the basket. She holds DEVRAJ's card in her hand. As she says the names of other women, DEVRAJ repeats after her.

IZZAT: Sure, *sahib*. Sure. Here. Veena, Budhiya, Kasturi, Shanta, Farida, Phoolmati, Babban, Meeta, Imarti, Roshni, Rani . . .

DEVRAJ: Not a word of that to Dr. Sonya. This is between you and me. Can you keep it that way?

IZZAT: My lips are sealed. I give you my word, *sahib*.

DEVRAJ leaves. IZZAT says blessings for him.

SCENE 2

A detention cell. Chief Minister JAGANLAL *is speaking to* SONYA *Labonté.*

SONYA: For kidnapping?

JAGANLAL: Yes, for kidnapping.

SONYA: Have you gone completely insane?

JAGANLAL: Is that the way you talk to the chief minister?

SONYA: Who is charging me?

JAGANLAL: Dr. Labonté, I trusted you. I gave you a seat on the advisory board of one of my most important missions. I even granted you privileges reserved only for Indians. How can you stand there and tell me with a straight face that you were not abusing the privileges I granted you?

SONYA: Abusing? I have simply been carrying out the research you—

JAGANLAL: We both know you've been doing a great deal more than that. You have lost your perspective and completely overstepped the boundaries of your study.

SONYA: I'm just trying to help the women in your city. It's obvious what the problems are. Karbide is poisoning the—

JAGANLAL: Doctor, these are unfounded, uncorroborated allegations and—

SONYA: Have you read my research? Did you read any of the interim reports? Can anyone in your office read?

JAGANLAL: Your research will be impounded until we get to the bottom of this scam.

SONYA: You haven't even looked at it!

JAGANLAL: Whether or not I have read your material is not the issue, Doctor. The issue is kidnapping. You have tried to smuggle two Indian citizens out of the country.

SONYA: I need to call my embassy.

JAGANLAL: You *need* to?

SONYA: I'm a Canadian citizen.

JAGANLAL: Therefore what?

SONYA: I am a field physician with a UN-sanctioned NGO.

JAGANLAL: I've seen many such missionaries from the West.

SONYA: Mr. Minister, you can't do this to me!

JAGANLAL: Yes I can. Poor, hungry, destitute they may be, Doctor, but the children of my country are sacred.

JAGANLAL exits.

SCENE 3

A detention cell. Canadian diplomat Pascal SAUVÉ enters.

SAUVÉ presents his business card to SONYA.

SAUVÉ: Pascal Sauvé, Government of Canada.

SONYA: They won't tell me who is charging me.

SAUVÉ: It's my duty to help troubled Canadians abroad.

SONYA: They're trying to bury my research.

SAUVÉ: Well, then let's get you out of here.

SONYA: These charges are completely trumped up. The minister or somebody close to him doesn't like the work I'm doing and they've invented this. My research points to some very serious problems and they think they can scare me and I'll just stop.

SAUVÉ: Doctor, all I want to do is get you back home safely.

SONYA: I don't want to go home. I want to get out of here, clear my name, and do my work.

SAUVÉ pulls some papers from his suitcase.

SAUVÉ: Well, first we need to work through some problems before we can say what will happen.

SONYA: You believe me, don't you?

SAUVÉ shows her a document.

PASCAL: This, I believe, is yours.

SONYA: What's that?

PASCAL: A requisition for two plane tickets.

SONYA: Okay.

SAUVÉ pulls out a visa document.

SAUVÉ: And a visa application for Izzat.

SONYA: Isn't that supposed to be confidential?

SAUVÉ: What? The application or the fact that you signed for her?

SONYA: Nothing wrong with that! She gave me the right to—

SAUVÉ: Nothing to worry about then.

SAUVÉ points at the photograph on the visa document.

So you know this woman?

SONYA: Izzat. Yes.

SAUVÉ: What is your relationship with her?

SONYA: She's one of my study subjects.

SAUVÉ: What did you tell her, Dr. Labonté?

SONYA: About what?

SAUVÉ: I need to know what you told her.

SONYA: (frustratedly) I told her I was doing a study on women's health. That I would be collecting data pertaining to women's reproductive health in the slum. I would be examining women and their babies.

SAUVÉ: And did you promise her treatment if she came to Canada?

Flashback: SONYA's clinic. IZZAT is lying on the floor. SONYA is giving IZZAT a pelvic exam. Members of the chorus have become SONYA's assistants. Zarina's basket sits nearby.

IZZAT: My stomach burns, feels hot inside.

SONYA: Are you menstruating normally?

IZZAT: I bleed a lot.

SONYA: Thick and dry?

IZZAT: A lot of mucky blood.

SONYA: Open your legs.

IZZAT: No, *doctorni sahiba*, no, my . . . this thing is a mess.

SONYA: I will have to send you to Dr. Bhalerao.

IZZAT: I don't need this thing anymore. Zarina's father is dead.

SONYA: That's okay. You may sit up. Dr. Bhalerao must see this.

IZZAT stands and picks up Zarina's basket.

IZZAT: Don't worry about me, *doctorni sahiba*; you help Zarina.

SONYA starts examining Zarina.

SONYA: And her lungs are . . . weak, Izzat. Her breathing? It's difficult, hard for her. I don't know—I can't tell right now if there's actual tissue damage to the lungs but . . .

IZZAT: Why, Doctor?

SONYA: Well, again it's difficult to say exactly, Izzat. There are any number of factors involved, many reasons. But given your own condition, the discharge, the cervical erosion—and its consistent with what I'm seeing in a lot of the other women—I think there's a contaminant, poisons, in your body that got into Zarina's body, and—

IZZAT: You help Zarina?

SONYA: Izzat, there's not much I can do here. Her arm is not going to grow. Her breathing . . . Give her clean water, Izzat, clean milk. Keep her close, warm, hold her. We can keep her comfortable. I can't promise—

IZZAT scoops Zarina up from the basket and moves away.

IZZAT: No. The company doctor says Zarina—

SONYA: What? Did you go to the company doctor? Hans Weil? Did you? Dr. Hans Weil?

IZZAT: Uh?

SONYA: Big hair, moustache?

IZZAT: No.

SONYA: Good.

IZZAT: He came to see me.

SONYA: Give me a straight answer, Izzat.

IZZAT: Sarthi *sahib* came by my hut. He said he wants to help me.

SONYA: Mr. Devraj Sarthi . . . the president of Karbide . . . he came to your hut?

IZZAT: To help me.

SONYA: Money?

IZZAT: God bless his soul.

SONYA: Oh yes, God bless his soul; he'll help you all right. He's the one making the poison.

IZZAT: How do you talk?

SONYA: You are forbidden to see another doctor. You come to me if there's a problem, Izzat. Go and wash up now.

IZZAT: I'm sorry.

SONYA: Just go.

> *IZZAT goes to wash her feet. SONYA follows IZZAT and shows her some photographs.*

Where are these women?

IZZAT: Hasina? Kasturi?

SONYA: And why haven't they come to see me?

IZZAT: They are not seeing anybody.

SONYA: But I want to see them. I need to examine their babies.

IZZAT: Women are not talking.

SONYA: Why?

IZZAT: That's what we do—we don't talk when we lose someone in the family.

SONYA: So the babies are dead? Their babies are dead?

IZZAT nods yes.

Where are the bodies? When did they die? Why didn't you come and get me? They are crucial to my study.

IZZAT: You never told me.

SONYA: Listen to me carefully, Izzat. What I'm doing is good for you. Understand? What I am doing for you is something nobody else would do. And it's the best thing for Zarina. Do you understand? That's what we talked about and you signed it.

IZZAT: Thumbprint?

SONYA: Right, and you didn't tell anyone, did you?

IZZAT: Plan to go to Canada? Zarina and me? Thumbprint. No.

SONYA: Good.

SONYA returns to her charts and files, making notes. The flashback ends.

SAUVÉ: Dr. Labonté, we didn't give you a grant to fly Izzat to Canada, did we?

SONYA: I did what's best for my patient.

SAUVÉ: She's not your patient. She is a study subject.

SONYA: She is my patient. These women, they don't have doctors. They don't have—

SAUVÉ: What about this company doctor?

SONYA: That doctor is ex-Pentagon.

SAUVÉ: Well, Doctor, we fund non-governmental organizations to promote Canadian values abroad, not to—

SONYA: You want me to ignore what is happening to these women? Is that a Canadian value? Karbide is violating more than one of India's laws! The Obnoxious Industry Law says companies like Karbide have to be at least fifteen miles from populous areas.

SAUVÉ: There are so many laws it is impossible not to break a few. But that's a matter for the Indian officials. Their laws are their business.

SONYA: I can show you my research—or I could if I knew where it was— Karbide is draining toxic waste into the lake, the pond. The children *play* in that water . . . people bathe in it and fall sick of diseases unknown to medical science.

SAUVÉ: Unknown to medical science?

SONYA: If you want to see a human baby that is not necessarily a human baby, go to the slum.

SAUVÉ: Dr. Labonté, I advise you to sign this.

SONYA: I'm not signing anything.

SAUVÉ: You are in serious trouble, Doctor. I can get you out of here and back to Canada if you sign this.

SONYA: So they can say I'm guilty? I'm not quitting. These women need me.

SAUVÉ: Well, I leave you to weigh your options.

SAUVÉ exits.

SCENE 4

The waiting area of DEVRAJ's *office.* SAUVÉ *enters.*

SAUVÉ: I'd like to speak to Sarthi Devraj.

MADIHA: Devraj Sarthi. I'm sorry, but he's not here.

SAUVÉ: When will he be in?

MADIHA: Tomorrow morning at eight a.m.!

SAUVÉ: Then I shall come back tomorrow morning.

MADIHA: Maybe I can help you.

SAUVÉ starts to leave.

SAUVÉ: No, thank you, I need to talk to him directly.

MADIHA: I am his executive assistant, you know. I sometimes know more about what goes on here than he does.

SAUVÉ stops.

So, what kind of trouble is he in?

SAUVÉ: Do you know a Dr. Sonya Labonté?

MADIHA: Yes.

SAUVÉ: Have you ever spoken to her?

MADIHA: Yes, many times. That woman keeps trying to destroy this company.

SAUVÉ: Pardon me?

MADIHA: She accuses us of the most outrageous things.

SAUVÉ: Such as?

MADIHA: All Mr. Sarthi does is help these people.

Flashback: DEVRAJ'*s office.* IZZAT *enters with her basket.* MADIHA *notices her with some annoyance.*

IZZAT: *Memsahib, memsahib, memsahib.*

MADIHA: I told you, don't call me *memsahib.*

IZZAT: I call *sahib . . . sahib,* so I should call *memsahib . . . memsahib.*

MADIHA: Is it a goat? What is it this time? A dog? A rat? We're not paying any more for your dead animals.

IZZAT: *Sahib* said . . .

MADIHA: *Chalo Raasta Napo.*

Beat. Her eyes on the basket, MADIHA *walks towards* IZZAT.

Let me see . . .

IZZAT: No! For *sahib!*

MADIHA: You probably kill them yourself just to get the money. You can dodge him but I'm not a fool.

DEVRAJ *enters.*

Oh, Mr. Sarthi . . . Mr. Sarthi.

IZZAT: *(to* DEVRAJ*)* I begged the *chowkidar, sahib,* because I wanted to show it to you right in your hand.

DEVRAJ: All right, show me what?

MADIHA: Another dead animal.

DEVRAJ: Miss Akram.

IZZAT: *(to* DEVRAJ*)* Look, look inside—

MADIHA: Which, I'm sure is not hers—

IZZAT: Getting worse, *sahib*. See one more time, please, *sahib*—

MADIHA: She probably picked it up from the street—

DEVRAJ: Wait, Miss Akram—

MADIHA: Don't pay her a *dhela*.

IZZAT: Oh, please . . . please . . . look.

MADIHA: She says the company kills their animals. They are doing it themselves.

IZZAT: *(to MADIHA)* No, no. You look.

MADIHA pulls away the rag covering the basket and is visibly shocked at what she sees inside. We hear Zarina's cry. IZZAT grabs the basket and runs to a corner. A hush sets in.

DEVRAJ: *(to MADIHA)* This is her baby.

(to IZZAT) What do you want me to do? Didn't you bring her to Hans? Dr. Hans Weil?

IZZAT: I did. But she's getting worse.

DEVRAJ: He will treat her. I am not a doctor.

DEVRAJ puts two one-hundred rupee notes in IZZAT's palm.

The flashback ends.

MADIHA: Mr. Sarthi goes out of his way to help these people and she tries—

SAUVÉ: Dr. Labonté?

MADIHA: Yes. She tries to twist it into something awful.

SAUVÉ: Does she?

MADIHA: Mr. Sarthi makes the company doctor available to these women and Labonté comes here, right into the office, and accuses the company doctor of stealing her patients, taking mothers and their babies from her clinic. Those women come here for money; they are very skilled beggars. It makes no sense. And she claims Karbide Thunder is poisonous. That the company is poisoning these people in their shacks around the factory. As if the company would do such a thing. We manufacture pesticides, you know. These chemicals, they improve the lives of everyone. If you could hear Devraj talk about how Karbide Thunder will change everyone's lives, you'd soon see that that woman has malice in her heart.

SAUVÉ: I see.

MADIHA: I see you're from Canada?

SAUVÉ: Yes.

MADIHA: Take her back, and keep her there. We have enough problems.

SAUVÉ: Thank you for your time.

SAUVÉ departs.

SCENE 5

Chorus members mill about as guests at a party hosted by JAGANLAL. Everyone is in a festive mood. DEVRAJ and MADIHA enter. JAGANLAL greets them with great enthusiasm.

JAGANLAL: Ladies and gentlemen, Mr. Devraj Sarthi!

DEVRAJ: Thank you, Mr. Minister. What have I done to deserve such an honour?

JAGANLAL: I want to shake your hand, Mr. Sarthi. You're a great NRI.

DEVRAJ: NRI?

MADIHA: Non-resident Indian.

JAGANLAL: Not really Indian! Har, har, har . . . and *aadab* to you, Madam? . . .

MADIHA shakes hands with JAGANLAL.

MADIHA: Madiha Akram, Mr. Minister.

JAGANLAL: How so very wonderful to see women acting as equals. You have no idea how much I have anticipated this dinner tonight. Are you prepared to make a speech?

DEVRAJ: Speech?

JAGANLAL: A little after-dinner speech!

MADIHA: Of course, do it!

DEVRAJ: On the People's Progress Zone?

JAGANLAL: How must I introduce you? People say you're blinded by your feelings for the poor.

MADIHA: No doubt about that.

JAGANLAL: And you're an animal lover.

MADIHA: In a strange sort of way . . .

JAGANLAL: How so? How can I point that out?

MADIHA: He created the Animal Charity Fund.

JAGANLAL: I've heard great things about that.

DEVRAJ: The Animal Charity Fund is a public service. Sometimes, especially now due to this drought, animals die and people leave the dead animals on the streets.

MADIHA: And when they start to rot they contaminate the drinking water.

DEVRAJ: Thank you, Miss Akram.

DEVRAJ turns to JAGANLAL.

Yes, in order to prevent disease from spreading, we encourage the people to bring the dead animals to Karbide International and we compensate them. That helps *them*, and certainly doesn't hurt our company image. That's what I call the Animal Charity Fund.

JAGANLAL: Animal Charity Fund, compensation . . . Brilliant! Just brilliant.

MADIHA: Charity.

JAGANLAL: Excellent. Until yesterday, America had sent India its hippies, druggies, and devotees. In you, Mr. Sarthi, I see a new man. An exceptional NRI who went to America to learn, design, and build, and then returned to heal his home country.

Flashback: DEVRAJ is being interviewed by ANDERSON for the post of CEO of the Indian branch of Karbide International.

ANDERSON: I know that, but what city in India?

DEVRAJ: From Lucknow, sir.

ANDERSON: And you've been with the company for eight years?

DEVRAJ: Yes.

ANDERSON: Now you want to go back home?

DEVRAJ: It's just the sort of challenge that I'm looking for. I was friends with the son of my family's maidservant when I was young. I used to give him half of my lunch at school. When we grew up, I got a business degree and he ended up pulling a rickshaw. It was winter when I left for the US and he came to see me off at the airport. I gave him my coat. As I walked through the gate I saw my mother, superior as always, walk up to him with a dirty look on her face and I'm sure an insulting taunt on her tongue. Right then and there, I swore to myself that I'd come back.

Beat.

ANDERSON: What are your thoughts on DDT?

DEVRAJ: In my opinion, sir, Karbide Thunder will replace DDT.

ANDERSON: You'd like to be known as the pest that killed DDT.

DEVRAJ: Because DDT has been found in bird populations.

ANDERSON: Aw, poor birds. *(testing him)* What about the millions it has saved from malaria?

DEVRAJ: But it's a carcinogen. I believe, sir, that Karbide Thunder is a superior product. Not only does it spare the bird population, it's also non-carcinogenic.

ANDERSON: I'm sure you're aware there are scientific studies that suggest there are other deleterious side effects.

DEVRAJ: I would put my faith in scientific studies if they truly prove the point they claim to be proving. But, we know, one study proves a product is a health hazard, another proves the contrary. So I plan to prove something that's beyond any doubt, and that is that Karbide Thunder is safer than DDT, cheaper to produce than DDT, and sure to tilt India's trade potential.

ANDERSON: And what about Karbide International, Mr. Sarthi? We are, you know, looking to improve our performance.

DEVRAJ: Sir, India offers us a competitive advantage in many ways.

ANDERSON: I have to tell you that India is looking more and more marginal to us, Mr. Sarthi. We need someone who will cut costs and improve productivity.

DEVRAJ: Sir, our offshore operations generate fourteen percent of revenue but account for twenty-three percent of our profits. I am confident that I can find ways to make our India operation more efficient and productive. Karbide Thunder is the key, sir.

ANDERSON: You think so?

DEVRAJ: I'm sure of it, sir.

ANDERSON: I like that, son. The heroes of this world are men who have a vision, and are willing to take risks.

DEVRAJ: If something can keep hungry millions from starving, it will more than make up for the risk. Believe me, Mr. Anderson, given the chance, I'll show you that Karbide Thunder will touch many lives.

The flashback ends. DEVRAJ *resumes his conversation with* JAGANLAL.

JAGANLAL: India needs more men like you.

DEVRAJ: India deserves a shot in the arm.

JAGANLAL: Shot?

DEVRAJ: Boost its production capacity.

JAGANLAL: All poor countries deserve a shot in the arm.

DEVRAJ: India is not poor, sir, it's simply forgotten.

JAGANLAL: It's about time somebody said that.

DEVRAJ: If we want the world to respect us, India's output must be increased tenfold.

JAGANLAL: Quite right!

DEVRAJ: Granted your approval, I am prepared to increase our production tenfold.

JAGANLAL: And reduce your costs, I believe?

DEVRAJ: We've discussed the People's Progress Zone. It's like a country within a country.

JAGANLAL: *Achha.*

DEVRAJ: Free of bureaucratic barriers, an area of deregulation.

JAGANLAL: Okay.

DEVRAJ: Such incentives are needed to increase the country's industrial base, to generate wealth, and, yes, to support our efforts to produce profitable chemicals.

JAGANLAL: Pesticides, you mean?

DEVRAJ: As you may have seen in my submission, pesticides have recorded a quarter century of sustained growth. Under the People's Progress Zone plan, we can manufacture upwards of five to ten thousand tons of Karbide Thunder a year. But the quantity is not the important thing.

MADIHA: It's the quality. Pesticides are peaceful. They are not like chemicals of war.

JAGANLAL: Right, they just war against pests . . . har, har, har . . .

MADIHA: Of course. The pests will not be given a chance to eat poor peoples' food and leave them to go hungry. But let me tell you one more thing, Mr. Minister. The life of an average Indian today, like myself, like yourself—we live better than the maharajas because of the kinds of chemicals Karbide produces.

JAGANLAL: Yes, yes. Although, Karbide Thunder is used for cotton, not for peoples' food.

DEVRAJ: But pesticides generally improve—

JAGANLAL: Of course. But I'm concerned. I've heard a rumour that Dr. Bhalerao is planning judicial action to stop the People's Progress Zone and Dr. Labonté's study is being cited as proof of—

MADIHA: That woman? She thinks Karbide Thunder is poisoning everyone. That woman just won't stop.

DEVRAJ: Miss Akram.

(to JAGANLAL) They are worried someone might drink Karbide Thunder.

JAGANLAL: Drink it?

DEVRAJ: As if someone would drink pesticide. But even if Karbide Thunder got into your body . . .

JAGANLAL: My body?

DEVRAJ: . . . it would only cause coughing, sneezing, and minor itching. Then it would be hydrolyzed.

JAGANLAL: *(sighs)* Aaah . . . *(thinking)* What?

DEVRAJ: Our company doctor, Hans Weil, confirms that it will roll out via the eyes.

JAGANLAL: Like tears?

DEVRAJ: Like tears!

JAGANLAL: Aaah! . . . Is your Bhopal plant identical to the one in the US?

DEVRAJ: Of course!

JAGANLAL: And Karbide Thunder will roll out of American eyes like ours, in the form of tears?

DEVRAJ nods affirmatively.

Any proof?

MADIHA: Mr. Minister, let us invite these people to this dinner and feed them Karbide Thunder.

DEVRAJ: Miss Akram?

JAGANLAL: What?

MADIHA: Yes! To prove that it will roll out of their eyes.

JAGANLAL: Brilliant.

DEVRAJ: Of course we wouldn't need to do that.

Transition to the after-dinner speech.

Mr. Minister, on the way to your office, I passed through the slum. It was filled with open garbage, the heat was suffocating, and the stench of human excrement was unbearable. I stumbled over drunken men, saw babies hanging from their mothers' breasts, and encountered stubborn seven- and eight-year-old boys with faces that said that if I didn't give them some change, they'd die of hunger. I met a woman, a poor woman, who told me that her first child died of worms that crawled out of its body. Why? How did this happen? There are those who will blame industrial development. Chemicals like our Karbide Thunder. Obviously, that is not the case; we always think of safety first. But environmental safeguards are irrelevant if we don't attack poverty first, for it is the poverty that is our greatest environmental hazard. Yes, my efforts aren't reaching the people yet. But with my plan in place, the benefits will trickle all the way down to the poorest of the poor. That's why we need the People's Progress Zone.

Applause.

JAGANLAL: That storm of applause is for you.

MADIHA: That was wonderful.

DEVRAJ: Really?

MADIHA: Yes.

JAGANLAL: Mr. Sarthi, that was a very moving speech. People in this room, my staff and dignitaries, froze as you talked, and we now know we want to hear more from you. Yes, you must boost production.

(announcing) Ladies and gentlemen, the first gift of the People's Progress Zone.

JAGANLAL sets his eyes on DEVRAJ.

Karbide will build seven hundred new houses!

DEVRAJ: Seven hundred new houses?

JAGANLAL: But of course! When you expand the Karbide complex . . .

DEVRAJ: But I don't remember promising seven hundred new houses . . .

Before DEVRAJ can answer, JAGANLAL walks up to him, stands face to face with him, and clasps both his hands in a traditional namaste.

JAGANLAL: That, Mr. Sarthi, must be the necessary gift of Karbide to my people.

JAGANLAL departs to loud applause from the chorus.

DEVRAJ: Well . . . in that case, I must name it Jaganlal Colony.

More applause from the dispersing crowd.

SCENE 6

The next day. MADIHA is in DEVRAJ's office. DEVRAJ enters and pulls her into his arms. She frees herself and steps away from him.

MADIHA: Did you see the look in people's eyes?

DEVRAJ: What people?

MADIHA: At the party!

DEVRAJ: People looked victorious seeing the look on my face.

MADIHA: What?

DEVRAJ: When Jaganlal volunteered me to build seven hundred new houses.

MADIHA: I'm not talking about that look.

DEVRAJ: What look are you talking about then?

MADIHA: The look that says, "Look at that slut."

DEVRAJ: Darling, don't start that one.

MADIHA: You know what people think about me?

DEVRAJ: Please!

MADIHA: I blackened my name for you.

DEVRAJ: We have talked about it many times.

MADIHA: So what are you going to do about it?

DEVRAJ: I have something for you.

DEVRAJ gives her a gift.

Open it.

Before she can open the gift, he opens it for her.

MADIHA: Devraj, what is this?

He puts a locket around her neck.

DEVRAJ: With this, I make you a promise.

MADIHA: Yes?

DEVRAJ: I'll be yours, I promise, but I can't handle marriage.

MADIHA: Then what's the promise?

DEVRAJ: Marriage like a sacred duty or marriage like a burden? What Mother wants for me? The way she married? It's not for me. We don't need to be married to be together, do we?

They embrace.

SCENE 7

One week later. JAGANLAL *visits the slum with his entourage. Reporters, cameramen, the members of the chorus as citizens and slum dwellers follow him.*

JAGANLAL: No, no, no. Don't take a photo yet. Over here!

Slum dwellers begin to assemble. JAGANLAL *notices* IZZAT *in the crowd.*

You, *bai!*

(calling) Would you? Yes, yes, please—come here . . . stand here . . . don't move.

He speaks in part to himself and in part to the media.

When I see a woman like you, *bai,* a voice inside me says, "Go hug her. Pick her child up in your arms, and give her your shawl."

He puts his shawl over her shoulders.

IZZAT: May God give you long life, *mantri ji.*

JAGANLAL: Okay. Now. Smile.

She does.

No, no, not like that, like this.

He models a smile and she imitates him.

Like that, okay.

Cameras start flashing.

I'm sick of having my photograph taken. If I catch any one of these photographers, I will shoot to kill . . .

IZZAT steps out of the photo shoot.

IZZAT: Me too, *mantri ji.*

JAGANLAL: I feel very close to you, *bai,* so close that I want to drink from your glass and eat from your plate.

IZZAT: Honour is all mine, *mantri ji,* but I don't have much on my plate.

JAGANLAL: Where is your hut, *bai?*

IZZAT: Do you see this *pagdandi?*

JAGANLAL: I'm standing on it.

IZZAT: This *pagdandi* snakes through garbage, shit, and dead animals.

JAGANLAL: Bad, very bad . . .

IZZAT: All the way to the pond. Do you see the pond?

JAGANLAL: *Haan, haan . . .*

IZZAT: From the pond one *pagdandi* goes this way—to the lake—and the other goes that way—to the company. There, my hut is there.

JAGANLAL: I have decided to demolish it.

IZZAT: Oh, no . . . oh no, please . . . I beg *mantri ji* . . . I'm a poor woman . . .

JAGANLAL: But I am going to do something about it.

IZZAT: *Mantri ji*, please, my husband lost everything to the bottle. And I ended up here. I made my hut behind the railway. The *chowkidar* . . . "hut *haramzadi*" . . .

JAGANLAL: Your hut—

IZZAT: Then, I made a home between the fences and the *mandir* and the *pundit ji* chased me, "*Chal bhag. Bhagwan kay ghar say.*" Then I go . . . under bridge . . . on sidewalk . . . by the gutter . . . "*bhaag, hatt bhaag.*"

JAGANLAL: Now, *bai*, your new house—

IZZAT: Finally I made this shack . . . my home . . . in shadow of *sahib's* company . . .

JAGANLAL: But having your home here doesn't make you legal.

IZZAT: In front of all these people . . . *mantri ji*, these people are my witness . . . I don't know rules and regulations. In front of all these people, *mantri ji*, I say I will not leave my hut even if you kill me. In the name of all these people, *mantri ji*, be merciful.

She shows him Zarina's basket.

I have a sick baby.

JAGANLAL: I'm sorry, this hut of yours will be replaced with a house!

IZZAT: What will happen to me, *mantri ji*?

JAGANLAL: You, *bai* . . . you will live in that house.

IZZAT: What?

JAGANLAL: Your hearing is fine, *bai*. You will own the house.

IZZAT: Me? House? Mine? But . . . but . . .

JAGANLAL: But what, *bai*?

IZZAT: It feels like a promise.

JAGANLAL: And didn't I promise a water tap in the *basti* last year?

IZZAT: We were hoping for some water from it this year.

JAGANLAL: Such life—such life here! You are the ray of hope.

(to media, crowd) This *bai* is right. I hereby announce—and you media people note me and quote me—through the authority vested in me as the chief minister and the head of the new Super Ministry for Trade Liberalization, I declare that Bhopal Lake, the connecting bridge, and the railway station—all this area surrounding Karbide International—to be known as the People's Progress Zone, a new, independent governing zone that will also be known as the PPZ.

IZZAT: PeePeeZeee . . .

JAGANLAL: The PPZ will be a model site. A country within a country with distinct rules! To help us help our people. To catch up on decades of under-development! As of today, all inhabitants of the Peoples Progress Zone will own the piece of land on which their illegal huts sit. *Bai*—

IZZAT: May God give you longest life, *mantri ji*; I'll have a real home. God be merciful, this means a ration card and right to vote!

JAGANLAL: This is not for your vote, *bai*. This is for real.

IZZAT: Oh?

JAGANLAL: You are the first citizen of the People's Progress Zone. Yes. And here is a sample of what your home will look like.

He distributes pictures of model homes to the slum dwellers.

This is for you. This, *maa ji*, this is for you.

IZZAT calls other slum dwellers. They are happy, comparing photographs of their prospective homes.

IZZAT: I live in this, in the paper. Imrati. Babu. Come here. Look, my home . . . window and indoor *snadas* . . . no more shutting the bowel from sunrise to sunset, no, noo . . . no more going behind the bush to do the business. And hey, look, a water tap.

SCENE 8

One week later. SAUVÉ, *who has just returned from the High Commission of Canada in New Delhi, visits* JAGANLAL. SAUVÉ *opens a document.*

SAUVÉ: Mr. Minister, may I be frank with you?

JAGANLAL: Please.

SAUVÉ: Either you free Dr. Labonté or lose India's preferred trading status.

JAGANLAL: One woman is more important than two countries?

SAUVÉ gives him a document.

SAUVÉ: As you know, our next bilateral trade summit is in Montreal.

JAGANLAL: I will say a line or two in French in my opening speech.

SAUVÉ: The problem is, sir, that Labonté is scheduled to speak at a parallel conference taking place next door to our trade talks.

JAGANLAL: Not if she's in my custody. I won't have anyone distracting attention from my presentation.

SAUVÉ: That's exactly what will happen if you keep her in jail. Protesters will throw themselves against the fences and throw tear gas at a time when the eyes of the world are set on our prime minister.

JAGANLAL: You want me to drop the charges against this doctor so your prime minister will have one less headache?

SAUVÉ: Quite frankly, sir, it is a trade headache.

JAGANLAL: I don't accept that.

SAUVÉ: Sir, it has taken years to prepare Canada for your trade mission. Our countries are setting an example in bilateral trade that will make the world envious. But when you and your trade delegation arrive in Canada, the media won't leave us alone, sir. Labonté is Canadian, after all, and her arrest is . . . dramatic. It will make things very difficult for us. Canada will be embarrassed and will have a hard time ratifying contracts and treaties signed with you.

JAGANLAL: Free a women who kidnaps mothers and children to badmouth my country abroad?

SAUVÉ: Sir, sooner or later the world will come to know that she wasn't kidnapping. She was just trying to bring a mother and her sick child to a conference in Canada. Forgive me for saying this—people would not only see her as a victim, but would also say that you caved in to Karbide.

JAGANLAL: That's nonsense.

SAUVÉ: Sir, I'm pleading for the success of our trade talks. If you don't sign her release, Karbide International will applaud you but Canadian trade and aid to India will not increase.

JAGANLAL: I do not appreciate blackmail from a trade partner.

SAUVÉ: Our government and transnationals don't want to have to answer embarrassing questions about the way a high-profile Canadian is treated by a trade partner. They'll be quite happy to invest in one of the seventy-five countries around the world whose GDP is less than their corporation's profit. You asked me to be frank; I'm being frank.

SAUVÉ retrieves the document and moves as if to leave.

JAGANLAL: What does the document say?

SAUVÉ: It contains an apology: she relinquishes all rights to her research and accepts a lifetime ban from working in India.

JAGANLAL: Bring her in.

SONYA is brought in forcefully.

Is this your first visit to India?

SONYA: First to a jail.

JAGANLAL: The children of my country are not your props.

SONYA: Nor should they be casualties of Karbide—

JAGANLAL: You have been here barely long enough to see a few malnourished kids and—

SONYA: And a lot of poisoned kids.

JAGANLAL: And you're in the habit of not seeing the millions of healthy kids.

SONYA: There aren't any healthy kids in the slums.

SAUVÉ: Well, madam doctor, Mr. Minister, I brought you both here—

JAGANLAL: I want to let this lady know something.

(to SONYA) Sit down.

She sits.

Maybe your research is accurate; maybe our housing project is a bad idea. Maybe the People's Progress Zone is a big mistake. Maybe the children of Bhopal are really unlike any human beings you have ever seen before. But I don't need a foreigner to exhibit a sick child of my country in a foreign land. Doctor, we can look after our sick. I resent white people showing me what's best for my people. Anyway, I didn't mean to say that. My last comment wasn't intentional.

SAUVÉ: We understand.

JAGANLAL: Mr. Sauvé has persuaded me to drop the charges against you.

SAUVÉ: You will sign this apology.

SONYA: Apology? For what?

SAUVÉ: That's the deal.

SONYA: Apologize?

SAUVÉ: And accept a lifetime ban.

SONYA: Are you out of your mind? I'll stay here.

SAUVÉ takes SONYA a few steps away.

SAUVÉ: Excuse me, Mr. Minister. Use your head, Doctor.

SONYA: Who would believe that bringing a mother and her sick child to Canada is kidnapping?

SAUVÉ: I don't think you live in the real world.

SONYA: Izzat wanted to go. She knew that it was the best thing for her and Zarina.

SAUVÉ gives SONYA an affidavit.

SAUVÉ: This is in English, Doctor! The woman didn't know what she was putting her thumbprint on!

SONYA: Bring her here and she will tell you.

SAUVÉ: She's the one who charged you.

SONYA: She did?

SAUVÉ: Look, Labonté, if you sign now, you can go somewhere else and carry on your research. Maybe—maybe you can find a way to get back to India and resume your work. On the other hand, if you want to be "principled," well, maybe the CBC will do a documentary on you, or environmentalists will circulate an online petition for your release, but you won't see daylight for fifteen years. Which one do you want?

SAUVÉ holds out a pen to SONYA, who is silent. He walks towards JAGAN-LAL. SONYA follows. SAUVÉ gestures for both to sign the deal.

SONYA: I'll sign this, but it won't shut me up. I'll sign this, but it won't silence me.

SAUVÉ: Mr. Minister.

JAGANLAL signs, then SAUVÉ adds his own signature. JAGANLAL extends his hand to shake SAUVÉ's, but SAUVÉ in return clasps his hands in traditional a namaste.

Marché conclu.

(to SONYA) This prohibits you from going near Karbide International and the PPZ. Your plane leaves December 3, 1984, at 0100 hours from Bhopal International Airport.

JAGANLAL: A government car will take you to the airport. My people will make sure you catch your plane with no inconvenience.

SAUVÉ: Congratulations, you are allowed to return to Canada.

SONYA angrily crumples the papers in her hands and exits.

SCENE 9

Outside IZZAT's hut. SONYA enters. Zarina's basket is absent.

SONYA: Izzat. How could you be so stupid?

IZZAT: *Mafi, doctorni sahiba!*

SONYA: How much did they pay you? What did you think would happen, eh?

IZZAT: Okay, okay, *doctorni sahiba*, don't shout.

SONYA: Do you know what they've done?

IZZAT: I'm sorry, *doctorni sahiba* . . .

SONYA: You're sorry! They stole my research. I have nothing to present at the conference. All my surveys, blood, urine, samples—everything—is destroyed. The clinic is bulldozed, and I'll be put on a plane tomorrow night.

IZZAT: You will go?

SONYA: Yes! Zarina would have received the best treatment of her life. Now she will get nothing . . . Where is Zarina?

IZZAT: She's sleeping.

SONYA: She's alone? I want to see her.

IZZAT: No! My man is back.

SONYA: Your man is dead!

IZZAT: Leave me alone, *doctorni sahiba*!

SONYA: Where is she?

IZZAT: She was my baby, my little angel. I don't want anyone to see her. She was my baby.

SONYA: She's dead?

Long pause.

Where is her body? They bought her body, didn't they? Money? How much? You sold your baby.

IZZAT: No.

SONYA: Like Hasina.

IZZAT: No.

SONYA: Like Kasturi.

IZZAT: No.

SONYA: You sold your own child.

IZZAT breaks down in tears.

IZZAT: Satan invaded my heart. Satan took money for Zarina. Devil in me did that. Devil lived in my stomach. I don't need this money.

IZZAT pulls a few rupees from her blouse and throws them towards SONYA.

Throw this away into the gutter; I don't need it.

SONYA: The devil lives in the company's poison . . . you fool.

IZZAT: Me, fool?

SONYA: The company killed Zarina and gave you some cash for her dead body and you came home thinking that the company did you an act of charity.

IZZAT: You don't know how I survive, *doctorni sahiba.* Why do you harass me?

SONYA: If money is all you wanted, this is nothing compared to what I could have got for you. You fool.

IZZAT: You? You cannot fool me! No clinic, no research, no treating, nothing, just a big mouth. What you want, huh? You want to take my daughter to a foreign country to show her. What will that say about my daughter? Huh? What will people say? What kind of mother is she, showing her daughter to everyone—her twisted hands, her heaving chest, her melting skin—shame on the mother who did that to her child. And who wants to look at my Zarina? How dare you? My daughter is in peace. I have peace. Why do you come between us? Please, *doctorni sahiba,* please, be merciful to me, be merciful to my daughter, let my daughter have peace.

SCENE 10

DEVRAJ's office. DEVRAJ enters. SONYA storms into the office after him.

SONYA: What are you doing? What the hell are you doing?

DEVRAJ: You're not supposed to be here, Doctor.

SONYA: Stop it, damn it, stop killing everything that lives around this factory.

DEVRAJ: *Chowkidar!*

SONYA: Your People's Progress Zone, your cover-up.

DEVRAJ: Get on your plane, white woman.

SONYA: Bloody coconut.

MADIHA: This woman does not stop.

SONYA turns to MADIHA.

SONYA: Do you know what his company has been doing?

(to DEVRAJ) Does she know your company doctor paid my patients for their babies?

DEVRAJ: Out! Out of here!

SONYA: Twenty-seven dead babies—

MADIHA: What is she talking about?

DEVRAJ: Where the hell is security?

SONYA: Was paying for Izzat's baby part of your Animal Charity Fund?

MADIHA: No, that woman is lying. Devraj?

DEVRAJ: *Chowkidar!*

SONYA: You bought Izzat's baby to destroy evidence.

MADIHA: It was alive . . . the baby was alive.

SONYA: They sold you their dead babies.

DEVRAJ: I want you to leave . . . now!

MADIHA: They brought dead *animals*.

SONYA: You are destroying evidence of murder!

DEVRAJ: To hell with your evidence!

MADIHA: The evidence? The evidence is right here, right inside me.

(to SONYA) I breathe more poison than any of those women in the slums. If what you say is true, then my baby must be ten times more deformed.

SONYA: You're damn right, Madam, because the company's poison does not discriminate.

MADIHA: Then I'll be a good test case for you.

SONYA: What?

MADIHA: Sign me up for your study. Why not?

SONYA: My study is banned.

MADIHA: I offer my womb regardless.

DEVRAJ: What's wrong with you, Madiha?

MADIHA: I'm helping you. I want to shut her mouth.

MADIHA turns to SONYA.

To see you posturing. *(imitating her)* "I have this evidence, I have that evidence!" Well *(pointing at her own stomach)* here is my evidence. When my baby is born, you'll see.

SONYA: *(to MADIHA)* I won't be around.

SONYA turns to DEVRAJ.

(to DEVRAJ) But how are *you* going to live with it?

SONYA exits. DEVRAJ turns to MADIHA.

DEVRAJ: What the fuck is wrong with you?

MADIHA: For the last two months I have been thinking about how to break the news to you.

DEVRAJ: What news?

MADIHA: I missed two months.

DEVRAJ: What does that mean?

MADIHA: Yes, yes! I'm pregnant. Aren't you going to say something?

DEVRAJ: How did this happen?

MADIHA: Is that all you can say?

DEVRAJ: That night was the only night.

MADIHA: Are we talking about a single night? Devraj, I just revealed to you the fruit of our relationship.

They speak over each other.

DEVRAJ: I thought we had /

MADIHA: I'm going to be the /

DEVRAJ: an understanding.

MADIHA: mother of your child.

DEVRAJ: What do you want me to say?

MADIHA: Say something nice.

DEVRAJ: Are you sure?

MADIHA: Aaaaah . . .

DEVRAJ: Please, how do you know for sure?

MADIHA: I'm hungry, I vomit—of course I know for sure. It's in my body, for goodness' sake.

DEVRAJ: How long has it been?

MADIHA: Stop talking to me like that.

DEVRAJ: Madiha, I think maybe—

MADIHA: What?

DEVRAJ: You could get an abortion.

MADIHA slaps him.

MADIHA: No. No! I would never do that. Never. Not on my life! This is your baby for God's sake, Devraj!

DEVRAJ notices the sound of escaping gas, but chooses to ignore it.

DEVRAJ: I'm sorry, I didn't know how to react to news like that.

MADIHA: Hold me in your arms, kiss me.

He kisses her.

DEVRAJ: It's just that I don't want to do something now that I can't handle later.

MADIHA: You can't handle a baby?

DEVRAJ: What if the baby . . .

MADIHA: What?

DEVRAJ: I mean . . .

MADIHA: What? Is not healthy? Like the babies of those slum women?

DEVRAJ: I mean I'm not prepared to be a father.

MADIHA: Why wouldn't the baby be healthy?

DEVRAJ: I didn't say that.

MADIHA: What is that woman's research about?

DEVRAJ: Her research is nonsense. The slum mothers are not dying of diseases caused by Karbide Thunder, but by poverty. I don't give a toss about Labonté, I'm just nervous at the thought of being a father. Afraid of your motherhood out of wedlock! Afraid of mudslinging! What will everyone say? How will you handle that?

MADIHA: I'm sorry I doubted you, but I only wanted to help you.

DEVRAJ: By betting your baby with that dreadful doctor?

MADIHA: I believe so much in your work, I don't mind betting my womb to shut her mouth.

DEVRAJ holds her in his arms and kisses her.

DEVRAJ: Oh, Madiha, you don't understand . . .

A deafening thunder starts.

(looking out) What the hell is that?

The sound of thunder rises like a massive earthquake. Sparks start going off in all directions. DEVRAJ's phone starts ringing. The sounds of chaos mingle and increase. People start running in all directions. The noise from the street turns into cries for help. DEVRAJ runs to the window.

God! The plant is burning . . .

MADIHA: Oh my God.

DEVRAJ: *(calling)* Rishi, Ashraf, Pooja! Wait! Wait!

(to MADIHA) Go with them. Take the southeast exit. The southeast exit!

(calling out) Raja! You stay here with me.

MADIHA: Aah! My eyes. I can't breath.

MADIHA runs back to DEVRAJ.

DEVRAJ: Cover your eyes, Madiha. Just run. Madiha, just GO!

Calling out.

Pooja, Rishi, help her!

He pushes MADIHA to escape. Complete darkness. We hear people whispering in the darkness.

What in God's name has happened? What do you mean exploded? What tank?

JAGANLAL: What?

DEVRAJ: The MIC?

"Ek Zahreeli Hawa" begins to play and continues, overlapping all that is being said on stage.

SONG: Khamosh cheekho say bhari
Yeay kahan say utha rahi haiaisi dardili hawa
Gaib say chalnay lagee jub
Ek Zahreeli Hawa.

MADIHA: My eyes.

JAGANLAL: Say it again. Where?

IZZAT: Run, *juldi, juldi chandalika bhago.*

MADIHA: I can't see anything.

IZZAT: Run, *chandalika*, run.

A loud clearing of a throat is heard. It's from ANDERSON. *We see him in the US while people continue in whispers.*

ANDERSON: Sorry, I've had the flu for a week. But I'm getting over it. Washington is damp as hell at this time of year. I wanted to get back to Connecticut. But Julie was invited to lunch with the first lady. What! How many? Over sixty?

The noise of a crowd in India.

SONYA: Oxygen. Amyl nitrate.

DEVRAJ: Mr. Minister, sorry to bother you.

SONYA: Thiosulfate.

ANDERSON: That's worse than Mexico!

SONYA: Oxygen. What do you mean you don't have any?

DEVRAJ: Damn it, Mukund, what about the scrubber?

JAGANLAL: Mr. Prime Minister, there is a problem . . .

MADIHA: Get out of my way! Move!

DEVRAJ: Move, Mukund!

ANDERSON in the US.

ANDERSON: Who's our guy over there? The minister. I want to talk to him.

JAGANLAL: Karbide International's slogan has come to haunt us.

SONYA: Body number on the forehead. One thousand five hundred and thirty-eight. One thousand five hundred and thirty-nine.

ANDERSON: What do you mean no one knows for sure what happened?

JAGANLAL: Why Bhopal? Why Bhopal?

As a deadly calm settles, lights fade in. We see ANDERSON *and* JAGANLAL *in their respective countries.*

SCENE 11

ANDERSON and JAGANLAL *are answering questions:* JAGANLAL *addressing the press in India and* ANDERSON *in the US. A tightly packed crowd stands some distance away from them.*

ANDERSON: You're ten times safer inside a Karbide International factory than in a slum.

JAGANLAL: Right, they all died on the streets, no one died inside the factory.

ANDERSON: Gentlemen, if any of you have been to India, you know how they live over there. They are desperate for jobs. There was no slum around the factory when we started.

JAGANLAL: What rubbish. Slums were there long before the factory. Not just the slum, the deputy inspector general of police's bungalow too.

ANDERSON: Look, the name of the game is not to nail me down; the name of the game is to provide for the victims. What they need is fair compensation.

JAGANLAL: That's so typical, so bloody typical of the West. The courts of India haven't even opened the case against him, and he's already telling us what's fair! Absconder of justice, that's who he is! Three deadlines have passed, Mr. Anderson, and you're still talking to the *American press* for a crime committed in India.

ANDERSON: I'm going to see to it that the suffering is adequately compensated; I will pay compensation—no question about that at all. But no, I don't think there is any criminal responsibility here!

JAGANLAL: Really? What do you think?

ANDERSON: Obviously I didn't have, I don't have, and I never will have a criminal intent! I am personally going to go to India to better understand the situation.

JAGANLAL: Thank you.

SCENE 12

SONYA's makeshift clinic. Scores of victims are lying on the floor. IZZAT is among them. Many victims have eye patches. SONYA brings a patient in.

SONYA: If you are sick, stay in this area. There are doctors here that can help you. If you're looking for someone, go behind the market square, by the lake . . . there's a big poster on the lawn that says "Unidentified Dead." Go there first. *Wahan jauw.*

IZZAT: Doctor Sonya.

SONYA: What?

IZZAT: My body aches. What will happen?

SONYA: I don't know.

IZZAT: You know, *doctorni sahiba.* You have my file.

SONYA: The situation is changing every day. We're waiting for medicine. I have nothing here.

IZZAT pulls out a handful of tablets.

M & Ms?

IZZAT: I want to live, *doctorni sahiba* . . . stop this pain.

SONYA: Oh God, who sold you these?

SONYA throws them away. The song starts while SONYA helps IZZAT. IZ- ZAT coughs up lumps of blood and tries to stop by shoving the edge of her scarf into her mouth. IZZAT convulses. SAUVÉ enters.

SONG: Kaisa bhabhka kaisi gandh
Ho rahi hai sans bandh
Roshni ankhon ki mand
Jismo jan main bus rahi hai, kaisi matmaili hawa
Gaib say chalne lagi jub, ek zahreeli hawa

SONYA: Izzat, no!

SAUVÉ: Dr. Labonté.

SONYA: I can't talk to you now. Help me get her onto the table.

SAUVÉ hesitates.

Help me! She's got fluid in her lungs!

SAUVÉ and SONYA help IZZAT onto the table.

SAUVÉ: Legally you can't help this woman.

SONYA continues to help IZZAT.

If something happens to this woman, you'd be personally liable.

SONYA: There is a bag on the table. Get me a bronchodilator!

SAUVÉ: I don't know what that is. You shouldn't be here, Doctor.

SONYA: It's grey plastic!

SAUVÉ: It's not safe to stay here.

He looks for it, holds it up.

Is this it?

SONYA administers a shot from the inhaler.

SONYA: Get me a rag.

SAUVÉ: You're on your own, Labonté.

SONYA: Attendant!

SONYA keeps helping IZZAT. SAUVÉ leaves.

SCENE 13

Amid sounds of protest, ANDERSON arrives in India. JAGANLAL receives him at the airport.

ANDERSON: Mr. Minister, I am so sorry.

JAGANLAL: Yes, Mr. Anderson.

ANDERSON: I really am sorry.

JAGANLAL: You don't have much time, Mr. Anderson.

ANDERSON: And I do appreciate your coming in person to meet me.

JAGANLAL: They are outside.

ANDERSON: Who?

JAGANLAL: The police.

ANDERSON: Am I being arrested?

JAGANLAL: You need protection.

ANDERSON: Where is Mr. Sarthi?

JAGANLAL: Well protected!

ANDERSON: May I see him?

JAGANLAL: You will.

ANDERSON: Is it a police escort waiting for us?

JAGANLAL: Don't worry about the photographers. Let them photograph you. Our people need to see you answering to authority. I'm doing you a favour. I will keep you under house arrest. Twenty-four-hour surveillance. Nobody will be allowed near you but Sarthi. That is the best I can do under the circumstances.

ANDERSON: I'm sure.

JAGANLAL: *Chalo.*

Both exit.

SCENE 14

JAGANLAL's office.

JAGANLAL: Dr. Labonté, we need your help.

SONYA: Pardon me?

JAGANLAL: The people of Bhopal need your help.

SONYA: You need my help? It's a little late. There isn't much I can do now. If you had listened to me earlier, if you had read my research, Mr. Minister. If— You're unbelievable. You're as bad as they are.

JAGANLAL: Dr. Labonté, I am asking you to please stay in Bhopal. I'd like you to work at the Hamidia Hospital.

SONYA: You want me to care for—to give palliative care to the victims of this goddamn disaster that you—*you* are directly responsible for. We have no supplies, no oxygen, we are using the same syringes over and over again, we have no antidote for Karbide's—

JAGANLAL: What do you need?

SONYA: Thiosulfate. Sodium thiosulfate for a start. For the cyanide poisoning.

JAGANLAL: I'll see to it that you get all you need. Please write it down for me.

SONYA: You'll understand if I don't fall over with gratitude.

JAGANLAL: I am grateful to you.

SONYA: What is this about? What do you want from me?

JAGANLAL: I want you to continue the work you've been doing.

SONYA: The work?

JAGANLAL: Your research.

SONYA: The research you dismissed two weeks ago. The research you banned.

JAGANLAL: The situation has changed, Doctor.

SONYA: I can continue my research without interference?

JAGANLAL: Yes. Yes.

SONYA: And if I agree to continue my study, what will happen to my findings?

JAGANLAL: As I said, the situation has changed. I am in a position to make your findings public. To let the world know.

SONYA: Montreal. You're going to the trade talks, the conference. You can present the material there.

JAGANLAL: Yes. Yes I can, Doctor.

SCENE 15

ANDERSON at DEVRAJ's, *under house arrest.* DEVRAJ *is sitting nearby.*

ANDERSON: *(on the telephone)* Yeah, how's the big snowstorm in Connecticut? Overnight? That makes me feel a helluva lot better. Oh no, beautiful, fine, fine, well, apart from being jet-lagged and under house arrest. What? Yes . . . I don't know . . . What? That much? . . . No. No. Fine. Get back to me.

He hangs up and turns to DEVRAJ.

We've lost eight hundred million in market capitalization in the last week; production is shut down worldwide, so we have no revenue; and our insurance may not cover us. What do you people get up to in this country?

He tosses a safety manual at DEVRAJ.

What is this?

DEVRAJ: Your safety manual.

ANDERSON: Our safety manual. Did you ever look at it?

DEVRAJ: Yes.

ANDERSON: You had a total of four safety devices. How many were working?

DEVRAJ: The refrigeration was turned off at your request to cut costs. The flare tower was shut off to cut costs. The scrubber had just been repaired, but still didn't function. The water hoses did not reach the tower.

ANDERSON: The book says at least two should have been working. How many were working?

DEVRAJ: They were certified.

ANDERSON: But were they working?

DEVRAJ: I don't know.

ANDERSON: You don't know?

DEVRAJ: None!

ANDERSON: Who certified them?

DEVRAJ: The minister's safety inspection team—we were *certified*.

DEVRAJ gives ANDERSON a logbook. ANDERSON flips through the pages.

ANDERSON: When was the last time they were certified?

DEVRAJ: Two weeks ago.

ANDERSON: When is the next certification?

DEVRAJ is silent.

Okay . . . if the plant hadn't blown up, when would the next one have been?

DEVRAJ: Two weeks from today!

ANDERSON: That means week four. But that's already been certified. So have weeks six, eight, and ten. What is going on here? You have clearance for periods that haven't even arrived yet?

DEVRAJ: This is India.

ANDERSON: My apologies, I didn't know.

DEVRAJ: We have to adjust to local conditions here.

ANDERSON: Which means?

DEVRAJ: We must bribe. There are only two certification officers for the whole state and they won't come every two weeks. So once they come for certification, we pay them to certify three months in advance. Corruption is culture here, sir.

ANDERSON: You had gas leaks before, didn't you?

DEVRAJ: Not this big.

ANDERSON: What was done?

DEVRAJ: We handed out flyers door to door.

ANDERSON: Flyers? Aren't people illiterate?

DEVRAJ doesn't answer.

How much did you save shutting down the refrigeration?

DEVRAJ: It was—

ANDERSON: And the scrubber!

DEVRAJ: Listen, sir—

ANDERSON: And on bribes . . . how much?

DEVRAJ: Mr. Anderson—

ANDERSON: Why wasn't I informed?

DEVRAJ: You were, sir. I have them recorded. Twenty-seven memos were sent to you.

ANDERSON: Twenty-seven memos?

DEVRAJ: Twenty-seven dead babies.

ANDERSON: What?

DEVRAJ: No, I'm sorry, eighteen; I sent you eighteen memos.

ANDERSON: How do I save this corporation?

DEVRAJ: We responded to all instructions sent by the head office.

ANDERSON: Just shut up.

ANDERSON picks up the newspaper.

This reporter here, Raj Kishore Keshwani; I keep seeing his name all over the place. How come he prophesied so much about the safety of the plant and I never heard about it?

DEVRAJ: Sir, he's been writing those ever since the plant opened.

ANDERSON: He mentions some clinic's research—about Karbide killing unborn babies!

DEVRAJ: A Canadian NGO doctor. She was doing research claiming that Karbide International has been poisoning unborn babies ever since its Bhopal plant was built.

ANDERSON: And you ignored it?

DEVRAJ: We had her barred from the plant.

ANDERSON: And what's this about a Karbide employee? Madiha Akram, who is apparently pregnant with the CEO's child?

DEVRAJ snatches the newspaper from him.

So you got an employee pregnant.

DEVRAJ: Yes.

ANDERSON: What a mess. I thought I sent India a man with a vision. I didn't know I was sending a fucking playboy.

ANDERSON pushes a flyer into DEVRAJ's hand.

What does it say?

DEVRAJ: *Zinda nahi murda.*

ANDERSON: Which means?

DEVRAJ: "Dead not alive."

ANDERSON: "Wanted. Anderson. Dead not alive!"

DEVRAJ: I'm sorry, Mr. Anderson.

ANDERSON: People are calling me the ghost of Bhopal. Look at these eyes—a total of nine hundred and two wrinkles under these eyes. Each wrinkle represents a Karbide plant somewhere in the world. I and my men and women have hung on to a single hope—that Karbide would be a good citizen in each of those nine hundred towns, and, as in Bhopal, would help to put an end to poverty. Help realize untapped potential. And you, Mr. Sarthi, have killed that hope. All nine hundred of us are fighting for our lives. Karbide is fighting for its life.

DEVRAJ: Mr. Anderson, the courts have not decided anything yet.

ANDERSON: Corporations don't lose in courts; they lose under public scrutiny.

ANDERSON gives DEVRAJ the flyer.

Merry fucking Christmas, Mr. Playboy.

SCENE 16

The Hamidia Hospital. Victims are lying on the floor in groups. IZZAT and MADIHA are among them. MADIHA's eyes are covered with eye patches. IZZAT has one eye patch. IZZAT is nibbling dry seeds.

IZZAT: Madiha *memsahib?*

No answer.

Bai? Memsahib? Madiha memesahib? You don't talk. Not a word. Eh.

MADIHA starts to cough. IZZAT offers her seeds.

Would you like to eat? A little bit. Not even for the baby?

IZZAT passes grain to MADIHA, who drops it.

Now you know where it is. You are saving it. You will need it later. Want to hear a story? Listen . . .

Aise kihis bhagwan
Badd devta patta pay bathis
Haath la mal kay nikalis maile
Maile say janmis ek kauwa
Kauwa la kihis bhagwan
Ja tai khoj key bhumi la laan
Aise kihis bhagwan.

Pher kauwa, makdi, auo kekda mun kachwa kay ghench la dabais,
Tub kachwa ha bhumi la ugal dees.

Paani ooper ghoom-ghoom kay
Jaal bicha dis makdi
Jaal kay ooper bade jatan say
Bhumi jama dis makdi
Bhum la pahchan
Aise kihis bhagwan.

Pher sab jan milkay nachay gaye bur bhidgay. Okhar baad badd devta apan
mudi kay jata say baal noach kay phakis. Okhar say pade bun gaye. Udi pade
la kaat kay hul banis. Jub hul chale la lagagay taub bhumi say anna upjis.

Anna la deemak kay banbee kay bheetar
Rakh do bhaiya
Sub munsay kay kaam yay aahi
Bolo ram ramiya
Kauwa, makdi, kekda, kachwa
Sab jan khais dhan.
Aise kihis bhagwan.

MADIHA: *Phir kya hua?*

IZZAT: *Phir?*

MADIHA: Yeah, what happened then?

IZZAT: Then the crop got infected by pests.

MADIHA: Then?

IZZAT: Then men began to search for chemicals to kill the pests.

MADIHA: What happened next?

IZZAT: That chemical killed my daughter.

SONYA enters. She shows signs of sickness due to the poisonous gas.

SONYA: *(to IZZAT)* She's talking?

IZZAT: Yes.

MADIHA: Sonya Labonté? Dr. Sonya Labonté?

MADIHA sits up and attempts to take off her eye patch.

SONYA: No, don't take that off.

MADIHA: Thank you. I know I have not been kind to you. I feel embarrassed.

SONYA examines her with a stethoscope.

SONYA: Don't be. Breathe.

MADIHA: I don't know how to thank you for giving me back my life . . . and my little baby.

SONYA: There is a heartbeat.

MADIHA: See, I told you.

SONYA: Yes, yes.

MADIHA: I need to see Devraj.

SONYA: Miss Madiha, there are some things you need to know. Bhopal is littered with deformed and stillborn babies.

MADIHA: That won't include my baby. No. Look, those women lie. They lie about everything . . . about their animals . . . about their families . . . about their babies . . .

SONYA: Miss Madiha—

MADIHA: Like Izzat. She lied about everything—her dead dog, her dead pig, her dead goat . . .

SONYA: The chemical that killed Izaat's goat killed her daughter; the same gas that poisoned you—is going to affect your baby.

MADIHA: I see what you're doing. You cannot stop, can you? You want to blame Devraj for everything. Why are you trying to scare me? Have you no shame?

SONYA: There was a baby born without eyes.

MADIHA: Why do you talk like that?

SONYA: I urge you to seriously consider terminating this pregnancy. I will not tell you what to do. I can't. But you need to know the facts.

SONYA starts to exit. She coughs and staggers as she walks. She stops, gasps for air, and then collapses slowly as the lights close on her. Dr. Labonté dies.

SCENE 17

ANDERSON and JAGANLAL at DEVRAJ's house.

JAGANLAL: This is the settlement you are proposing?

ANDERSON: Yes.

JAGANLAL: This is not just.

ANDERSON: Mr. Minister, there is always an element of speculation in these arbitrations. The point is—the dead have stopped dying.

JAGANLAL: What?

ANDERSON: The dead have stopped dying.

JAGANLAL: The dead have stopped dying?

ANDERSON: Look—

JAGANLAL: My people are dying faster than the insects your chemical was supposed to kill.

ANDERSON: Well, your casualty numbers don't match ours.

JAGANLAL: Two hundred thousand and counting.

DEVRAJ: There have only been two thousand recorded deaths.

JAGANLAL: Only?

DEVRAJ: We ought to be precise about the numbers.

JAGANLAL: Thirty-seven wards are affected.

DEVRAJ: That's the entire city.

JAGANLAL: And the poison clouds are not clear yet.

ANDERSON: Mr. Minister, we'll provide compensation. We'll look after the gas victims, but first of all, you have to determine how many.

JAGANLAL: What?

ANDERSON: Who was living in the affected wards at the time?

JAGANLAL: And how should I determine that? Should I go to every dead body and ask his home address?

ANDERSON: Well, don't you have census records?

JAGANLAL: As if they had homes.

ANDERSON: So what are we supposed to do? Pay for every patient you happen to have in your hospitals?

JAGANLAL raises a file.

JAGANLAL: Three hundred fifty thousand registered medical files, two hundred thousand temporary disabilities, one hundred fifty thousand possible permanent disabilities.

DEVRAJ: How many of them are faking?

JAGANLAL: How does one fake death, Mr. Sarthi?

DEVRAJ: Half the dead wouldn't have been alive in the first place, had it not been for the wealth the plant provided.

JAGANLAL: For goodness' sake, Devraj; I bent over backwards to grant you the People's Progress Zone. Bent over backwards to give you concessions that are unmatched in the history of India. You could at least think a little before opening your mouth. *(imitates him in repulsion)* "Half the dead wouldn't have been alive!"

DEVRAJ: I'm sorry, Mr. Minister. You go on forgetting this was an accident!

JAGANLAL: An accident?

DEVRAJ: Do you think we'd do it purposefully? It was an accident—a chemical, a chemical got too hot and exploded.

JAGANLAL: What chemical?

DEVRAJ: What?

JAGANLAL: Spell the name.

ANDERSON: What?

JAGANLAL: Spell that chemical, methyl isocyanate. It decomposes to hydrogen cyanide and carbon dioxide. It burns the skin, eyes, and respiratory membranes. It penetrates the skin and is lethal in very low doses.

ANDERSON: Look, Mr. Bhandari, our scientists know perfectly well what they—

JAGANLAL: MIC, the gas that killed my people!

ANDERSON: We acknowledge the damage this explosion has done. But it was an acc—

JAGANLAL: You knew you had a problem.

DEVRAJ: No!

JAGANLAL: No? Buying dead animals?

DEVRAJ: That was the Animal Charity Fund.

JAGANLAL: Charity?

ANDERSON: Mr. Minister, we have charities in all corners of the world. This was an accident. It could have happened in the US.

JAGANLAL: Then why didn't it? It didn't happen in the US because you don't store enormous quantities of MIC at your American factory. It didn't happen there because you have automated monitoring systems: you don't rely on your workers' noses to tell you when there's been a leak. It didn't happen there because you have extra safety measures in place—measures you didn't bother to install here.

A long silence.

ANDERSON: I believe we all share the same philosophy—

JAGANLAL: Aaah, so there's a philosophy to killing people?

ANDERSON: *(to DEVRAJ)* Show him our figures.

JAGANLAL: Your figures?

ANDERSON: These are generous amounts and my final offer.

JAGANLAL: Shouldn't the courts of India determine what's final?

ANDERSON: I have shareholders, insurance companies—they are throwing Molotov cocktails at the factory in Stuttgart. The company's bonds are on credit watch. You have no idea of the scope of my problems.

JAGANLAL: Regardless of your problems, you can't be your own judge and your own jury. This happened here and an Indian court must settle this.

ANDERSON: If you want to wait that long—but your people need help *now*! Give him our figures. Please just listen carefully.

DEVRAJ: Eight thousand per death, four thousand per partial permanent disability, and two thousand per partial temporary disability!

ANDERSON: Not in rupees, in American dollars!

JAGANLAL: This is what an Indian life is worth?

DEVRAJ: These figures are based on the Indian standard of living.

JAGANLAL: How American, Indian boy!

DEVRAJ: You had nothing here. We brought you a world-class plant.

JAGANLAL: A world-class plant? I licensed you to manufacture mega-quantities of Karbide Thunder and agreed to an outrageous extension of the People's Progress Zone. Why? Because my country is poor. We are not competitive on the global market. We are *always* in the position of trying to catch up to *you*. But the price *we* pay for trying to catch up leaves us *victims* of your progress, your technology, and your crimes against humanity.

ANDERSON: We are not criminals.

JAGANLAL pulls out SONYA's research.

JAGANLAL: Really? All right, you don't want to wait for an Indian court, fine; you will go to a US court. I will negotiate with this.

ANDERSON: What's that?

JAGANLAL: Dr. Labonté's research.

DEVRAJ: That can't be admissible.

JAGANLAL: Because you purposely hid information?

DEVRAJ: This is ludicrous.

JAGANLAL: And coerced mothers to abort and to bury deformed dead babies, according to this study.

DEVRAJ: Oh, please.

ANDERSON: Let him speak.

DEVRAJ: Mr. Anderson?

ANDERSON: You be quiet.

JAGANLAL: *(reads the front page)* Significant amounts of methyl isocyanate have been detected in the blood of pregnant women, causing birth defects, birthing abnormalities, and deformities. Karbide International manufactures this product. This study shows that, while long-term health risks are not conclusive, Karbide International has increased the production and . . .

DEVRAJ: A woman you charged with kidnapping has done this research!

JAGANLAL: We have dropped the charges. She is now working in the Hamidia Hospital, and I have decided to lift the ban on her study and have asked a special commission to examine her findings.

JAGANLAL starts to leave.

DEVRAJ: Mr. Minister?

ANDERSON walks towards JAGANLAL, *motioning for* DEVRAJ *to leave.* DEVRAJ *exits.*

ANDERSON: Mr. Minister, perhaps there is one area of our settlement that we could actually begin to discuss in depth.

JAGANLAL: Yes, there is an area we may talk about substantially.

ANDERSON and JAGANLAL *talk. They are very animated but their words are inaudible to the audience.*

SCENE 18

MADIHA is at the clinic. DEVRAJ *enters.*

DEVRAJ: Madiha?

MADIHA: Just say hello.

DEVRAJ: Hello.

MADIHA: No, like when you would come bursting through my door Sunday morning, so full of life, "Hello, Madiha," and run into my arms . . . "Hellooo Madihaaa!"

DEVRAJ: *(trying)* Hellooo Madihaaa. I thought you died.

MADIHA: Me too.

DEVRAJ: It's my fault. I told you to run. If only you didn't run; it's my fault, all my fault. You ran right into the gas . . . I'm sorry, I'm sorry.

Pause.

Say something . . . something . . . just say it.

MADIHA: I love you.

DEVRAJ: No.

MADIHA: I love you.

She touches DEVRAJ, *then kisses him passionately.*

DEVRAJ: I have been thinking.

MADIHA: About what?

DEVRAJ: About us.

MADIHA: Yes?

DEVRAJ: I should go back to the US.

MADIHA: You should?

DEVRAJ: And you must come with me.

MADIHA: Yes. When? How soon can we go?

DEVRAJ: That depends.

MADIHA: On what?

DEVRAJ: What Jaganlal does with Labonté's research.

MADIHA: Labonté isn't in the picture anymore.

DEVRAJ: But do you have any idea what Labonté's research was about? Do you?

MADIHA: Some nonsense about the factory? About the factory!

DEVRAJ: What about the factory?

MADIHA: I don't know . . . about animals, women, babies. I don't know.

DEVRAJ: Why do you think we paid for all those dead animals?

MADIHA: It's becau— the Animal Charity . . . Oh my God.

DEVRAJ: My nightmare is growing in your belly.

MADIHA: You lied to me.

DEVRAJ: It was a mistake.

MADIHA: You told me—

DEVRAJ: Can you forgive me?

MADIHA: Forgive you? Forgive you for what?

DEVRAJ: This baby—

MADIHA: Forgive you for your own baby?

DAVRAJ: Madiha, please understand me.

MADIHA: That night, I thought I'd die. I was running . . . I couldn't breath . . . I couldn't see. I fell and my hand touched something. It was a dead body. Oh God, I had never touched a dead body before. I never prayed before but that night. I prayed, "God save me and the life of my baby." I wanted to prove to myself that what you had told me before the accident was true.

DEVRAJ: Madiha, I'm sorry. It was a mistake. I didn't think this accident would happen until it happened. I thought I was doing something good. I thought I would be a bringer of prosperity. I really thought that. Now I look at you . . . Madiha, I'll make it all up to you. We can start over again in America.

MADIHA: What will America do for me? Will it give me back my eyes? Will it heal what's growing inside me?

DEVRAJ: What's growing inside you will have to be aborted.

MADIHA: Will have to be?

DEVRAJ: Madiha, I don't want to leave you alone.

MADIHA: So it's that simple. If I don't abort, I'm left alone.

DEVRAJ: That's not what I said.

MADIHA: Then why do you want me to abort this baby?

DEVRAJ: It's not a baby.

MADIHA: What is it?

DEVRAJ: You saw Izzat's baby.

MADIHA: I am not Izzat.

DEVRAJ: You don't understand.

MADIHA: What do I not understand?

DEVRAJ: Imagine how that creature would suffer. Every day would be a reminder of the mistake I made. Imagine if the child lived . . . knowing that his father . . . that I was responsible. I want us to be together. I want to marry you . . .

MADIHA: You have really mixed me up.

DEVRAJ: I really do want to marry you, Madiha. I know that now . . . But we can't . . . we won't last with such a burden in our lives.

MADIHA: Labonté told me that all abortions in Bhopal will have to be recorded. It's government regulation.

DEVRAJ: We will go outside of Bhopal.

MADIHA: Izzat was saying that a woman died a horrible death at the hands of a doctor outside of Bhopal.

DEVRAJ: Don't be afraid, darling. Are we poor, uneducated clods who would leave such matters to some two-cent clinic outside of Bhopal?

DEVRAJ holds her hands.

Hans will take care of you. I think you have made a good decision.

MADIHA: Stop—

DEVRAJ: We'll leave all this—

MADIHA: Stop, please, I haven't made a decision . . . I want to think about it.

DEVRAJ: Shussssh . . . Sleep . . . We need to sleep.

MADIHA: I haven't made a decision.

DEVRAJ: Shusssss . . . You will see the sense of it in the morning.

MADIHA rests, her eyes closing with drowsiness. DEVRAJ sits besides her.

SCENE 19

ANDERSON on the phone.

ANDERSON: I thought we had an understanding. I don't have the luxury of only having one thing to worry about. I'm turning my attention to other things. I can't think about Bhopal one hundred percent of the time.

My hands? My hands shake hands of heads of state and men at the White House. My hands provide for a million employees around the world and give scholarships to bright Indian students. My hands were trying to build the future of this country. My hands are clean. I was ten thousand miles away.

We both know your charges are absurd. Well, they'll have to find me first, and then they'll have to drag me into court. I've got a plane to catch. Good luck.

SCENE 20

Action takes place in three locations: at the Montreal conference, at a graveyard, and at DEVRAJ's *home where he remains under arrest.*

At the Montreal conference where JAGANLAL *is preparing for a speech.*

JAGANLAL: Dear delegates, good people of Canada, and business leaders of the world assembled in Montreal, *je veux vous dire*—I want to tell you—*il n'y a pas d'amour*, there is no love left in Bhopal. There are ten thousand sick babies. Dying babies, orphaned at birth. What can I do? Seek to lay blame? Cry for one baby? No. Do I mourn the dead? No. Sad as it may sound, I cannot afford to mourn for the dead. It's useless. Because we know that for every child that dies, a new baby is born. The time for mourning has passed; we must now pave the way for the future.

Song starts.

Kya Zamin kya aasman *[What on earth what heaven]*
Ek kohra ek dhuan *[One is fog and one is smoke]*
Ek kayamat ka sama *[The time has come for our fate]*
Gaib say chalne lagi jab *[When it starts to move unnoticed]*
Ek zahreeli hawa. *[This poisonous gas.]*

At the graveyard, where IZZAT *is sitting by a mud grave with Zarina's empty basket beside her . . .*

IZZAT: Doctor *sahiba*, Zarina died the day she was born. One leg, one arm, no fingers . . . there was nothing right with her. Her tiny little heart was like dried rubber . . . I could see it under her skin. Doctor *sahiba*, can you understand me? The night Zarina died, I saw her in a dream, standing. Looking like an angel. "Free me from my pain," she said. "Why am I like this? I am already dead . . . " That night I felt something had changed. I woke up and turned to look at her. She had stopped crying.

She takes out flower petals from the basket and drops them onto the grave.

She has peace. You have peace.

At DEVRAJ *and* MADIHA*'s, where they are under house arrest.*

DEVRAJ: *(to* MADIHA*)* What are you thinking?

MADIHA *doesn't say a word, walks away from him, and then tears the airline ticket in two.* DEVRAJ *is stunned.*

MADIHA *looks at* IZZAT*, who is at a distance.* IZZAT *looks at* MADIHA*. Both women start walking towards each other and meet centre stage.* MADIHA *takes* IZZAT*'s hand in hers. The women have resolute expressions of defiance.*

BOYS WITH CARS
Anita Majumdar

I am one of the lucky people in this country who have seen *The Fish Eyes Trilogy*, which is quite a feat because the three plays live in Anita Majumdar, so the only way to see them is to see Anita inhabit them. More people will have experienced *Fish Eyes* than any other, because Anita danced that play into existence in 2004, and it has travelled the world since. *Boys With Cars* and *Let Me Borrow That Top* premiered in 2015, and together they give us a glimpse into the delicate negotiations of young women with their histories, their cultures, and the power structures within which they live.

While I have been enchanted by the sparkling *Fish Eyes*, and *Let Me Borrow That Top* challenges its audiences to enter dangerous territory, *Boys With Cars* is my favourite of the trio. For me, *Boys With Cars* interweaves the complications of living together on this land called Canada, remembering who we are, and using that knowledge to empower us, not to shackle us to a past that can be used to oppress us.

Naz introduces us immediately to the complicated, conflicted world of the play. Dressed in an Indian dance skirt and the ubiquitous uniform of the Canadian teenager—a hoodie—she dances classical Indian dance to the contemporary music of Imran Khan *on* the roof of a red Mini Cooper, the iconic British car that itself colonized the world, eventually produced in Australia, Spain, Italy, Belgium, Chile. The car belongs to Lucky Punjabi, Naz's erstwhile boyfriend, a Bhangra-dancer wannabe who has—with his friends and classmates—participated in slut-shaming Naz.

Violence dances around the edges of *Boys With Cars*—the violence visited upon women, on women of colour, who are already so imperilled by the societies in which they live: India, Canada, high school. The "honour killings" of India about which Canadian citizens tsk-tsk and shake their heads suddenly seem uncomfortably close to home. The slut-shaming of Naznin, delicate Naznin, engenders physical violence, terror, and her eventual banishment from school and her only remaining community.

Dance tells as much of the story as text in *Boys With Cars*, and the dance is by turns classical Indian, Bhangra, and ultimately Naz's own, informed by her history and transformed by her experiences. The fierce dance of the final moments of the play is how Naz reclaims her honour from those who would take it from her. Naz—which means pride—dances for herself, reclaiming all that is beautiful and powerful from her history, infusing it with the reality and strength of being a twenty-first-century woman of intelligence and grace. She walks away from small-minded Port Moody, away from boys with cars, under her own power towards a larger, evolving, inclusive Canada.

—Yvette Nolan

Boys With Cars premiered in a double bill with *Fish Eyes* at the Great Canadian Theatre Company, Ottawa, on October 16, 2014, with the following cast and creative team:

Choreographer and actor: Anita Majumdar
Director and dramaturg: Brian Quirt
Producer: Rupal Shah
Stage manager: Sandy Plunkett
Lighting design: Rebecca Picherack
Set and costume design: Jackie Chau
Sound design: Christopher Stanton
Production manager: Simon Rossitor

CHARACTERS

Naznin
Gustakhi
Lucky
Buddy
Candice
Miss Flemming
Mr. Peter Nicholas Smyth

In the dark, Imran Khan's "Amplifier" plays. Two headlights appear and the spill of light reveals NAZ *standing on the roof of a red Mini Cooper. The lights of the parking lot show* NAZ *in detail; she's dressed like a Mughal courtesan in a glittering peacock-blue Indian dance skirt and Indian jewellery, all covered by a hoodie. On the roof of the car,* NAZ *dances a full-body version of the Fisherperson Story. Her dance retains a traditional grace, but is distinctly sharp and vengeful. A fury pulses through* NAZ, *and yet with every spin her skirt flairs upwards, and for a moment she appears like a shimmering teardrop. By the end of the dance she notices she is being watched and immediately stops dancing. She puts on a pair of large sunglasses and sits on the roof of the Mini Cooper with her back turned to the audience and hides her face.*

Present: May 2014, Victoria Day weekend.

Noises from a nearby reception are heard. NAZ *notices her watcher hasn't left yet.*

NAZ: You know who wears sunglasses at night? Assholes. But most people hate talking to assholes and I hate talking to most people, so it works out. You here for the wedding? Duh, right? Are you with the bride or the groom? Me too.

NAZ fiddles with her iPod earbuds and puts one in her left ear. Chris Brown's "Kiss Kiss" underscores.

I have this thing where I listen to the same song over and over again. I'll be listening to that song when something kinda big's happening in my life, but then I'll stop listening to it, but then I'll hear it again and all of it . . .

She listens for a moment.

. . . comes back again . . . So I try not to listen to those songs anymore.

NAZ takes the earbud from her ear. "Kiss Kiss" stops playing.

People get mad when I say I like Chris Brown . . .

She rolls her eyes.

. . . because he hit Rihanna. People don't get there's two sides to every story. Chris is really sorry . . . and HOT. And he's making it all about the music now, so I don't know why people don't just get over themselves, so . . .

Gustakhi's supposed to be here by now. Oh, yeah, she's looking for parking. Did YOU have to look for parking? Of course not, because this school has more parking spots than it does textbooks. Gustakhi was supposed to be here ten minutes ago. We're the dance company for tonight. I love dancing . . . except for the part where people have to look at me. At every one of these things, I dance-dance-dance, the crowd watches me, and for a split second I think he might be there. "I don't even want to see him!" I say that to trick God.

She holds up an Allah pendant hanging around her neck.

Because *God's* always giving me the opposite of what I want. And then I wonder when he's coming back . . . because he HAS to come back, right? My dance set's pretty easy; dance *Slumdog Millionaire* songs for white-people weddings.

"Jai Ho!" from Slumdog Millionaire *plays. NAZ dances on the roof of the Mini Cooper, lightly kicking up her feet and putting graceful attention*

into her hips. In the middle of an intricate Indian hand gesture, NAZ *turns the song off abruptly.*

Fucking "Jai Ho!" Sorry, but I really hate that song. It's like the Le Château national anthem, and other AWESOME stores like that. When I first started performing weddings, it was all like:

"Jai Ho!" plays from the beginning again. NAZ *dances to the same choreography as earlier and exaggerates her enthusiasm for the dance. She abruptly turns off the song at the same place as before.*

But one year later it's more like:

"Jai Ho!" plays from the beginning again. NAZ's *eyes widen and she dances like she's being held hostage by the Russian militia. The song abruptly stops again.*

I don't have a studio, so I practice here in the school parking lot. It's the only square footage in Port Moody that's mine . . . and it isn't even. Not the car, not the lot. I don't even have a licence to drive myself out of here. You think Port Moody's *nice*? Port Moody has this inlet of water, mountains, trees, but do you notice any of that? Nope. You look at the motherfucking stacks of the YELLOWEST sulfur—UNSECURED—piled up over there on the Barnet Highway! Speaking of acidic compounds, where's Gustakhi?! She's not my mom. She's like my *Toddlers & Tiara's* show mom, so not like a mom who loves me or anything? I don't have parents. I mean, I HAVE parents, but not ones I can see in front of my face. And no, I'm not like the grade-twelve girls who lie about having dead parents to be deep and not wash their hair. I live with Gustakhi. And work with Gustakhi.

Flashback: GUSTAKHI *appears in her home.*

GUSTAKHI: We're like a *Mughal-e-Azam* courtesan business, Naznin; you dance for the whites, I keep their dollars. Just like old-time India . . . before England showed up and gave us AIDS.

Present: NAZ *sits down on the roof of the Mini Cooper.*

NAZ: Our usual gigs are in Vancouver. After driving us back to Port Moody, Gustakhi helps me out of my costume because the hooks are at the back.

NAZ tries to unhook the back of her blouse but can't reach. Flashback: GUSTAKHI appears and sits behind NAZ, undoing the hooks of the blouse from behind.

GUSTAKHI: If only you wore all your clothing with buttons in the back, Naznin. Then it wouldn't be so easy to take it off for every boy who offered you a bag of Timbits!

Present: NAZ dangles her feet off the roof of the car.

NAZ: Gustakhi's not a dancer. She's barely HUMAN most of the time. But I keep living with her and she keeps letting me . . . as long as I keep dancing. She moved here from Punjab after her kids died. After high school ended, I needed a new place to live and work . . . I met Gustakhi at the mall and we really hit it off—

Flashback: June 2013. NAZ approaches GUSTAKHI in the Coquitlam Centre parking lot.

Hi, *Aunty*—

GUSTAKHI: Don't do that; I hate that. All you Indian kids, I don't know who told you every person you meet on the road to turn them into family. I'm not your family.

NAZ: Sorry, *Aunty*, or, um—

GUSTAKHI: Eh! You look like a giraffe. What's wrong with you? How come you stand so tall? You look like you're proud of yourself.

NAZ: I'm not proud. I'm an Indian dancer, so—

GUSTAKHI: Eh! You see this Shanta Claush operation over here in the food court? Huh! Christmas in July! What a pile of horseshit! So any time is the right time to teach small girls if you want nice things, just sit in an old man's lap?! Every year I enter His temple at the Coquitlam Centre Mall Centre and I say, "Shanta-*ji,* make this life a little easier . . . with a new samosa maker . . . and a bigger mirror. I can't see myself properly in my one at home!" But *Shanta's* a regular Sherry Seinfeld: "Well maybe if you ate less samosa you fit into existing mirror"—"Ha ha ha"?! And then his *kameeni* Mrs. Claush says it's little Suzy's turn. So I told little Suzy, "YOU WAIT YOUR TURN, LITTLE SUZY!" You're a girl; get used to being served last from now, only!

Back to the present.

NAZ: *(points to the car)* This is Lucky's car. Lucky Punjabi? He's my boyfriend. He's coming back for the wedding tonight. When we were still in school, Lucky'd park in Top Lot parking along with the other "cools" from our school. Middle Lot's teacher parking and Bottom Lot's for the rest of the kingdom. This car is like Lucky's religion . . .

Flashback: One week before Victoria Day weekend, May 2014. GUSTAKHI, *in her living room, approaches* NAZ.

GUSTAKHI: What happened to Lucky Punjabi? Did Calgary "stampede" our Lucky out of town? You never told me that part of the story, Naznin.

Present: GUSTAKHI *is nowhere to be seen but* NAZ, *rattled, looks to see if she's arrived.*

NAZ: I still hang out here when I'm not dancing. Port Moody Senior Secondary. PMSS for short. Oh, I suggested alternate names. Like name it after Albert Street down the hill: *ASSS?* But Principal Shaker said I was in enough trouble and mature PMSS girls should know better.

I'm not nervous. I never get nervous. I mean, the last time I felt like *this* was Golden Spike Fest 2012.

Ever since July 1886, Port Moody celebrates trains stopping in Port Moody— *on purpose*—by watching locals perform by day and teens ODing on drugs by night. My dance teacher forced me to do this Indian dance—

NAZ demonstrates a version of the Natraj statue pose with the hand gesture for "one with eyes like a fish" by her left eye.

—which got seen by a ton of the "cools" from my school. None of them even knew my name. How could they, they never saw me. But now these guys parked their SUVs around Rocky Point stage and pressed their eyes into me while licking ice cream cones.

Flashback: Golden Spike Days Festival, July 2012. NAZ performs a classical dance to the song "Laal Ishq" from the film Goliyon Ki Raasleela Ram-Leela *on a makeshift stage in the middle of the park. In between quick spins and angular arm movements lies an entrancing softness. NAZ's genuine joy for the dance bursts from her and pulls the watcher's gaze even closer. NAZ ends in a traditional Kathak/North Indian dance posture that demurely hides her face. Upon the end of the dance, NAZ turns away from the audience and looks down.*

(avoiding eye contact) I get off stage and I look down because if I can't see them, they can't see me, right? But then I feel someone coming up to me; Buddy Cain and me meet eyes as he walks over with Candice Paskis trying to catch up behind him in her red bikini and cowboy hat, until, thank God—

Akon's "Chammak Challo" plays. NAZ turns sharply. LUCKY Punjabi appears on the Golden Spike Festival stage and dances like a sincere but mediocre America's Got Talent contestant. But what LUCKY lacks in dance skills, he makes up for in self-assured bravado. The song ends and LUCKY addresses his public while noticing NAZ standing in the crowd.

LUCKY: Name's LUCKY PUNJABI! And I'll be signing autographs by Pajo's Fish & Chip Hut with my bro from another ho, Buddy Cain. YEAH, BUDDY!

LUCKY sees NAZ trying to leave.

Hey . . . Oh . . . no . . . what have I done? I've Axe Body Sprayed-a-nated myself. For the fans. Ladies. Love it. Hey, Naznin! Did you know I am a founding member of the Coventry School of Bhangra? Yeah! I invented the "Bhangra burpee." You know?

LUCKY *dances a Bhangra move while hopping on one leg and pumping his arms in the air. He then pounces to the ground into a push-up and jumps back up.*

BURPEE! Naznin, yeah? Pretty good back there. I love watching your hands.

NAZ *shouts over the crowd, looking up at* LUCKY *on the stage.*

NAZ: *(shouting, looking up)* Everyone has hands.

LUCKY: You Indian dance pretty good, Naznin.

LUCKY *appears to leave nonchalantly but then immediately turns back to* NAZ *and takes out a Keg Steakhouse mint.*

It's from the Keg. The steakhouse? It's my "Lucky mint," but I want you to hold it for me because that's how good you dance.

NAZ: *(to wedding guest)* Lucky says he's moving to PMSS in the fall and that I should remember the name:

LUCKY: LUCKY PUNJABI!

He does his dance move again.

BURPEE!

LUCKY *throws the Keg mint into the air and* NAZ *picks it up. The Pussycat Dolls's remix of "Jai Ho" plays as* NAZ *looks at the mint for a moment, then dances with genuine enthusiasm to the song.* NAZ *spins into the first day of PMSS grade twelve, September 2012.* MISS FLEMMING *appears in the PMSS gym.*

MISS FLEMMING *blows on a whistle while bouncing a basketball.*

MISS FLEMMING: All right, girls, let's kick off Miss Flemming's Gym 12 by getting sex-ed done and out of the way! But keep dribbling your balls: NO WATER! Now, I've heard a lot of you doe-eyed gazelles talk about date rape. "Oh, Miss Flemming, he raped me. He did this horrible thing!" and then you bat your eyelashes like a . . . *gazelle*—PASS!

She passes her basketball to one of the girls.

Rape is a two-way street, ladies. When you decide to kiss a guy for a certain amount of time and then you stop because you "changed your mind," well, that poor guy's gonna get blue balls. *Blue balls*—PASS—is where a guy needs to release the stress *you* caused him. If a deer gets hit by a car, well what was the deer doing in the middle of the street? At night? BY HERSELF? So girls who get date raped just rape themselves. Girls? Man up, and let's end date rape forever!

MISS FLEMMING holds her basketball and starts nodding and clapping loudly.

Woo! Yeah! PASS!

MR. PETER NICHOLAS SMYTH appears and addresses his classroom.

MR. PETER NICHOLAS SMYTH: All right, ladies and gents, welcome to this year's English 12. I'm your "commando" in chief, Mr. Peter Nicholas Smyth, but you can call me P-N-S, P-N-S, P-N-S, P-N-S, P-N-S, P-N-S, P-N-S— Say it real fast and what do you got? You got penis! Now we're going to start off with *Mother Courage*, or as they say in the theatre—

He acts out the famed Mother Courage *silent-screaming gesture.*

"Silent-scream," that's what I was doing there—our way through *Mother Courage*. God. What a bitch. Am I right, gents in the back? But don't worry, everyone gets to read the screenplay I wrote this summer: *The Never-Ending Story: My 5 Seasons on MacGyver*. Working title. Now it won't be on the provincial exam, but great to get your feedback.

NAZ walks through the hallways of PMSS.

NAZ: Senior year at PMSS. Before I could have had a pet iguana, named it Fluffy, and walked it on a leash of banana peels, and still no one would see me. But *Paradise Lost*. Lucky drives his red Mini Cooper straight into Top Lot parking. I move past him and Buddy Cain in front of the rainbow-colour lockers PMSS painted to make the ethnics feel welcome. I brush Lucky's hand with his Keg mint in my hand . . . the heat from his hand makes a knot. A knot that's one end me, one end Lucky.

NAZ pulls both ends of the Keg mint wrapper like a bow.

A knot so tight no one can loosen it.

LUCKY appears across from NAZ in the hallway in front of the rainbow-coloured lockers.

LUCKY: Everyone! She just stole my lucky Keg mint that I've had ever since the first time I *went* to the Keg! Lucky Punjabi just got violated on by Naznin! And don't try and deny it. You girls are like natural-born liars. Like those La Senza bras that make your boobs bigger . . . LIES! Like, I asked out this A-cup last week because she made me *believe* she was a D-cup! Uh, an A to a D? That's witchcraft! Watch out for Naznin! She's a witch who belly-dances for men. Just look at her Egypt necklace!

NAZ: I dance *Indian* classical, and hello?

She holds out her Allah necklace.

Muslim? I'm Ismaili—

LUCKY: No, you're not! You're not "smiley" at all! You're all "frowny" and droopy—

NAZ: *IS*-maili. It's a branch of Islam—

LUCKY: I don't think so. Like I watch Fox News—like, A LOT—and they're always showin' your lot talking in "Egypt"—

NAZ: What about you, Lucky *Punjabi*? Shouldn't you be marrying your eight-year-old cousin right now? I guess hanging out in Surrey and gang-shooting people as they come out of the SkyTrain station keeps you pretty busy, huh?

(to wedding guest) And then it happens. The "cools" laugh. Not at me. For me. Even Buddy and Candice, they all clap and cheer for me. Lucky comes up to me all grown-uppy and pinches my cheek and smiles.

From then on, kids started to *see* me. I was the girl Lucky liked. So I started to look down a lot. Not in an "Indian woman" way, just in a "staying out of the way" way. Lucky writes this note saying we should go out, just him and me, Friday night.

Flashback: LUCKY *and* NAZ *sit in his Mini Cooper. Chris Brown's "Kiss Kiss" plays from the car stereo.*

LUCKY: I hope you don't mind. I listen to just, like, one song over and over again. I'm weird like that.

NAZ: Lucky buys us a box of doughnuts for dinner and we listen to Chris Brown's "Kiss Kiss" on repeat while we drive out of Port Moody in his red Mini Cooper, past the yellow sulfur on the Barnet Highway, over the bridge, and park in front of this West Van mansion.

LUCKY *points to the house outside the windshield.*

LUCKY: This house has, like, the biggest telly! We can watch through the living-room window! Like a drive-in, yeah?

NAZ: We watch the Friday lineup through Lucky's windshield; no talking, no sound, except for Chris Brown's "Kiss Kiss." I see him staring at me from the corner of my eye. And can see him thinking, "Whoa, her eyelashes are so long." And then he says:

LUCKY: *(staring at NAZ)* You have, like, the longest eyelashes!

NAZ: And nothing feels better than someone thinking you have long eyelashes. Then he hugs me. The CW Network never prepared me for . . . hugging. I let him because there's something in Lucky's arms . . . but then Lucky turns back to the TV.

LUCKY: Miley Cyrus is licking a hammer! Oh! When she does it, it's "art." When I do it, it's, "Oh, Lucky Punjabi's drunk!" and "Lucky Punjabi, get out of this Canadian Tire!"

NAZ: I kiss Lucky. And from then on it was every Friday night. Lucky and Naz. I stopped dancing. And wearing my Allah pendant.

NAZ takes off her Allah necklace.

Rehearsal never started on time, and . . . people looking at you all the time . . . there was no point when I just hit the PMSS jackpot! After school, we'd all hang out in Top Lot next to Buddy's Hummer, which always took up two parking spots. After Buddy and Candice left, it was finally just me and Lucky driving past the yellow sulphur on the Barnet, going anywhere but here. Listening to songs on repeat—

Present: From the PMSS parking lot, NAZ hears Destiny's Child's "Survivor" blare from the gym.

Is that "Survivor"? I'M JUST GOING TO KILL MYSELF! Fuckin' Port Moody! I HATE YOU SO HARD! Of course those PMSS *assholes* would play "Survivor" for their wedding. Fuckers! PoMo fuckers! This town's such a joke! Wait. You're going in? Why? You *like* this song? *Really?* No, I should stay out here, for Gustakhi. Are the bride and groom in the gym? No, I just really hate that song.

Beat.

Flashback: Early March 2013. NAZ slowly walks into the PMSS gym for a student assembly.

Just before spring break, we're at one of those dorky school assemblies PMSS holds to give the teachers a break from doing their jobs. I wore a skirt that day, for Lucky.

NAZ appears in a skirt that sits halfway up her thigh.

But I forgot Lucky was driving "the Cooper" to Calgary to audition for *Bhangra Idol*. We all file into the gym and Buddy's sitting by himself in the top bleachers. He fake yawns and pats for me to sit next to him, as a joke. Chris Brown's "Kiss Kiss" is playing on repeat in my head when:

NAZ sits next to BUDDY in the bleachers while tugging down on the hem of her short skirt.

BUDDY: So you got into UBC, huh? That early acceptance bullshit or whatever? Guess you're leaving Port Moody, then? That's mean . . . Leaving us behind? You're mean. Huh, you cold, meanie? Maybe if you weren't so mean, I'd share my jacket with you. Whoa, your legs look like a gazelle's. My dad and me hunt deer, so I know. Remember when we were at Golden Spike together? I even told Candice, "That Indian chick dancing, she looks like a gazelle."

NAZ: *WE* weren't at Golden Spike together. *LUCKY* and me were performing at Golden Spike.

BUDDY: Lucky? Lucky who?

Destiny's Child's "Survivor" plays.

NAZ: Buddy moves his jacket over both our knees when we start watching Candice and friends dancing to this, like, out-of-nowhere Indian dance by the girls' gym class—

I'm focusing on Meena, the one Indian girl who actually looks like she knows what she's doing, when Buddy grabs my hand under the jacket . . .

NAZ's right hand grabs her left wrist and remains frozen in this wrist-lock dance gesture.

. . . and moves it . . . on him . . . on his . . . private . . . on his body? Do you . . . understand what's happening? Because I don't. I don't . . . understand. I keep watching the school-assembly dance while trying to pull my hand back, but Buddy squeezes it there and rolls it in waves, which makes the jacket move. And it's damp— Every time I go over it in my head, I always ask myself, "Why didn't you use your free hand to pull the other hand away?!" That would be a practical application of Indian dance training! One quick— I keep watching the school-assembly dance. I laser-focus on Candice because there's something in my hand that belongs to her. But watching Candice Indian dance, I feel angry because there's something in her hand that belongs to me. Why couldn't that be me down there? I wish my name was Candice right now and I was down there and she was up here— Why didn't I fight harder? Why didn't my face . . . my face looked like nothing! Like I was just watching this school-assembly dance like it was nothing! Like nothing was happening!

The "Survivor" dance ends and thunderous applause rises from the gym bleachers.

The dance ends and Buddy throws away my hand—

NAZ's right hand throws away her left hand, releasing the wrist lock, and her hands transition into clapping along with the rest of the audience in the bleachers.

—and stands up clapping. And I'm just sitting there. I just sit there while Buddy whispers in Candice's ear. He spins her around by her waist and kisses her and calls her his bitch—

NAZ clasps her hands and stops clapping.

I'm so stupid! Stupid for just sitting there, stupid for wearing this skirt, stupid for thinking I was one of "them" because my boyfriend was! Stupid for sitting with Buddy, stupid for not using my hand, for not . . . STUPID for just— Where was Lucky? Why did he have to leave that day? Why would he leave me there alone with Buddy?! Why would he— When I needed him the most . . . WHERE WAS LUCKY?!

Flashback: Akon's "Chammak Challo" plays. LUCKY *appears centre stage in a high-school gym for the* Bhangra Idol *auditions in Calgary.*

LUCKY: Hello, *Bhangra Idol!* This is LUCKY PUNJABI from Port Moody, BC. And THIS? Is for YOU, Calgary! . . .

LUCKY lip-synchs and dances with full gusto, but is still mediocre at best. His high-energy, bouncing dance moves reach their peak and his audition ends.

Lucky Punjabi OUT!

LUCKY swaggers out and the Akon vocals transitions into the Hamsika Iyer vocal section of "Chammak Challo." NAZ *stands alone in an empty high-school gym. She steps into the centre spot where* LUCKY *was.*

NAZ: Lucky was in a gym somewhere, and so was I—

She replicates some of the moves from "Survivor" in time to "Chammak Challo." The dance is a true homage to the Mughal courtesan tradition, with seductive floorwork and the glittering fabric of her encircling skirt. NAZ *eventually dances to her feet and at the end she thinks she sees* LUCKY *and turns in a circle with him.* LUCKY *exits away from her.* NAZ *watches him leave. The music has ended and* NAZ *returns to the PMSS gym.*

After the school assembly.

Buddy's hanging all over Candice and looks at me like, "I don't know what you're talking about." Then it starts. At first it was "Naz-ty plus Buddy" in sharp pencil hearts all over the boys' change-room door. Then pictures of me with words next to them.

Without ever looking at it, NAZ *opens a locker door that has the words "Would you* FUCK *this* CUNT*" written in red paint and a hand-drawn penis below it.*

Lucky gets back in time for the test in Mr. Peter Nicholas Smyth's class, and I'm trying to answer "Name that Quote": "I am too far away from you now, talking to you from a land you can't get into with your quick tongue and your hollow heart . . . "—*Antigone*—when the "cools" at the back rub out lit cigarettes into my neck and hair and cough, "Ashtray." I don't know why "Penis" can't see, or SMELL, but I keep writing. "I am too far away from you now . . . " And Candice. Candice Paskis corners me in front of the lockers PMSS painted to make the ethnics feel welcome?

CANDICE *appears in the company of her girlfriends and corners* NAZ *against the lockers.*

CANDICE: Are you retarded? You weren't even good enough for Lucky; you thought you'd be good enough for Buddy? When Lucky first started talking about you, I was all like, "Who is that? I don't even know who that is." But that you made a move on MY BOYFRIEND? That you thought Buddy'd want to eat out mud when he could lick a snow cone? Before me and Buddy, I offered to go down on Lucky . . . like a couple of times? And he said no 'cause he's hard-core *noble*. But you just look like a bitch. You have a face that looks like a bitch. So shut it off . . . Nazu . . . Nazi—what's your—what's her— *(aside to her friend)* WHAT'S HER NAME, AGAIN?

CANDICE *vanishes.* NAZ *is alone in the hallway.*

NAZ: We start volleyball in Miss Flemming's class and there's Emily Johnson, who I was in ensemble dance with just before Christmas break. We danced to "Beep"? The Pussycat Dolls's "Beep"? I showed Emily how to dance a deer with her hand.

NAZ *demonstrates the bharatanatyam hand gesture for deer,* "Simhamukha."

But Emily's tight with Candice Paskis and throws a volleyball at my head now, but says "oops." Miss Flemming pretends not to see. I say "bitch" softly because it makes me not cry. Miranda Parks smears up against me, "Did you just call Emily a bitch? That's not very nice to say about my *best friend*."

And I say, "Well she is. She's a bitch." Emily thuds another volleyball at my face. Harder. After school, Candice's Top Lot friends chase me with lighters and I run. You're not supposed to run in the halls! I don't know why anyone isn't coming out and saying, "Hey! You're not supposed to run in the halls!" I love my eyelashes. They're awesome. They're thick and long and great. My eyelashes are . . . they're really great. Emily thwacks me into a door and my eyelashes get two of my teeth stuck in them. And blood. And bits of door. But it's a red door, so at least it matches.

Adults are always talking about bullying because of annoying girls who cry about being shit-talked on Facebook. But I never said anything because I'm cool like that! Principal Shaker was NOT cool like that. After they take me to the ER to put back my teeth and cauterize my nose bleed, Principal Shaker brings ME into his office for the fifteenth time that month, and along with PNS and Miss Flemming, Principal Shaker tells me I've been become a "distraction" to the other kids, and with provincials coming up, they decide it'd be best for the school if I finished the rest of my year at home, which super-thrills my parents. After school ended, my parents sold our house on Heritage Mountain and left for Dubai. They couldn't look at me anymore. Everything in Port Moody reminded them of me.

There were only another four weeks left till provincial exams started! Eight weeks till graduation! No one gave me a chance to tough it out! *Mother Courage* it out! I could have "silent screamed" my way to graduation, kept my home, my family, my savings, and then I'd be at UBC right now! But instead I'm stuck in this fuckin' Greek tragedy called Port Moody: " . . . talking to you from a land you can't get into with your quick tongue and your hollow heart . . . "

Flashback: One week before Victoria Day weekend, 2014. GUSTAKHI, *in her living room, approaches* NAZ.

GUSTAKHI: What happened to Lucky Punjabi? Did Calgary stampede our Lucky out of town? You never told me that part of the story, Naznin. I'm only asking because Lucky phoned me. Lucky's getting married and wants you to dance.

NAZ: LUCKY . . . WHAT? LUCKY . . . WHAT?!

GUSTAKHI: When Lucky left, what song was playing? Which song do you think our Lucky would appreciate—OH GOD! Look at your face, Naznin! *Waah, isey kehte hain ishq.*[1] Relax, *yaar.* Lucky didn't call.

NAZ: ARE YOU KIDDING ME?!

GUSTAKHI: No, it was Buddy. Buddy phoned to ask you to dance for his and this Candice Pakeezah's wedding at your old high school, but the Lucky part I made up. You should use that shock face for dancing; we'd get more tips—

NAZ: You act like me knowing Lucky means *you* knowing Lucky. You *don't* know Lucky! As if I'm going to be all like, "Oh Gustakhi-*jaan,* can we make s'mores and talk about my feelings?" We're not friends like that, so why can't you stop talking about Lucky and just shut up about Lucky?!

GUSTAKHI: BECAUSE I WANT IT TO HURT! STOP AND FEEL IT HURT, Naznin! I've seen you walking around here for the last year, "Oh, I didn't do nothing and see what they all did." But remember: who didn't just pull her hand off his crotch? Who forgot she's a grown girl? A girl who forgot herself; you don't forget that.

NAZ: Then don't you forget to go get yourself laid so you can finally stop masturbating to me and Lucky.

GUSTAKHI: My daughter had a toilet-brush mouth like you too. All modern-thinking, small, thin, look like you can't do, but see what y'all do? My son's engagement day. My daughter gallivants in announcing, informing me in front of everyone, that she too will be getting married . . . to some low-class boot-polish boy she met at college. Bride's family cancels marriage with my son. Good dowry that we needed? Gone. Then village stops talking to us.

---

1 Translation: This is what they call love?

Any chance anyone wanted to marry into my family? Do business with my family? Gone. We needed a clean slate. So I told my son, "You take your late daddy's gun, and take your sister into the field."

The Jagjit Singh ghazal "Unke Dekhe Se" plays in the distance.

That morning . . . that old Jagjit Singh ghazal was playing over and over from my neighbour's place when they brought *two* bodies to the village yard . . . Saying it was both murder and suicide? My son too soft and my daughter too loose. The ghazal keeps playing and their bodies just lie there. My blood in dirt. You know what it is to see your own blood lying in dirt? How it is to have the blood in your veins ache and scream at same time? *The cry of the gazelle when it's cornered by the hunter and knows it will die?* My village wouldn't even give them last rites! So *I* built the pyres and watched my children burn. I gave my blood back to Him so their ashes could feed the earth and vegetables. But how could I watch my village eat my family's skin and eyes? So what? Before summer, I was gone.

NAZ: You . . . killed your children? You murdered your . . .

You killed your own blood! And you think you did the RIGHT thing? Was God sitting in your lap saying, "Hey, Gustakhi, do God a solid and kill your daughter for me?!"

GUSTAKHI: Don't YOU talk about God! Don't YOU talk about God like you're chummy-chummy! You know, if you lived anywhere other than here you'd be dead by now. Oh, so sad for "Lucky"? Naznin, you just remember you're the one who's lucky.

NAZ: DON'T SAY HIS NAME! Don't YOU . . . EVER say his name! EVER! Your awful mouth on his name! Don't talk to me like you and me are somehow the same! Like ANYTHING between us is the same!

GUSTAKHI: God, you're so Canadian, Naznin. *Haan*, you study classical dance, dance your "Jai Ho!," but you think because you live here you're different than the rest of us when someone takes away everything and you lose *everything*?

You know, our ghazal in India isn't just some song the third world made up to kill time. It's the cry of the gazelle when it's cornered by the hunter and knows it will die. So before that happens, I want you to think, Naznin. Eh, Naznin? Are you listening? Naznin?

> GUSTAKHI *snaps her fingers in front of* NAZ's *face.* NAZ *jolts as though waking from a deep sleep.*

NAZ: Buddy and Candice are getting married THIS weekend? Lucky's coming back! He wouldn't miss his best friend's wedding! I don't know if I'll feel like dancing for the people who took away everything I ever had . . . THIS weekend.

GUSTAKHI: Did you hear anything I just said—

NAZ: In the Middle East, you cut off a man's hand when he steals something from you? An eye for an eye?

> NAZ *assumes a version of the Natraj statue pose for a moment while maintaining the hand gesture for "one with eyes like a fish" by her eye. Imran Khan's "Amplifier" begins playing in the distance.* NAZ *places her Allah pendant around her neck again. Present and past tense begin to bleed into each other.* NAZ *approaches* LUCKY's *Mini Cooper.*

You tell Buddy and Candice I *will* dance for their wedding. Then you and me will meet at Lucky's Mini Cooper in Bottom Lot just before the reception is supposed to start. You bring out Buddy.

We'll tie him to the car door. And Candice. Candice Paskis. You bring that bitch out here. You bring her and I'll bring all the cigarettes I have. I'll sit in front of Buddy tied to Lucky's red car door and I'll light one and then another and then another, right close to his eyelashes, just to fuck with him. And then when he's good and scared, I'll light a fistful and ASH them in his stupid hand! The cry of the gazelle when it's cornered by the hunter and knows it will die!

GUSTAKHI: Naznin, stop and hear yourself for even a minute—

NAZ: I won't touch Candice! Even though all I want to do is throw her in a pile of sulphur till her "You weren't even good enough for Lucky, you thought you'd be good enough for Buddy?!" bitch face burns off! I'll just make her watch. Even if I have to hold her by her Shoppers Drug Mart–yellow hair and HOOK open her Aryan blue eyes—she's going to SEE ME.

GUSTAKHI: Justice doesn't make living easier, Naznin. I promise it doesn't—

NAZ: I'll keep those cigarettes in that fucker's hand till Buddy's in so much pain he'll do anything for it to stop, but not so much pain that he can't talk. And then Buddy'll tell everyone at the PMSS wedding what really happened. Whose hand was *where*, doing *who*, and *what* and *where* and . . . WHAT under that jacket! And then everyone'll know! And Lucky.

NAZ lies on the hood of the car. "Unke Dekhe Se" faintly plays from the car stereo.

Lucky will touch my face, and stroke the hair away from my face, and kiss— Buddy and Candice's wedding limousine will be parked in Top Lot, and Lucky'll pick me up in his arms and put me in the limo and we'll just go. And everyone will just watch. We'll sink into the back seat, I'll put my head into that place that fits perfect into Lucky, and we'll *kiss* . . . for all the time we lost . . . for all the time we could have been *kissing*. We'll drive past the sulphur on the Barnet one last time and go.

She holds her Allah necklace.

"I am too far away from you now . . . "

Present: NAZ is in a half-dream state lying on the hood of LUCKY's car.

There is no God in Port Moody. So I started wearing this again to call Him back. Even when I sleep. It always somehow swishes over to my left boob, which made me think maybe God was ready to hear my side? That if He could just *hear* my heart, and *feel* my heart, God would stop punishing me and bring back Lucky?

NAZ suddenly opens her eyes wide, as if waking up from a nightmare. The music is gone.

ENOUGH! I'm done. I'M DONE. Enough "Jai Ho!" and Top Lots and Bottom Lots and the same song over and over and over and licking the UBC course book like a puppy in a window! How is this fair? Does this seem even a little bit fair, to *you*?! Buddy and Candice are getting married tonight. They're in the gym feeling the happiest they've ever felt . . . And I'm going to take that away!

At long last, GUSTAKHI arrives in the PMSS parking lot.

Gustakhi?! Where have you been? I've been waiting all night—

GUSTAKHI: Lucky isn't here. He didn't come for the wedding.

NAZ: You're lying!

GUSTAKHI: Lucky isn't here! Go see with your eyes! Thank God. Now you can cancel this *duffer* plan of yours. What I did was for my family. My name. You want to do this for a boy who gave you a Keg mint?!

She takes LUCKY's Keg Steakhouse mint from her pocket.

NAZ: It was his LAST Keg mint! From the Keg! Like, you can't just get those! You actually have to eat a full steak dinner at the Keg! And he told me to hold on to it!

She dances the "knot" hand gesture.

We made a knot! You don't just forget that!

GUSTAKHI: You want to right the wrong, punish Buddy and Candice? But what about Lucky? You're not Romeo and Juliet. Where is he? Has he called? Written? You know what Gustakhi thinks? Gustakhi thinks when Lucky came back from Calgary and everyone believed *you* put your hand on Buddy? He believed it too.

Flashback: Early March 2013, in the evening. LUCKY, *freshly returned from auditioning in Calgary, sits in his car with* NAZ *in the parking lot at PMSS.*

LUCKY *is in the driver's seat.*

LUCKY: Buddy told me everything last night. Candice too. While I was singing in Calgary, you were . . . I can't even look at you, Naznin. Dubee was sitting right behind you and Buddy in the top-row bleachers.

NAZ: You're not even going to let me tell my side?!

Present.

GUSTAKHI: Tell me your side, Naznin! Your side, his side, but tell SOME SIDE! Scream, yell, abuse him, but really look back and remember what—what really happened—

Flashback.

LUCKY: Are you going to tell me that you *didn't* have Buddy's cock in your hand? That the second I left you alone . . .

Beat.

I should have known—the way he looked at you—

NAZ: The way HE looked at ME! Let's just go for a drive. And then we can talk and we can go for a drive—

Present.

GUSTAKHI: What drive? You have to dance now, Naz! But get this out of your system. Burning Buddy's hand with duty-free smokes won't fix nothing—

NAZ: You know how everyone was super stressed out about Rihanna and Chris Brown and how maybe they hooked up again? But looking from the outside doesn't mean you know! You don't know anything! Even if everyone else says so, you have to hear both sides!

Flashback.

LUCKY: I don't have to hear any sides. I know. I kissed Candice tonight. She's a really good Indian dancer. Better than you. She was telling me how she's going to the Coventry School of Bhangra. And I kissed her, but then I stopped because—

Present.

GUSTAKHI: Where was Lucky when those ugly girls threw volleyballs at your face, Naznin? When Lucky's boy-friends ashed their cigarettes in your neck and hair in class—

Flashback.

LUCKY: I loved you, Naznin. In Hindi, the word for "trouble"—it's feminine. You're *taqleef*, Naznin. You tricked me into kissing my best friend's girl.

She pulls out the Keg mint.

NAZ: But we made a knot!! You don't just forget that and make a knot for nothing. A knot makes us family! Lucky?

NAZ reaches out to touch LUCKY.

LUCKY aggressively swats NAZ *away.*

LUCKY: SLUT, DON'T TOUCH ME!!

NAZ: *(shocked)* LUCKY . . .

Present.

GUSTAKHI: Family isn't just driving around in a car and "*main yahaan, tum wahaan.*"[2] Family is for when things get tough.

Flashback.

---

2 Translation: "I'm way over here, and you're way over there."

LUCKY: I should have known better! You prostitute-dance for men!

NAZ: I stopped dancing for you!

LUCKY: I have to get away from you!

LUCKY gets out of his car. NAZ rushes out behind him to the middle of the parking lot.

NAZ: PLEASE, LUCKY! STOP! YOU HAVE TO STOP! I CAN'T . . . I don't know what . . . YOU HAVE TO STOP . . .

Present.

GUSTAKHI: Things got just a little tough, and Lucky ran? Have some "Naz," Naz! *Some* pride! See what you became with Lucky?

Flashback: LUCKY is outside of his car.

LUCKY: I have to get away from you. I don't think I'll be back for graduation. My car broke down on the way back from Calgary. Barely rolled it up the hill, so I'm leaving it here in Bottom Lot.

NAZ sinks down to the pavement.

NAZ: Please, Lucky. Please don't do this! Don't punish me! I'M SO STUPID! I wore a skirt that day! At the school assembly? I wore a stupid skirt that day because I forgot you weren't going to be there. I'm so stupid! I sat next to Buddy! I should have known better! When he took my hand—

NAZ's right hand grabs her left wrist, assuming the dance position she took to tell the story of what happened in the bleachers during the school assembly.

I should have fought him harder. I should have tried harder. I should have thought about you! I should have thought about how much I love you and then I would have fought harder! I'm sorry! I don't know what else to do! I'm so sorry, Lucky . . . PLEASE!

Beat.

Can I at least look after your car for you—

LUCKY: Look after my car?! Look after— You can't even drive, Naznin! And even if you could . . . My car is my God. I'd never trust you with my God.

Present.

GUSTAKHI: You're wearing your Allah necklace again? Keep wearing it, so you know God hasn't forgotten you. I wish He'd remember me. It's been twenty years since . . . my children. And ever since my life has been a constant Ramadan. Going without my whole life. But I'm ready for Eid, Naznin. I'm not even Muslim but I'm ready for Eid. I want my feast and forgiveness.

Flashback.

LUCKY: I have to go . . .

Present.

NAZ: I have to go.

GUSTAKHI: What? You have to dance. Do your job then go back to the house.

NAZ: No, I mean I can't dance for these weddings anymore. I can't look at that sulphur anymore. I was supposed to go to university! How did I get here? How did I get myself here? I have to go. Sorry I'm not giving you two weeks notice, but you killed your daughter so . . .

GUSTAKHI: Don't run like Lucky. Be proud like Naz. Do your job then leave. Go. They're waiting.

Imran Khan's "Amplifier" begins playing as NAZ *walks up the steep hill to the PMSS gym lit by the glow of parking lights and street lamps and wet pavement.*

NAZ: Here we go. When we get in there, can you maybe stay with me for a bit? Thanks. Yeah, all I have to do is walk up the hill. Past Bottom Lot. Past

Middle Lot. Past Top Lot. Funny, from here, doesn't it look like the gym's being surrounded? Like all these boys with cars have her backed in and she has nowhere to run? . . . Cornered by the hunter . . .

NAZ enters the PMSS gym where BUDDY *and* CANDICE's *wedding reception is in full swing. The lights are dim, the decorations are cheap, and a disco ball turns in the background.*

This is it. The PMSS gym. I see Candice Paskis, who's nine months preggers. And I see Buddy got a stupid haircut . . . that makes him look stupid.

BUDDY steps up on a makeshift riser while holding a glass of sparking wine to address his wedding-reception audience. He taps the side of his wine glass with a plastic fork.

BUDDY: I don't know if you all know, but Candice is pregnant. And at first I was all like, "Fuck!" But then I was all like, "Fuck!" Candice? Babe? After you have our little Buddy burger, you're gonna be totes hot again. Some of you all know, because of the baby, my dad took back my Hummer. But it's okay, guys, because me and Candice are taking turns riding my sister's mountain bike— Yeah, Top Lot rules! Candice? Babe? The universe threw us a curve ball, but we will rise again, 'cause nothing's gonna get us down. Not even a broken condom.

NAZ watches BUDDY's *speech from the side.*

NAZ looks at the crowd around her.

NAZ: Look at these PMSSers! Do you see these Top Lot douchebags listening to this like, "Oh my God, that's love!" And they all have stupid haircuts too! It's like these assholes got a Groupon to get stupid haircuts! But I don't see Lucky. And yet I see him so clearly now. And I hear . . . The cry of the gazelle. I should get on stage— Buddy?

BUDDY: Hey! We're all super excited to see you dance. You still look, like . . . like you really stayed in shape and stuff. Too bad Lucky's not here, right? I just wanted to say . . . about last year? I wanted to say sorry . . . for Candice. She said some pretty nasty stuff and then you had to drop out . . .

NAZ: You want to say sorry . . . for Candice?

BUDDY: Yeah, and Emily and them too; they were really out of line. But are we cool?

Beat.

NAZ: No, we're not cool. You're a bitch, Buddy. You have a face that looks like a bitch.

NAZ looks to the audience.

Let's do this!

Chris Brown's "Kiss Kiss" begins to play and the lights shift to a spotlight on NAZ at centre stage. NAZ unzips her hoodie and takes it off to reveal a sparking saree blouse underneath. NAZ jumps off the makeshift stage and the spotlight follows her as she approaches the crowd, who circles around her. She stares at each of them directly in the eyes and then begins moving. NAZ dances for BUDDY and CANDICE's reception with power and distinction because she is dancing for herself. The dance is a true demonstration of NAZ's skill because her movements are as precise as they are wild. She plays with Chris Brown's set rhythms, sometimes working with them and sometimes against, but it is clear that she is calling the shots, not the music. Kicks and jumps and footwork are laced with tight spins that make NAZ's skirt glitter in the air, but ultimately the dance ends with simple Kathak footwork directly in front of the audience as NAZ stares each audience member in the eye. With one last stomp, the song ends and NAZ exits the gym through unanimous, thunderous applause without taking a bow.

NAZ walks outside and spots a heavily decorated bike that has a bright "Just Married" sign on it and some tin cans and streamers trailing off the back. NAZ looks at the bike. "Unke Dekhe Se" starts playing in the distance. NAZ *takes* LUCKY's *Keg mint out of her pocket, unwraps it, and pops it into her mouth as she peacefully looks across the horizon of sulphur. Abruptly,* NAZ *spits the mint out onto the pavement.*

Ugh! How old is this mint?

NAZ *gets a backpack and slings it over her shoulder.*

NAZ *goes to the bike and rips off the "Just Married" sign, throwing it to the ground. She looks down the length of the Barnet Highway in front of her and then walks the bike urgently towards it, leaving Port Moody.*

Blackout.

End of play.

A BRIMFUL OF ASHA
Asha and Ravi Jain

To family

ACKNOWLEDGEMENTS

A special thank you to Andy McKim, who gave me the first chance to present a fifteen-minute version of the play in front of an audience. I'd also like to thank Richard Rose for taking me in as part of the Urjo Kareda residency program and having the courage to invite my mother into the playwrights unit. Thanks to Andrea Romaldi, Deborah Pearson, d'bi.young, Anna Chatterton, and Andrew Kushnir, who were all part of the development of this play in the playwrights unit. Thanks to Daniel Brooks for his artistic mentorship and support, especially in the days before opening.

Thanks to all the people who stay and tell us their own stories after each show.

I met Ravi Jain in the summer of 2007, during a workshop he organized that was led by two members of Complicite. Like most people who meet Ravi for the first time, I was taken by his boundless enthusiasm and desire to engage with others. We got along like a proverbial house on fire, and I knew that Ravi and I would soon be friends.

Around the same time as the workshop, I went to see Ravi's production of *Hamlet*. The direction was compelling, fresh, and aesthetically imaginative. We went out for coffee to chat about the play, and we spoke a little about what worked and a lot about what didn't. It was clear to me that there was little room for Ravi's ego to get in the way of making the show better. That's when I knew that Ravi and I would soon be collaborators.

It's no exaggeration to say that my work with Ravi has changed the course of my career. I'm a better writer because of him.

Ravi first spoke to me about *A Brimful of Asha* when he was planning it as a one-man show, detailing his parents' scheme to arrange a marriage for him. When he told his mother about it, she challenged him: "If they hear my side of the story, they'll agree with me." Thankfully for us, it was a provocation that Ravi was unable to resist.

The first time I saw *A Brimful of Asha*, it was an experience of pure magic. Mother and son are there to greet us, the audience, as we enter the theatre.

We are welcomed with a handshake and a warm samosa. As Ravi and Asha share their story with us, it is hard not to imagine ourselves transported into their living room, complete with family photos . . . and their odd binder brimming with biodata.

A Brimful of Asha is funny, warm, and touching. It is driven by the truth of its central relationship: Ravi and Asha are the beating heart of the show, and the reason it's been such a success. Their affability and wit are integral to the story. Nothing can quite substitute for Asha's shrug and hand wave when she forgets a line or Ravi's sudden fit of the giggles when Asha invariably says something outrageous during a performance. (Don't tell Ravi, but she's the real star of the show.)

The show's flexible and spontaneous nature is deceptive, because it is a finely crafted script. Though Ravi's background is in physical theatre, his understanding of and insight into text is exceptional. I can attest to this, as his work on the *Fault Lines* triptych made each play better. With *A Brimful of Asha*, Ravi and Asha have transformed an anecdote into a heartwarming piece of art. It has touched audiences across Canada and around the world, and that is no small feat.

—Nicolas Billon

A Brimful of Asha, A Why Not Theatre Production, premiered at the Tarragon Theatre in Toronto in January 2012 with the following cast and crew:

Actors: Asha Jain and Ravi Jain
Director: Ravi Jain
Set design: Julie Fox
Video and lighting design: Beth Kates (Playground Studios)
Stage manager: Sarena Parmar
Script coordinator: Jenna Turk

This script reflects the show as it was performed in January 2014. It has been updated by Andre du Toit from the original script. The play has gone on to tour all around the world, with dates continuing through to June 2017.

RAVI and ASHA welcome members of the audience as they arrive. The stage is set with a kitchen table and a large flat-screen TV above the table. The audience is invited to help themselves to samosas and to chat. When the appropriate moment arises, RAVI calls ASHA to the stage to start the show.

RAVI: Okay! Ladies and gentlemen, thank you so very much for joining us this evening.

RAVI introduces the front-of-house person, who then gives an introduction, if required.

Most of you have met my mother, Asha.

ASHA: Hi, everybody!

The audience usually responds by saying "hi" and clapping.

RAVI: Oh, you hear that? You got a big "hi"! There you go. My name is Ravi. Hi.

The audience says "hi."

Oh, you got more "hi's" than I did.

ASHA: I told you. It's called *Brimful of Asha*—not Ravi.

RAVI: Oh yeah. I should have thought of that. So tonight my mother and I are going to have a little conversation, and we are going to tell you all a story. A very true story of something that happened to me in 2007.

ASHA: Hey! It happened to me too, so I will start.

RAVI: Right, I'm sorry. That's why you're here.

ASHA: I welcome you all to my home. It's not my home, but let's pretend for tonight. I thank you all for coming. You have not come here to see a play. You have come here to help me sort out a dispute with Ravi. Dispute is generational, and it's existing as long as this world is existing. Younger generation always thinks that it is smarter than their parents, and I don't doubt it for a minute.

RAVI: Good. We're off to a good start.

ASHA: They are the future. They are the *IT* generation. But they do not have any common sense.

RAVI: Hey. They have a little bit . . .

ASHA: Second dispute is cultural dispute. I'm Indian. Ravi's Canadian. So we don't speak the same language, and this dispute became so big that we had to fly all the way to Vancouver[1] and invite all my good friends here, getting their honest opinion, telling Ravi he is wrong.

RAVI: Hey, Mom! You're influencing the jury here. You can't do that!

ASHA: They are all smart people: how can I influence them? They can see.

RAVI: Yeah, but you just told them I'm wrong.

ASHA: You are wrong.

RAVI: Well, we'll get to the end and then let them decide.

ASHA: I am not an actor. I've never been on the stage before. I am a dedicated housewife and abused mother.

---

1   Or whatever city in which the play is being performed.

RAVI: Oh come on. Abused mother? Why would you say that?

ASHA: They will see from the story I am abused by you.

RAVI: Hey. Now let's be clear who the victim of the story is here. Don't be fooled by any of this.

ASHA: As I said, I am not an actor, so sometimes I go blank in the middle of my talking. If I do that, please have patience and try to hear my heart crying.

RAVI: You need so much sympathy? You're nervous today.

ASHA: I'm not nervous.

RAVI: Oh, come on: you say you're going blank, but there's no lines to memorize here. We're just speaking the truth. So how can you go blank if we're just telling the truth?

ASHA: That is very true, but the stress of dealing with you every day has brought this condition on me called senile.

RAVI: So it's my fault?

ASHA: That's why I can go blank in the middle of my talking. And sometimes I just sit alone and talk to myself.

RAVI: Well you won't have to do that tonight. Because we have a lot of people here to talk to!

ASHA: Yes. I feel very comforted by them.

RAVI: Okay. Fine. So tonight everything you hear is absolutely true. Exactly what happened in our lives. Nothing has been made up or edited or deleted.

ASHA: True, but before we start, I should warn you about this clever Canadian. He is going to twist the story and bend the truth, so be very careful. And when he is doing it, I am going to point out.

RAVI: You are not going to twist anything?

ASHA: Nothing.

RAVI: Whole truth and nothing but the truth so help you God, Asha Jain?

ASHA: Yes, exactly.

RAVI: Yeah, right. Okay.

ASHA: So now you have permission to begin.

RAVI: Okay. I need it? Great. Thank you. So our story begins in January of 2007. I arrive back from living abroad—I was working as an actor and teaching at a university in Athens, Greece. Because I had just finished my graduate studies in theatre. I was—

ASHA: Theatre! What a proud profession for Indian parents.

RAVI: It's going to be like this all night. So I come home to my proud parents' kitchen in Toronto, and I'm sitting with my mom and my dad, and my mom turns to me, and she says, "Okay, so what's your plan now?" So I say, "Well, what do you mean?"

ASHA: I mean, you have finished your studies; you've got your profession, now it's time for you to get married and settled.

RAVI: That makes sense. And I wanted to, but I didn't feel like it was the right time for me yet, because as I said, I'd just graduated from school, and I was going to start this theatre company. So I say to my mom and my dad, "You know what, give me two years."

ASHA: Two years? It was 2007 we are talking, and now it is 2014.

RAVI: I'm taking my time getting there! At the time, I said two years was a reasonable amount of time to meet someone, fall in love, and get married. Right?

ASHA: Right.

RAVI: So then my mom says, "Okay, well, do you mind if we introduce you to girls?" And I say, "Yeah, sure! Why not? You're my parents. I love you guys . . ."

ASHA: Big liar.

RAVI: Why?

ASHA: If you loved us, why we are sitting here?

RAVI: What? If I loved you, I would be sitting at home now married?

ASHA: Yes.

RAVI: No, that's not how it works. I love you; that's why we are sitting here telling this story!

ASHA: Different definition of love.

RAVI: I like mine way better.

ASHA: I like mine.

RAVI: But I mean, yes—I'm open to the possibility of my parents introducing me to a girl, and that might be the person I end up marrying. I mean, why not? But before we go through this, I have a couple of base rules I have to get us to agree to. Because I have an older brother who went through a similar process to this—that's a whole other play unto itself. So I say, "You know, look. I want us to agree to a couple of rules just so I know that we're staying on the same page through this whole time." So I say, "Rule number one: there is no lying. Absolutely—"

ASHA: Hey, did I ever lie to you or taught you to lie?

RAVI: No, you never taught me to lie . . .

ASHA: Then?

RAVI: They'll see from the story too, you know, and this might happen in your families, right? Because, kids—let's face it—when parents want things, they might conveniently forget to communicate important information. Or maybe bend the truth just to make something fit a certain way in order to get what they want. So, you know, I wanted to make sure that between us we had an open and honest communication, and there would be no chance of anyone being on different pages.

ASHA: We agreed.

RAVI: We agreed. Rule number two: I won't marry just anybody. I—

ASHA: That is the stupidest rule I have ever heard. What do you think? I'm just going to pick up anybody from street and say, "Ravi, marry her"?

RAVI: Yeah. We just did a show in Calgary, and she saw this girl in the audience and said, "Oh, she's really cute. Are her parents here?" So they know what you are capable of. And at least now I have the rules to protect me. To make sure I have a say in who I'm going to marry.

ASHA: Yeah, we agreed.

RAVI: We agreed. And rule number three: I want to do this in my own time. I need to be sure—

ASHA: Own time?

RAVI: What is—

ASHA: Ravi has no idea how time works. I have so many stories about his time, but I do not have time to tell you all those stories.

RAVI: Yeah, let's go on . . .

ASHA: But I have to tell them just one.

RAVI: No . . .

ASHA: Just to give them an idea. So one Friday evening, my brother is over for dinner, so I call Ravi and say, "Ravi, will you be home for dinner?" "Yes, Mom." "What time will you be home?" He says, "Six o'clock." So we sit down at six o'clock. I don't see Ravi anywhere, no word from him. So I called Ravi, "Oh, Mom, I am running a half-hour late." And by now we have enough experience of his half-hour—it could be midnight. So I told my brother, "Let's eat, there's no use waiting for him." But my nephew was over—he is a big fan of Ravi's—and he says, "I'm going to wait for Ravi." Poor guy went home hungry! Ten thirty! Ravi never made it home.

RAVI: That is not fair.

ASHA: What is not fair?

RAVI: And this has nothing to do with the story at all. Can we move on?

ASHA: This is important information so they know what kind of time I'm dealing with.

RAVI: Okay! But at the time you agreed to these three rules.

ASHA: Did I have any choice?

RAVI: Right. So my parents agree to these rules, and I go out into Toronto and I'm meeting as many people as I can. I'm starting this theatre company, so I am meeting actors, directors, artistic directors—I'm trying to network and collaborate in order to get my work out there. So while I'm doing that, I meet someone from Calcutta who is teaching workshops at my old high school. We hit it off, and he's like, "I really like your energy—I love what you do! Listen, you should come to Calcutta and do a workshop for my theatre company." And I was thinking, wow, that's exactly what I wanted to be doing. Because, as I said, I had just come back from living abroad after a number of years, and part of coming home was wanting to reconnect with my family, my culture, and my roots. So here's this perfect opportunity to go to India to do just that. So I rush home to tell my parents about this plan. And they approve. And now the wheels are in motion for me to go to India in November and December of that year. Now . . . April 2007: my father takes a trip to India. He goes every year. And while he's there, he sends me an email saying, "Hey Ravi, I know you wanted to do workshops in Calcutta, but I'm here in Delhi, and I just met someone from the National School of Drama." It's the largest theatre school in the north of the country. He says, "Why don't you get in touch with them and you can do workshops here?" And I'm thinking, "Wow, Papa, for the first time you're taking an interest in my career, trying to get me more work. This is so out of character." I read on. "So why don't you send me a bio and resumé and I will make sure that it gets into the right hands." Okay, so some of you know where we are going with this. But for those of you who don't, there's nothing to suspect, right? That's how you would get a job. You send a bio and a resumé, and then maybe you would get an interview for that job, and then maybe you would get that job. But! at the end of April 2007, when my father comes back from India, he doesn't come back with any job interview for the National School of Drama. Nor does he ever mention the idea of the workshop ever again. But what he does come back with is the biodata of a girl named Neha who lives in Bombay. Now for those of you who don't know what biodata is, let's just take a look over here, shall we? *(referring to the biodata on the screen)* So actually this is a mock biodata of a Bollywood star named Aishwarya Rai. And, actually, if you had come home with this we would be set! There'd be no contest—you'd have five or six grandkids running around everywhere—you'd be so happy.

ASHA: She is already married. I checked.

RAVI: So you considered it?

ASHA: Yes.

RAVI: Yeah, right. So the biodata is this real piece of paper. It's got your picture on it and all of this information about you. It's got things like your date and time of birth, which is important.

ASHA: That's very important. Because Indian society is a really superstitious culture. What we do is we match the stars of the kids with the time of birth, place of birth, and date of birth, and what we believe is if your stars match, you will have less trouble in the marriage and less chance of divorce. If sometimes the stars doesn't match, we don't even go for the proposal.

RAVI: Somebody was telling me this great story the other day where the mother checked the stars of her son, and in his star chart it said that he would be married twice in his life. So what she did was she took him and had a little secret ceremony, and she married him off to a tree. So that way when the second marriage happened to a person, it would stick. So Indian parents are very into skirting around the fates and destinies of their children. They are very pro-that. No?

ASHA: Yes.

RAVI: So we scroll through, and it's got things like your education, where you went to school, your degree. You know, it's got hobbies. Some know karate and kung fu and speak German. Whether it's true or not, I have no way of knowing.

ASHA: No, they don't lie on the biodata.

RAVI: Right. Foolproof. Then there's this wonderful category called Features where you have words like "fair, beautiful, smart, submissive, smiling in nature." You know, all the important qualities that any man or woman is looking for in a life partner. I think on mine it said something like "soft, good-natured, and . . . "?

ASHA: Accommodating.

RAVI: Right: accommodating. I'm just really glad it didn't say submissive. As we scroll through, there's a whole section that describes your physical appearance: your height, your eye colour, your hair colour. And then a final section dedicated to your family information. Your father, what job he does, your mom, your uncles and aunties, your grandparents, all of them listed. What their professions are . . .

ASHA: That information is very important because we consider marriage not just between two kids. It is considered between the families. So what both sides of the families are doing with this information is seeing the compatibility between the kids and the families.

RAVI: They want to make sure the other family has a lot of money. Because that's going to keep the kids together through the good times and the bad, right?

ASHA: Right.

RAVI: So the biodata, it's this real piece of paper—it's got your picture on it and all this info and your parents hand it out at parties, trying to get you together, and, actually, if you think about it, it's not really all that different from, like, Facebook. Because Facebook is this online profile, where you put on all this information about yourself—all these photos of you that you probably took yourself—and if you read between the lines, it says a lot about your class, your culture, your background. People get online, check each other out, and people have even gotten married through Facebook.

ASHA: It is not the same. First of all, Facebook is very recent and new, whereas biodata has existed for long, long time. Secondly, the parents get biodatas first, and they get a lot of them and go through them and then pick the best one and interview the kids. Where on Facebook, we can't even go and see what you are up to.

RAVI: Don't you think I can go online and see if she would make a good match myself?

ASHA: No. We have to find out first—the parents—because we know best.

RAVI: You don't think I know best?

ASHA: No, we know best.

RAVI: So because my parents think they know best, my contention here is that my parents make up this idea of the National School of Drama job in order to get my bio and resumé. From that they make a biodata for me! And that's how we get Neha's biodata.

ASHA: No, it's not true. His biodata was for the school job, but my husband's priorities changed when he got this nice girl's biodata. There were two things to get excited about that girl. First, we always wanted Ravi to get married to an Indian girl from India, so he will have his connection open to India. Because once we are gone, he will have no connection left to India. That's very sad. This girl was from our community. We are Jain; she was Jain.

RAVI: Jain is our religion.

ASHA: Our family in India knew the girl's family really well. So that was very comforting. The girl was average-looking, okay for Ravi.

RAVI: What? You see what I'm dealing with? You're setting the bar pretty low, Ma! What's wrong with you? Okay for me?

ASHA: And she was working in CNBC TV Bombay. So we thought she would be compatible with you, and she will understand your profession.

RAVI: Because you don't understand my profession.

ASHA: No.

RAVI: No, yeah, because someone should, right? May as well be my wife.

ASHA: Yes.

RAVI: So with shaky hands my parents hand me Neha from Bombay's biodata across the dining-room table and say, "Please make an introduction. Please, just a little introduction." So I'm like, "Fine. Okay, fine." So I take the biodata, and I go downstairs to my dad's computer, and I write an introduction email—

RAVI leans on the table.

ASHA: *(whispering)* Uh-uh-uh, Ravi! Don't sit on the table. Sit on the chair.

RAVI: *(whispering)* I'm not sitting on the table.

ASHA: *(whispering)* There's food on the table. Sit there. *(nodding towards the chair)*

RAVI looks at her. Eventually, he walks to the chair, pulls it out, and sits on it.

RAVI: So I go to make an introduction to Neha and I type an email and I say, "Hey Neha, I'm Ravi, nice to meet you. Look, I'm going to be in India in November/December, if you're around, maybe we can meet up." Enter. Send.

The very next morning I get a short reply from Neha. She says, "Hey Ravi, nice to meet you. I might be travelling around that time, so if my schedule permits, perhaps we can connect." Great. Two very short emails to each other. I felt like we were on the same page. No response from her saying, "Hey, really looking forward to being your wife!" Meanwhile every day my mother's going, "Did you write to her? Did you send her an email? What did she say? I want to know. What's going on?"

ASHA: I just wanted to make sure you were communicating with her.

RAVI: First of all, it's none of your business. Second of all, I told you I would email her—you should trust me and leave it at that.

ASHA: I cannot trust you. You are such a big liar.

RAVI: I wrote to her. How do you want me to prove to you that I emailed her?

ASHA: Just cc me on one email.

RAVI: Yeah, right. It's so easy. Why don't we make a joint account so you can monitor everything?

ASHA: No, I don't have time for that.

RAVI: You'd probably forget the password anyway. So fast-forward to November 2007, and it's one week before I'm about to take this trip to India. Now the trip to India turned into a bit of a bigger deal because my best friend Andrew, who's from Toronto, he and I planned a whole five-and-half week adventure where we'd travel all around India—see the whole country—and we spent the whole year planning it. Now one week before I am about to set off on this adventure that we had been planning all year, my father comes up to me and he goes, "You know, your mother and I, we have decided to take a trip to India."

ASHA: Hey—we go every year at that time.

RAVI: That's what he said! "We go every year! The weather is perfect! Me and your mother, we are going to relax." "But hey, Papa, hang on a second. You go every year, but you don't go twice a year. You just went in April—you never go twice a year." "Oh, yes, I know, but everybody is telling me to take time off from work and relax, so your mother and I, we are going to go and do just that." So I'm like, "Sure, great. Have a good time. Papa, you know I'm not spending very much time in Delhi. Andrew and I are going to be travelling around India, so, like, don't expect to spend any time with me." "You? Who are you? We are not going for you! Please! Me and your mother are going to relax and have a wonderful time. You always think it's about you." "Great. Okay. As long as we're on the same page, I'm cool." So I take off from Toronto to Delhi, and I arrive three days before everyone. Before my parents, before Andrew. And I'm hanging out in Delhi catching up with my cousins and some of my friends. And I don't know what it was, but I was twenty-seven at the time, and every single person I met, whether they were friends, whether they were family, whether they were complete strangers on the street, the very first question that everyone would ask me? "Are you married?" "Are you going to get married?" "Is it going to be an arranged marriage?" "Is it going to be a love marriage?" Marriage, marriage, marriage is coming at you 24-7. Before you can say, "Hi, my name is . . . " they want to know if you are married.

ASHA: What do you think we get when we go? And we go every year. You don't even go every year.

RAVI: Right.

ASHA: As soon as we reach there, first question is what is Ravi doing nowadays. We have a business, why is he not working with us in our business. Second question is when is he going to get married? Is he going to get married to a girl from India? Is he is going to marry a Canadian? And I have no answer for them.

RAVI: You should say it's none of their business.

ASHA: I would love to say that, but I have to go back again next year!

RAVI: There's probably lots you could say . . .

ASHA: Yes. And they make me feel so unfit mother. Somehow in our culture, it's mother's job to get the kids settled. She has power to make kids do whatever she wants. Pick a partner for them. Get them married. But when I tell them I don't have that power, they don't understand that. And then they give me all of their suggestions: how I can bring Ravi around to the business. I should set up an office with a secretary. He will come to the office.

RAVI: Like that's all I could ever want, right? An office with a secretary. And I would just come rushing back to the business. Like, what do they think I do all day?

ASHA: That's what they really want to know. And then they show me nice girls. I like them too, but I can't choose for Ravi. I'm stuck between two cultures. One side is my Indian culture, which I love and respect and want to hold on to for as long as I can. But when I come to Toronto, I'm dealing with Canadians. Our conversations are over in one sentence only: "It's none of your business." No further discussion. And now I made it worse for myself. Everybody in my family, deep down in their hearts, thought Ravi would starve in theatre, so he would have no choice but to join our business. Since I am working with him in this play with him, they are not very thrilled at all. They think I'm encouraging him to stay in the theatre.

RAVI: I win! I made you my employee: that's the best possible relationship.

ASHA: I am his only and lonely employee. And I've never seen a paycheque.

RAVI: Hey! So I'm in Delhi and my dad arrives. And as soon as my dad arrives, he comes to me and he goes, "Okay, so we have to go to Bombay." "Wait. What are you talking about?" "You said I could introduce you to the girl. She lives in Bombay, so let's go. Come on, we need to make an introduction." And I said, "Yeah. Okay, sure, yeah, I did say that. I'm a man of my word." So I'm like you: I'm stuck between two cultures. And when this was happening, I thought, yeah, I'm open to it. Because my parents could introduce me to a girl, and maybe this could be, you know, how I meet my wife. There's nothing wrong with that. But now, before I can go meet her in Bombay—and I didn't know this—I have to meet her parents.

ASHA: He needed their approval—to see if he has enough money or is good-looking enough to meet her.

RAVI: Or average looking is apparently your standard tonight. So the very next morning, my mother arrives.

ASHA: At three in the morning.

RAVI: And then at ten a.m.—they don't waste any time—they all come over to my auntie's house. And it's her mom, her dad, my mom, my dad, her auntie, her uncle, my auntie, my uncle, and me all at a dining-room table with tons of food. And I'm jet-lagged, and my allergies are going crazy. I'm trying to keep up with the conversation because everyone is speaking in Hindi— and they're all speaking in Hindi about me. Saying things like, "Oh, how's his Hindi?" "Does he understand what we're saying?" "Is it going to get any better?" And I understand Hindi, but I don't speak so well, so I'm chiming in very awkwardly. I'm like, "Ha, ha *(RAVI speaks some badly pronounced Hindi.).*" Yeah, it's that bad. And then there's her uncle, who's the middleman of this whole thing. Now the middleman has actually become a profession in India of these people who match people together, and then they will get a percentage of the dowry. So these people are in it to win it. He's not messing around. Very serious people.

ASHA: But this uncle was not a middleman. He is doctor by profession. Only thing he is making sure it is a nice boy and a nice family for the niece.

RAVI: Yeah, yeah, all right. So this uncle doesn't take his eyes off me the whole time we're sitting at this breakfast.

RAVI stares at the audience, demonstrating.

And it's awkward. People are meeting each other for the first time; they don't really know what to do, and so my dad decides to tell a joke. And in the middle of my father telling this joke, the uncle cuts my dad off and says to me,

"How much money did you make last year?" And I go, "Actually . . . I didn't make any money at all." And then my mom goes, "No, no, no, no, no, no, no, no, no, no, no, no! He's only joking! My son is such a comedian."

ASHA: Actually, I had to step in at that point. Because he was blowing the deal at the very first step. If he is not making any money, he will not be able to see the girl. So I said he is just joking.

RAVI: I said, "Look, I made a little bit of money on a show I did last year, but, like, let's face it: I have a theatre company, all right. I'm not going to make the kind of money that my father makes. I'm not even going to make the kind of money I would if I worked for my father. So, like, I don't even know why we're talking about this." And then the barrage of questions start: "Why don't you take over your father's business?" "You can support a family on that business!" "Don't you want to live comfortably your whole life?" "Why do you work so hard for such little money?" And everyone is throwing this at me, and even my parents are like, "Yes, listen to him." "He's got the right idea." "Very smart man."

ASHA: Yes, exactly. We couldn't talk to you direct, so you might listen to—

RAVI: So you just throw me under the bus?

ASHA: He is telling you right thing to do.

RAVI: I should be taking notes? He's rich, so he must know what he's talking about.

ASHA: Yes.

RAVI: So I interrupt them and say, "Look, it's really lovely to meet all of you. Thanks for the career advice. Uh, I'm feeling a little jet-lagged; I'm just gonna go have a nap." As I am going upstairs, before I can leave the room, her father stops me and goes, "No, wait, please. You can go to Bombay."

ASHA: He got their approval to meet the girl.

RAVI: So the very next morning at seven thirty a.m. my dad buys two tickets, and I am on a plane with my father going to Bombay to get an introduction to Neha. And this is all happening so ridiculously fast—like in the period of three short days. Back to back to back. It's absurd how fast it's happening.

ASHA: That's how it happens in India. They don't waste any time: they catch you at the airport and by the time you leave, you are married.

RAVI: Why are you telling me that now? You should have told me that then. You've got to get them while it's hot?

ASHA: Yes.

RAVI: Like a samosa. Well, it's all happening too fast for me, so if you don't mind, let's just put a hold on our story there. And Ma, I would love for you to share with these lovely people the story of your marriage and how fast all that happened.

ASHA: Okay. I am the number third child in a family of seven kids. I had a very comfortable life. Everything was taken care of by the parents. Only thing we had to do was concentrate on our studies and a little bit help in the house. My father was very strict. We could never talk back to him say that "it's none of your business." He would never let us go out late at night or let us take participate in extracurricular activities like drama and dance and all that. I have a brother who was the baby of the house—he was a polio victim.

RAVI: *(referring to a photo on the TV)* That's him in the middle.

ASHA: I really got attached to him and thought to myself, once my parents are gone, who is going to look after him? So I built up this dream in my head. My grandparents had big land—I would take land from them and open up a school there, buy a tractor, do some farming, and take care of my grandparents and my brother at the same time. Keeping my dream in my head, I was working towards a degree so I could open up a school. I was twenty-one at the time. As soon as I was finished my master's, my mother told me, "No more further studies. You have to get married and move on." That's the time I told my mother, "I do not want to get married—I have this plan." So my mother said, "Our culture is such that even a king cannot keep his daughter unmarried in the house." Because whole city talks about it. Some people will blame the parents: they are misers; they don't want to spend money for the daughter's wedding. Some people will blame the girl: there is something wrong with her; that's why she isn't getting married. So who wants to live their life with such gossip? Plus, parents want their children to get married and be happy. So my mother said, "You don't have to worry about your grandparents and your brother; you just get married and move on. They will be taken care of." So I said, "Okay, if I have to get married, I would like to get married to someone who is living abroad." Because in those days, it used to be very exciting for us. Whenever any of our friends, their sisters, or anyone we knew got married and moved to foreign countries, we would talk about it: "Wow, look how lucky she is—she is going to America, to Canada." So my mother said, "That is okay. That is no problem—we can find somebody who is abroad." And my father had a friend whose brother-in-law was living in Toronto.

RAVI: My dad had immigrated to Canada a few years earlier, then came back to get married.

ASHA: So he reached Delhi on January first. We met the second of January—hardly for two hours. That was also with my whole family. My brothers and sisters, my mother and father, my aunts and uncles. And he came with his brother-in-law. January third we were engaged. January twenty-eight we were married. Eighth of February I left the country with a completely strange man. I did not know anything about him. Spent ten days in Europe, and eighteenth of February landed in Montreal. Got my immigration papers there. Moved to final destination: Toronto. When I reached Toronto, what a strange land for me. No family. No friends. A lot of . . . a lot of snow on the ground, which I never saw in my home. The next morning, my husband got up to go to his job. When I got up, I didn't even know how to turn on the stove because I never saw that kind of stove back home: there are a lot things different in Canada than in India. So I waited for him to come back. He came; he showed me how the stove worked. Once he showed me, I started to cook, clean, and take charge of my life. From very next day, I started to go out. Started to learn some English. Very soon, I got myself a part-time job working as a hotel clerk. Life was moving. I was happy, but I was lonely. By the time I knew it, I was blessed with a son.

RAVI: I have an older brother named Anu. *(referring to a photo on the TV)* How old are you here?

ASHA: Twenty-two and half. So now my job was increased—taking care of the baby, cleaning, cooking, working the part-time job. I was very happy. And as I said, we did not have any family or friends, and there were not many Indian people around, so whenever we meet someone with Indian face—at bus stops, grocery store, or on the street—they became our friends and family.

RAVI: So, like, when I was growing up, every weekend without fail everybody would go to one person's house, cook potluck style, and there would be singing and dancing and storytelling and playing cards till like three or four in the morning. We'd call all the adults Auntie and Uncle. All the kids became cousins. Everybody would get up in our business. Every weekend without fail, we'd be celebrating someone's birthday as part of this huge extended family.

ASHA: Yes, because all the immigrants were in the same boat. So lonely. Working very hard to settle. We were working two jobs sometimes. And that was the only entertainment we could afford. So life was moving forward.

RAVI: Okay, get to the good part.

ASHA: Life was moving forward.

RAVI: Yeah?

ASHA: We were very happy. And by the time I know, I was blessed with another son. We named him Ravi. His name means "sun": S-U-N. He was born very early morning. That is the time the sun comes out. That's how we named him Ravi. Ravi was a born artist. He didn't talk for two years. Once he starts talking, he was singing Michael Jackson songs: "Billy Jean." And then he fell in love with a Bollywood star, Amitabh Bachchan.

RAVI: Amitabh Bachchan is Bollywood's hugest star of all time.

A clip from an Amitabh Bachchan movie plays on the TV.

And to this day, he's the reason I became an actor. I watched every single one of his movies over and over and tried to be him. I dressed like him. He was my idol. I mean, can you blame me? *(referring to clip)* Check this guy out. And I would watch his movies and copy every single one of his gestures, just like he did. And at these parties I would hide behind the curtains, they would throw on the song, and I'd bust out and perform them exactly like he did in the movies, right? And then we have this thing in our culture where when you perform, people will come and they'll spin money around your head when you do a dance, and then they'll give you a dollar. So think about this, I'm five years old and I'm making good money from being a professional actor. And so as a kid I had good business sense! So you should have known I was going to become an actor!

ASHA: If I had knew, you would have been banned from all these videos.

RAVI: But come on, Ma, I get to live out my dreams in front of all these people.

ASHA: You have enough lived out your dreams. Come back to reality. Wake up.

RAVI: Okay, let's stay on dreams for a second. You were telling us about your dreams. You're twenty-one; you have this dream of a school and taking care of your grandmother and your brother. But then you got married, and then you had to give up your dreams. Don't you feel sad that marriage made you lose your dreams?

ASHA: Not really, because when I got married I moved to a new country, and it was a whole new life. Time went by so fast, I didn't even realize I had a dream. Plus, my half dream was accomplished because I brought my brother from India who is well-settled with me in Toronto.

RAVI: What about your grandparents?

ASHA: My grandparents made me feel really bad. Still they were alive; they kept crying, kept begging me move back, because they could never come to peace with the idea that they had fifty-six grandkids why I was the only one who moved away. But I knew deep down I could never go back, because my life was in Canada. Now they are gone. I don't want to repeat my mistake. I have two sons. One is married and settled.

RAVI: Yeah . . .

ASHA: When you get married and settled, I will move on to my dreams. So it's you, Ravi, who is holding up my dreams.

RAVI: No way. I'm holding you from your dreams? That's garbage. I get married and you will get back to your dreams?

ASHA: Yes.

RAVI: When?

ASHA: Very next day.

RAVI: So fine, I want to get married, but why does it have to be when you say? It's like in Indian culture we have an expiration date. Like, as soon as you turn twenty-seven—POW—you have to get married. If you're a girl it's twenty-three/twenty-four. Why can't I get married when I know I'm ready, like at thirty-seven? Or forty-seven? Or when I feel like I'm ready? Not when you tell me to.

ASHA: Again, Indian civilization is one of the oldest civilizations, and what our forefathers have done is divided our life into four stages. The first stage is Brahmacharya, or you can call it Student Life, where you start a profession, achieve it, come home—

RAVI: What professions?

ASHA: Of course, doctor, lawyer, engineer—

RAVI: Actor?

ASHA: Actor is not profession.

RAVI: Just want to make sure . . .

ASHA: You come home and you enter into the second stage of your life that is called Grihastha, or Married Life. Where you select a partner, get married, start your own family, and your parents are reaching third stage of life, which is Vanaprastha, or Old Age. They retire, take life a little bit easy. Enjoying playing with the grandkids. Pass their wisdom and experience to second generation.

RAVI: Is that what's happening right now?

ASHA: Yes, exactly. Now comes the last stage of life, which is Sannyasa, where you denounce your worldly possessions. No attachments left to anything. You spend most of the time praying and meditating. What this does is bring peace and completeness to your life. We believe in reincarnation. When you die in peace, in your next life you are born in a higher state of life. If you don't follow this system, you mess up the whole cycle.

RAVI: Okay, that's how you think, but, like, that's not how I think. It's so outdated to have these four stages laid out for you. The world has changed. Because where's love in that equation? Love happens when you least expect it—it's not planned. It's like the song goes: "First comes love, then comes marriage, then comes Ravi with the baby carriage." That's how the song goes.

ASHA: That's why we do not sing that song.

RAVI: How does your song go?

ASHA: Our song goes: "First get a profession, then find a suitable partner—"

RAVI: Don't you think I should fall in love first? Take your time to fall in love. That will keep us through the bad times.

ASHA: Love is not something that happens overnight. It's a process. It happens over time. When you get married you make a home; you have kids together. Love grows together, every day. Look at me and Papa. We are forty years married. We built a business together. We raised two kids together. We love each other more than day before.

RAVI: Really?

ASHA: What do you mean, really?

RAVI: Just want to make sure . . .

ASHA: Sure, we fight and argue, but that is the best part of marriage.

RAVI: Okay, fine. But you make time for each other. You see how busy I am with my career? I barely have time for you. Like, I need to establish my career first. Then, fine, I can make time for somebody else, get married, and then I can have kids. But my career has to come first.

ASHA: No, sometimes it can take your whole life to establish your career. Because if you wait for that, you can miss on a very good opportunity. I have a video to prove it. Show them the video.

RAVI: Okay—hold on. So my mom wants to show an old commercial from Indian TV. It's for an insurance company or something. Um, in it a guy is at dinner with his girlfriend. He is about to propose to his girlfriend . . .

A commercial from Indian television plays on the TV and RAVI *translates the parts in Hindi. In the commercial, the camera cuts back and forth between a man and a woman at a restaurant table.*

WOMAN: So, you wanted to say something?

MAN: Yeah, I wanted to say something really special today.

WOMAN: Yeah?

MAN: I was wondering . . . *(continues to speak in Hindi)*

RAVI: *(translating)* You and me . . .

MAN: Not right now. Just, uh, maybe after I get my house, then . . .

WOMAN: Bolo?

RAVI: *(translating)* Say it . . .

MAN: And I get my promotion, because that's, uh, really important to me . . .

WOMAN: Bolo na?

RAVI: *(translating)* Say it now . . .

MAN: And life is just moving in the right direction . . .

WOMAN: Bolo . . .

RAVI: *(translating)* Say it . . .

MAN: After that . . .

WOMAN: Bolo, na . . .

RAVI: *(translating)* Say it now . . .

MAN: I was wondering, maybe you would like to . . .

The man reaches back to his jacket to grab a ring. When the camera cuts back to the woman, she is older and has another man and two kids with her. She waves and speaks in Hindi.

RAVI: *(translating)* Say goodbye to Uncle.

VOICE-OVER: Life comes at you fast.

The commercial fades from the TV.

RAVI: I'll explain. He's about to propose, but he keeps delaying the proposal—he's saying, you know, I need my house, my promotion, everything has to be moving in the right direction. So in the time it took him to delay the proposal, she went off and got married and had two kids of her own. That's her family saying "goodbye to Uncle" at the end. Which is my mom's amazing point. Basically what she's saying is if you like it, then you should put a ring on it. But what if that doesn't make me happy? I feel like if I got married, you would be way happier than I would be. And whose happiness is more important here? Yours? Or mine?

ASHA: It does not matter.

RAVI: Of course it matters.

ASHA: We are two sides of the same coin. Your happiness is my happiness, and my happiness is yours. Since you are born, I'm doing everything to make you happy. Why do you think I would do something now to make you unhappy?

RAVI: Just stay out of it and leave me alone. You don't change my diapers anymore—I'm a grown man, I do a hundred things a day that I know make me happy—I can take care of myself. I know what makes me happy.

ASHA: You do not know what makes you happy.

RAVI: And how is marriage going to make me happy?

ASHA: I know it.

RAVI: How?

ASHA: I know it because I'm your mother.

RAVI: So, all right, let's get back to our story, shall we? Now if you remember, I am on a plane with my father heading from Delhi to Bombay in order to have this introduction with Neha. So now, we are only in Bombay for three days. Day one we arrive and unpack our things. And that night my dad takes me to a fancy hotel where I'm supposed to go meet Neha. We get to the lobby doors, and I say to my dad, "Look, Papa, like, I've seen her picture. I'm pretty sure I can spot her in the crowd. I don't need you to come with me. I've got it." "No, no way. Listen, this is how it works, these are the rules—I have to come with you. I have to do this introduction . . . So come on now, let's go, let's go. We're already late. Go! Go! Get in there, man! Go!" And he pushes me into the lobby—we are indeed late—and there's Neha waiting for us. And we're walking up to her, and I am expecting my dad to make this grand introduction because that's what he said he was going to do. And I can feel he is really nervous, and as we walk up to her he's got this big grin on his face, and he looks at me, looks at her, looks at me, looks at her, and then leaves! Without even saying a word! He just bolts it out of the hotel! And I'm like—?

ASHA: Hey, you told him not to say a word.

RAVI: I told him not to say anything; I didn't think that he would actually not say anything!

ASHA: We get in trouble when we listen to you; we get in trouble when we don't.

RAVI: So then he chose to listen to me? It's common courtesy—you should say hi. Come on. So I say, "Hi, Neha, I'm Ravi, nice to meet you. That blur over there is my father." So Neha and I go out, and we have like an awkward first date. Nobody mentions marriage once. And we end up going to this pizza place called Not Just Jazz by the bay. And we're sitting there having pizza and drinking Coke, and for about fifteen minutes or so I'm thinking, yeah, she's smart, pretty, we have a lot in common. Yeah, I can do this. I can totally see myself marrying . . . her!? But then as I have this thought, my heart starts to palpitate; I start sweating; the room starts to spin because there's no possible way you can ever decide to marry someone in such a short amount of time. So I start to scrutinize all these insignificant details about her. I'm like, oh my God, she ordered mushrooms on her pizza! I could never marry someone who orders mushrooms on her pizza! What will that do to our kids? So I'm literally starting to sweat like a madman. My heart is pounding and I'm like, "Neha, I'm having a really good time and all, but, you know, I'm not feeling so well. Do you mind if we call it a night?" And she's like, "Yeah, no problem. What are you doing tomorrow?" And I say, "Well, my dad and I are going to do some sightseeing, see a play. You're more than welcome to come if you want. No pressure." And she's like, "Well yeah, I'm pretty busy, but I'll text you and let you know if I'm going to make it to see the play." Great. We say good night. I go home. Go to bed. Day two. I am awoken by the auntie that we're staying with. "Ravi!!!! Wake up!!!! Tell us all about the date!!!!" *(referencing projected photo)* That's Sujatha Auntie—the auntie we're staying with—the best alarm clock in Bombay. And I come out to the dining room, and there's my auntie, my uncle, and my dad all sitting there having breakfast, and my auntie goes, "So . . . ? How did it go?" And before I can say anything, my father cuts me off and goes, "Ravi, please, let me. Sujatha, I met the girl. And I have to say, she is so punctual!" And I was like, "Yes, Papa, absolutely. She's very punctual. That is absolutely the reason to marry her. Very good observation. Thank you." Then I say, "Well, Auntie, she's very nice, whatever, it was fine, but I just didn't feel a spark—I just don't think this is going to happen. So can we just leave it." But my dad says, "Come on, you only have one more day in Bombay so just give it a shot! Try to see her again. Give it a shot!" So I send Neha a text with our plan for the day, and my dad and I go see Bombay. It's my first time to Bombay, so I'm thrilled to be experiencing the sights and smells. And while I'm doing that, I get a text from Neha that says, "Sorry, I'm busy—I can't make the play, but have a great rest of your trip." Thank God. I don't have to see her again. So my dad and I finish up our day and go home. Go to bed. Day three. Last day in Bombay. I wake up and I go into the living room, and my dad goes, "Okay, so what's the plan?" "What are you talking about, Papa?" "You didn't meet her yesterday, so today's our last day in Bombay, so let's make a plan! You have to give this a real shot!" And I'm like, "Papa, you know, she texted me, and she told me that she was busy. And frankly I'm feeling pretty busy myself. I think we should just cut our losses, go home, go back to Delhi. Andrew's arriving tomorrow. I'm really looking forward to taking this trip around India. So let's just kind of end it here." And he says, "Oh yeah, sure, sure. Why don't you go pack your things, have a shower, and then we'll plan our day." Great. So I hop in the shower and I think, wow, that was so easy! I only had to meet Neha once! That was so easy. That was . . . way too easy! No, no, no, that's not how it works with my dad. So I get out of the shower, towel off, throw on a shirt, and go downstairs to the living room. My dad says, "Okay. It's all set." "Sorry, uh, what's all set?" "Oh, she lives near the airport, so we're going to have dinner with her on the way there." "What do you mean? How did you do that?" And he says,

"Don't worry. I called her." "No, Papa, you did what? Don't you see how she was busy? She didn't want to go. So you're my dad. She can't say no to you, so if you call her, you are forcing something to happen that's not supposed to happen." "Oh stop it! You are being so dramatic!" "No! No, Papa, listen! Like, even if I were to marry this girl, that's my dad calling a girl for a date! Do you see how messed up that is?" "Oh stop your crying. Come on, let's go!" So that night I get to go on a date at a noodle bar. And it's me, Neha . . . and my dad. Now I should mention here that my dad is a very good business-man. Our whole lives he's provided for our family. And he's done quite well. I mention this because in this moment he is going for the sale. Because he knows that nobody has talked about marriage, not even mentioned it once, and he's getting nervous, saying things like this: "Oh, Neha, you are going to love Toronto. Toronto's such an amazing city! We have so many Indians there; you'll fit right in! And she could get a job on Indian TV, couldn't she, Ravi? We only have to contact the right person. And you're an independent girl, and you've been living on your own for so many years. Ravi's an inde-pendent boy. He's been living on his own for so many years. We thought this would be a perfect match." Neha and I are dumbstruck. Like, all we can do is just slurp our noodles. We're like *(mimes slurping noodles)*. Because we can't actually believe that these words are coming out of my dad's mouth. It's in-sane! So somehow we get out of this awkward night. We say good night at a distance. And my dad and I get into a cab on the way to the airport, and he says, "Okay, Ravi, listen. So the ball is in your court." And I say, "Yes! Please! Yes, Papa! I've got it right here. Go play in that court five miles away! I've got it. Thank you." So we get on this plane and go two and a half hours back to Delhi, and I'm sitting there thinking, what the hell am I going to do with this ball in my court? And as soon as we land in Delhi, I go to my cousin's computer and write Neha a very long email. "Hey Neha, it was really nice to meet you. You're a really lovely person, but we are not going to get married. Okay? I only met you as a favour to my parents. Please don't get upset. Uh, it's not you, it's me." Enter. Send. The next morning I get a timely reply from Neha, and she says, "Thank God! You're the seventh guy I've met. Don't wor-ry about it. One day we'll all have a good laugh about this." Great. Again, I feel like we're on the same page. Now the morning when I read that email, Andrew arrives from Toronto, and he's hanging out with my family, getting to know them, and I go upstairs with my mom and my auntie to help my mom pack, because my parents are heading back to Toronto the next afternoon. And my auntie turns to me, and she goes, "Ravi, what's the matter with you? Just get married! Get it over with! We'll have a party. We'd all be way happier if you'd just get married." And I turn to my mom and say, "If I were going to marry someone I would need to know them for, like, I don't know, at least six months. Six months seems like a reasonable amount of time to get to know them and choose if that's the right person to spend the rest of my life with."

ASHA: You don't get to choose anybody.

RAVI: Why?

ASHA: Did I get to choose you?

RAVI: What? God gave me to you!

ASHA: God trusts me, and you don't trust me.

RAVI: I'm stuck with you. My wife is the one person that I get to choose.

ASHA: I'm just helping you choose.

RAVI: So I leave the room because who can argue with logic like that? In the living room Andrew is showing my dad a map of India of all the places we are going, and my dad says, "Oh, you're going to Jaipur?" And I say, "Yeah, why?" And he says, "While you're there, you should stay with uncle so-and-so." And I say, "Who is uncle so-and-so?" He says, "Actually he is the grandfather of Neha from Bombay who you've just met." And actually, that wasn't that bad an idea, because Andrew and I were travelling around India on the cheap; we were staying in some pretty shady places, and so in our itinerary Jaipur was the perfect stop to stay at a fancy house—you know, have a couple of fancy meals, do some laundry. So I took him up on the offer. So the next morning, my parents are all packed because they're going back to Toronto that afternoon, and my dad's driving Andrew and me very early to the airport, and he's saying, "Okay, so you have enough money? You have the phone numbers that you need? Okay, perfect. By the way, your mother and I, we have decided to extend our stay in India by one week." I say, "Why? Why, Papa? What's going on?" "Oh, you know, we are having such a good time relaxing. Don't even worry about it." And I say, "Okay, sure, have a great time. I just want you to promise me that you're not going to do anything stupid, okay?" "Whoa? Is that any way to talk to your father? I just drove you to the airport! I gave you money! Oh, go! Go have a good trip, big actor man! You think you're so important!" So Andrew and I get on the plane, and we head off to Udaipur in Rajasthan. Now the plan here is we're going to be there for five days in Udaipur, and the next stop on our trip is Jaipur. But Andrew and I have such a good time in Udaipur, and we make such great friends while we're there—it's so beautiful—that we decide to stay an extra day. A sixth day. And upon making that decision, my dad calls me in a bit of a panic, and he's like, "Hey, what's going on? Why are you staying in Udaipur for an extra day? Aren't you still going to Jaipur?"

ASHA: Ravi—I should tell them . . .

RAVI: No, it's fine. I'm telling them now.

ASHA: But I need to tell them what was happening.

RAVI: Wait, wait, wait, no . . .

ASHA: Because the grandfather—

RAVI: No, no, no, no! Don't! It doesn't come now.

ASHA: But it is very important for them to know about this—

RAVI: I know! But not now! No, no, no, no!

ASHA: No, you are taking too long.

RAVI: No, no, no, no, no. I tell my part, and then you tell your part. That's how we're doing it.

ASHA: Are you sure?

RAVI: Yes. I'll give it back to you in a second.

ASHA: Okay.

RAVI: Okay. Do a play with your mom!

ASHA: Udaipur.

RAVI: Yeah, thanks. Udaipur. So I finish up with my dad. I tell him we're only staying one extra day, and Andrew and I take a train to Jaipur. We take a fourteen-hour train all the way from Udaipur to Jaipur. I don't know if you've ever been on a train in India, but it's like the most exhilarating experience you've ever had. And as I said, I'm on this romantic getting-back-to-India trip, so I've got my Salman Rushdie book on my lap; I'm watching the desert pass in the distance. So thrilled to be on this train that I don't sleep a wink for the fourteen hours. The grandfather sends this beautiful, fancy car to pick us up at the train station. And that fancy car takes us to an even more beautiful, fancier house. With a gate. The gates open and I get welcomed in by the grandfather. *(mimes shaking hands)* "Hello, hello, so nice to meet you." "Oh, yes, your friend is so tall, hello, hello." We get welcomed into this beautiful lobby. There's this big chandelier. And there's a big lineup to greet us. "Namaste, nice to meet you, Namaste." We walk into the living room, and I turn the corner, and at the dining-room table is Neha eating a bowl of Cheerios.

RAVI is stunned. ASHA sips some tea. RAVI mouths "What the fuck!"

I walk up to her, about to ask her, "What the heck are you doing here?" And as I approach her, out comes her dad! "Hey, Ravi! So good to see you. You must be hungry! Come, come! Sit! Sit! Sit!" And before I know it, her grandma, her grandpa, an auntie and uncle, her mom, her dad, and me and Andrew are all sitting at this dining-room table with tons of food that was probably cooked three or four days before I even got there.

ASHA: Hey! They don't serve old food! They prepare everything fresh.

RAVI: Okay, thank you for that. Sorry, it was very fresh food—apparently—prepared for my arrival. And I'm freaking out. I don't know what to say. Thank God for Andrew, who is fielding all of the questions, saying things like, "Oh yes, I really love India. The food is spicy. Everybody wants to know if I'm going to get married." My heart's pounding. I'm freaking out. Finally, I gather up the courage to say to her dad, "Hey, Uncle! Wow . . . it is so good to see you . . . here. But what are you doing here?" And he says, "Oh, you know, we haven't seen my father in such a long time . . . and we heard you were going to be here . . . and your parents are going to be here at three!"

RAVI leans back in his chair.

Now you can tell your part of the story! Now is the time to tell it! If you tell it before, it doesn't work.

ASHA: It's okay. Dowry is a big part of our weddings. And especially in our community, it can be very high. We made it sure and clear that we are not looking for any dowry or big wedding. We are just looking for a nice, homely girl. The family was very interested, and they—

RAVI: Never mind that the boy is handsome and charming. There's no dowry? This is just a really good deal.

ASHA: It was double deal.

RAVI: It's so romantic. It's like zero-percent financing on a car.

ASHA: And there they are so quick. They don't waste any time. They have checked our references in Toronto. They found out we are a very well-established business family. So they really wanted to make the relationship. When they like the boy, they will go to any extent. They will find a common relative or friends that can put pressure on you. In this case, they found the grandfather. We respect the elderly, so they thought that grandfather could bring all of us to meet. As soon as Ravi accepted the invitation to stay in Jaipur, my husband extended his stay by one week. My husband was constantly in touch with the grandfather, and they were making plans to get everyone together at the same time. So that's why my husband extended our stay by one week. Sometimes this kind of pressure can turn into a wedding. So when Ravi was changing his plans, that's why my husband was getting very tense, because we were leaving the next day, and if Ravi stayed in Udaipur an extra day, he would have messed up the whole plan.

RAVI: So I find out my parents are coming at three, and I'm pissed. I turn to Neha and say, "Neha, do you mind if we get out of here?" And she says, "Absolutely. Why don't you go upstairs, unpack your things, and then we'll go take a tour of Jaipur." So, Andrew and I head up to the bedroom that we're staying in upstairs, and we're sitting on the bed, and I'm pissed. And, well, first I have to explain to Andrew what's going on because he has no idea what the hell he's walking in on! And as I explain it to him, I get really, really sad, and I sit there and I'm like, "You know what? I give up. Like, look at how far my parents are going to get me married here. Like, this is crazy. I don't even know why I'm fighting this. Like, maybe I should just give up, get married, take over my dad's business. It would make my parents happy."

ASHA: Very happy.

RAVI: It would make—as far as I'm concerned, it would make this whole country happy. I'm so selfish here, stopping the flow of happiness. Everyone wants a parade, and I'm just being so selfish. And Andrew's my best friend, and he says, "You know, I hear what you're saying, but I have to say that is the stupidest thing I've ever heard you say!" And like an angel, Andrew comes down from—

ASHA: Like a devil. He broke your right-thinking.

RAVI: No, he's my angel! He saved me.

ASHA: No, if I find him, I don't know what I will . . .

RAVI: He was my angel rescuing me from the pit of despair that you put me in. He shook me out of it. So Andrew, Neha, and I get in the car, and as soon as we get in the car, I'm still so angry that I'm on the verge of tears. And I'm like, "Neha, this is a trap! It was set up. I had no idea you were going to be here! You got my email, right?! You know I don't want to marry you! My parents are crazy!" And she says, "Whoa, whoa, whoa, calm down. Look, I didn't know you were going to be here either. I'm pretty pissed myself, but like, we're here now—there is no need to get this hysterical. The only thing we can do right now is just go and have a good time. Okay?"

ASHA: See, it was not just any girl. She was a smart girl.

RAVI: Right. That's what we did. We went to this fort in Jaipur. And if you wanted to set me up, that's how you should have done it! You should have just let us go on our own and have a good time. We actually got to know each other, and something could have come out of it.

ASHA: But we did not have much time. We were flying the next day.

RAVI: Yeah. So all the fun that me and Neha and Andrew were having had to come to an end at three because my parents had arrived in Jaipur. So we go back to the grandfather's house for a very boring formal lunch. And it's her grandma, her grandpa, her auntie, her uncle, her mom, her dad, my mom, my dad, me, and Andrew—all at this dining-room table with tons of food. And she's not even sitting with us because she's in from out of town, so her little cousins are thrilled to see her, and they're in another room eating food and watching cartoons. So, at this table, all eyes are on me. No one knows each other, so no one has much to say. So awkward. And all that's on anybody's mind is, "Is this happening? Can we sign the papers, break out the laddus, and call it a day?" So boring lunch turns into boring tea in the other room. Finally Neha emerges, and it's time for her and her family to leave. My parents are spending one last night in Jaipur before they head back to Toronto. So as soon as Neha's family leaves, I ask my mom if we can go upstairs and have a little conversation, which goes something like this: "What the fuck are you doing here, Mom?"

ASHA speaks in Hindi.

"What are you doing here? You just show up and lie to me?"

ASHA speaks in Hindi.

"I don't care! You couldn't call and tell me you were going to be here? This is a trap! What is this?"

ASHA speaks in Hindi.

"No, no, Mom! I'm going to go downstairs right now and scream at the top of my lungs and swear and tell these people that this is bullshit. That I had nothing to do with that. I don't want to marry these people."

ASHA: "Please, I beg you . . . "

RAVI: "No, stop. You know, this isn't ever going to end, okay? This is not going to end until I kill myself. All right?"

ASHA: "No, no."

RAVI: "And I don't want to die, so you and Papa should just consider me dead."

ASHA: "No, we can't consider you dead till you get married."

RAVI: So we had a very serious fight, and the very next morning my parents head off to Toronto. They go, and I don't say goodbye to them. I'm so furious. Andrew and I stay a couple more days in Jaipur, and then we head off to Calcutta. We go there. I do the workshop. And it's a hit. We make some friends. I tell my story. They tell me better stories—they tell me worse stories. Everybody's got a story. And on the last day in Calcutta—we're going to go to Bangalore the next day—we're having a goodbye party with some friends at a café—and as we're exchanging emails and saying our goodbyes, my phone rings, and there's a man on the phone: "Hello, is this Ravi?" "Yeah. Hi, who's this?" "You don't know me, but I just spoke to your parents, and they told me you are going to be in Bangalore."

RAVI looks at his phone, stunned.

"Um, yeah—sorry, who is this?" "Well, my daughter lives in Bangalore. Why don't you go meet her there and then come meet me in Delhi." And they did it again.

ASHA: Hey, what do you mean, "They did it again"?

RAVI: You set me up again.

ASHA: Not me.

RAVI: Who?

ASHA: Papa.

RAVI: Papa did it? And you had nothing to do with it?

ASHA: Nothing.

RAVI: You were in another room, with your fingers in your ears?

ASHA: No idea.

RAVI: You couldn't, like, call me and tell me what was going on?

ASHA: I did not have your number.

RAVI: She's the next person to call in the story. If you don't have my number, how did you call me then?

ASHA: Papa dialed the phone and gave it to me.

RAVI: You're just in the habit of taking pre-dialed phones from Papa?

ASHA: Yes.

RAVI: Come on.

ASHA: It's true.

RAVI: So they did it again. We just had this huge fight in Jaipur, and I'm being set up in Bangalore, and I'm so furious. Two hours later my mother calls—apparently my father dialed for her—"Oh, hello, Ravi! How are you?" "Hi Mom. How are you doing? Why are you calling? Are you calling because you set me up again?! You told those people I was going to be in Bangalore! Ma, I don't want to marry these people!" She starts shouting, "You stupid kids! You don't know what kind of pressure that we're under! You have no idea! You need to get married!" So we start shouting and fighting with each other on the phone for about an hour. And I'm on the streets of Calcutta with the phone. It's not like this.

RAVI *demonstrates how you would normally hold a phone to your ear.*

I'm just standing there shouting in the receiver.

He motions yelling into a phone, holding the phone out in front of him.

We're fighting for an hour, and it sounds exactly like this:

A recording of their phone conversation plays.

So when Papa comes to you, why do you then call me, or why do you even give permission, like, you should be sticking up for me. Like, it's, it's . . .

ASHA: No . . . no, no, no, Ravi, you don't understand. You know what? He—he called Papa, and I noticed Papa—Papa, he—hundred times—because—and he gives your number, and he—and I told, uh, Papa told him that "Ravi's visiting, he's not in Tor—Delhi, he's visiting—"

RAVI: So, so fine, so when he says, "Let's get on a plane and go to Jaipur," why don't you—why do you say yes, why do you go? Even if you have a headache, you said you didn't want to go . . . and then you go? And then you show up in Jaipur? And then you do things like this? And—then—even though—even Jaipur, we, we sit there—and we have our conversation—

ASHA: Okay, Ravi—

RAVI: We have a conversation—

ASHA: Okay—I've had enough with you. You better get married or not, I don't even care at this point, okay?

RAVI: Mom—

ASHA: Okay?

RAVI: Mom—

ASHA: Okay—I don't want to talk about it anymore. You don't believe me, and I, I don't carry on with you anymore.

RAVI: Fuck them.

ASHA: Okay—that's enough, Ravi. That's enough—I cannot take any more.

ASHA starts to cry, trying to speak, but it's unclear what she's saying.

RAVI: So my mom starts to cry *(the phone cuts off)* and it is like the worst, most horrible sound I've ever heard in my life. I feel like such a jerk. I was swearing at my mom. Being disrespectful. She is sobbing terribly on the phone. So I start to apologize, I'm like, "I'm so sorry! I'm so sorry! What can I do?" And as I'm apologizing, the phone clicks exactly one hour, and then it dies. My mom is in Canada bawling her eyes out, and I'm on the streets of Calcutta, so there's nothing I can do about it. I'm so pissed. My blood pressure peaks, and I smash the phone on the sidewalk because I can't understand how I got myself into this stupid, ridiculous nightmare. I feel like such an idiot. And actually, before we continue, just tell them all the story of the recording of that phone call.

ASHA: When this really happened, I was really crying. We did not make any recording or anything, because we didn't have any idea that one day we would be making a play out of it. So when we are decided to make the play, this piece was very important. We needed that recording. So we tried to record it in the house. So Ravi is in the basement and I'm upstairs in the kitchen. Ravi starts to push me, "Mom, you have to cry. You have to cry." Suddenly, I start crying. As soon as I start crying, Ravi came running upstairs—and his face is white as a ghost, and he's all apologetic to me. "Sorry, Mom. I'm very sorry. All right? Please don't cry!" And I was laughing at that time.

RAVI: I didn't know if she knew that we were pretending, right? It sounded so real. You lied at the beginning. You are an actor.

ASHA: I have seen enough Bollywood movies.

RAVI: But no, you were really crying on the phone that day.

ASHA: Because I'd had it with you by then.

RAVI: Yeah, so had I. So I ran into the café and grabbed my friend's phone and say, "This is going to cost you a lot of money." And I call my parents and my dad, he answers, "Hello?" And he's got this, like, fake crying voice on—it sounds nothing like my mom. I can smell right through it! "Hello?" And I'm like, "Uh, Papa, can you put Mummy on the phone, please? I really need to talk to her." And he says, "My wife can't come to the phone right now." "Papa, please put Mummy on the phone right now. You know why? Because I can't talk to you right now. You want to know why? Because we are in this shit because of you! Because you keep setting stuff up behind the scenes! Because I'm sure you—" "Wait, wait, wait a minute. Why are you making me out to be the villain, huh? Listen, I told Neha's family that you would be ready to marry her in six months!" "What? No! Papa! What are you talking about? First of all, that was a conversation I had with Mom and Auntie, and in that conversation I said that if I were to marry anyone I would need to know them for six months. Not that I would marry Neha and her family in six months! So don't you see how when you twist the truth—you lie—you make people think something is going to happen when it's not going to happen?!" "Oh, stop twisting my words! I'm not a villain! Oh, just talk to your mother!" He puts my mom on the phone, and she's still crying horribly, terribly. And I'm apologizing profusely saying, "Ma, please, if you stop crying I will marry whoever you want, whenever you want, just as long as you stop crying."

ASHA: And I fall for his trap and stop crying.

RAVI: And after forty-five minutes, you finally stop crying, and then what did we agree on?

ASHA: That we will sort it out when you get home.

RAVI: She said that we can't talk about it on the phone, that when I come home we're going to sit down as a family and talk about it. Great: we agreed. So I finish up my trip in India, and I'm flying back on the plane to Toronto, and I'm really preparing all of my arguments, because it's really important for me that my parents understand why I'm so upset and why I don't want to do it their way. And, you know, we've agreed to talk about it. And now, this might be true in your family as well, but in true Jain family fashion, we've agreed to talk about this, and, Mom, what happens when you pick me up from the airport?

ASHA: I do not want to bring the subject up because I'm scared you are going to shout at me again.

RAVI: Nobody mentions it once. It's as if it never even happened. But for two weeks at my parents' house it goes like this: "Hi." "How are you?" "Good." "I'm hungry?" "Good. Here's some food." "Food was good." "Great." "I'm going to go to bed." "Okay, good night." "Good night." Verbatim. So one day I come home and I'm like, "Ma, are we going to talk about this? We said we were going to talk about this!" And like she was waiting for it; she's like, "You stupid Canadian! You don't understand our culture. You have no idea of the pressures that we're under. Why don't you listen to us?" And we start shouting at each other in the kitchen. My dad comes home from work, takes off his jacket, puts on his boxing gloves, and gets in the boxing ring for round two. Ding, ding, ding. "You're a liar!" "Don't call me a liar." "Don't talk to me that way." "Don't talk to your mother that way." Screaming and blaming and accusing each other for three and a half hours. And then, by the grace of some miracle, at the end of three and a half hours, my mother turns to me and says:

ASHA: I'm sorry.

RAVI: My father turns to me, and he says, "I'm sorry." And then I turn to them both and say, "I'm sorry." And it was the most incredible feeling I've had in my whole life. Because it is so rare for a family to actually go through their shit like that—to sit at the table, say everything you wanted to say, get everything out openly and honestly. Leave nothing behind. And at the end of it, actually feel like you've resolved things. Pretty amazing. So we're sitting at the dining-room table, *Wheel of Fortune* is playing in the background, and my mom turns to me and she goes, "You know, I'm really glad that we had that conversation." And I say, "Oh my God, me too. I feel like a big weight has been lifted off my shoulders. I feel like, like . . . I feel so happy." And my mom goes, "Yeah, me too, I'm happy too. Because there's this other girl that we want you to meet." And she hands me the biodata of a girl named Deepika who lives in New York! Shameless. Look at her.

ASHA: What's there to be ashamed of? I asked you, "Ravi, do you have a girl-friend?" And you said, "No."

RAVI: Right . . .

ASHA: So here's this nice girl. She is Jain.

RAVI: Uh-huh . . .

ASHA: She lives in New York. You can take your time to get to know her.

RAVI: Sure . . .

ASHA: Plus she works for Citibank: she can finance all your projects!

RAVI: Of course—what was I thinking? You were just looking out for me. But wait—that's more for you, right? Because if she finances my project, then you don't have to anymore.

ASHA: It's for both of us.

RAVI: So then, a couple weeks later, I come home, and my mom is lost in her thoughts, sitting having tea at the table. And I go, "Ma, are you okay?" And she goes, "We were lied to!" "Sorry, what, Ma? What happened?" "You know Neha from Bombay? She's getting married." I say, "That's good, right? Should we send her sweets or a card?" "No, she's getting married to her boyfriend. She had a boyfriend the whole time! Her parents, they lied to us." "No, no, no, no, Mom. Nobody lied to you. I could have told you that she had a boyfriend. I knew that it wasn't going to happen, but instead you tried to insist and force it to happen. And if you think about it, you could have ruined my life."

ASHA: No, it wouldn't happen until you both said yes.

RAVI: You brought us to the grandfather's house and tried to force it to happen.

ASHA: But it didn't happen.

RAVI: But that's just your dumb luck!

ASHA: It's over now, why are you crying?

RAVI: The point is, whether it's an arranged marriage, or love marriage, or meeting someone on Facebook, you can never really know someone until you take the time to get to know them.

ASHA: No, we have our system. We have family and friends who let you know so that it doesn't happen.

RAVI: So you think that would be the end of the story, but it's not. Because one month later, my parents put an ad for me in an Indian newspaper to get married. Let me clarify: my parents put an ad in a newspaper in India to get me married.

ASHA: You came home one day and looked so sad. I asked if you had a girl-friend, and you said, "No." So I asked, "Do you mind if I put an ad in the paper for you," and you said, "Yes, go ahead."

RAVI: No! That is not how it happened! You asked me like fifteen times, "Can I put an ad in the paper?" "Can I put an ad in the paper?" I said no every time, and then I said yes on the sixteenth time, just so you would stop asking me.

ASHA: So that was "go ahead" for me.

RAVI: You know why I don't tell you if I have a girlfriend? Because if I told you I had a girlfriend, you would say, "Stop everything right now and go marry her."

ASHA: Yes, that's what you should do.

RAVI gets up and leaves the stage.

RAVI: No, it's not the right thing to do.

ASHA: What are you waiting for?

RAVI: You're not listening to anything.

ASHA: You are not listening to anything.

RAVI: What, I'm so desperate that you have to put an ad for me in the paper?

ASHA: Not desperate, but where am I going to find a girl for you?

RAVI: *(from off stage)* Okay, fine, so you put an ad for me and then what happened?

ASHA: We got some responses.

RAVI returns to the stage with two large binders and places them on the table.

RAVI: Well, actually, we got about a hundred and fifty responses. These are the responses that came from the ad. I call them my "binders of women." They're labelled "Ravi's Matrimonials." Thankfully these binders were put together by my dad's secretaries. And they've been, you know, itemized and numbered. They have, uh, different-coloured sticky notes just to tell you which ones are the more interesting ones. Highlighted Xs for the ones that are not. And it's filled with pictures of—I'm sure they're lovely people—it's got biodatas like the one you saw earlier. Yeah, it's real. And it's got wonderful emails that go like this: "Dear Mr. Jain, many thanks for sending details and photographs of

Ravi. The profile of Ravi is really very impressive and interesting. I hope that you have also gone through the particulars and photographs of"—fill in the blank with any one of the girls' names in any one of the two binders—"would highly appreciate if you would please accord and confirm your interest so as to proceed further in the matter." Hallmark doesn't write them this good. "With best, best wishes to you and your family. Regards"—fill in the blank with the name of any auntie or uncle trying to marry off their daughter to me from an ad in an Indian newspaper. So, one hundred and fifty proposals.

ASHA: Yes. Just imagine if you would have been a doctor how many I would get.

RAVI: We're just scraping the bottom of the barrel here. India's a big country and we only got one hundred and fifty. Sorry to let you down. So it's never going to end, is it?

ASHA: It will end when you get married and settled. Please, I beg you.

RAVI: Nobody wants to be begged to get married. Leave it alone.

ASHA: No, I can't leave you alone.

RAVI: Why do I have to get married?

ASHA: What are you waiting for? You're getting old. Please! It's my one last wish.

RAVI: And then what?

ASHA: Then I'll be free.

RAVI: I set you free, in front of all these people. Go.

ASHA: Just saying it does not make me free.

RAVI: I think you're just bored. Can't I just get you a puppy?

ASHA: No!

RAVI: You would have so much fun with it! And it would have more puppies—

ASHA: Once you are married, I will get a puppy. All kidding aside, think seriously because before I go, I want to see you settled and happy. Can you do that? Will you do that little thing for me? Just a little thing I am asking for.

RAVI motions to cut her off with a blackout and the lights start to fade.

RAVI: Shh. Stop talking. Mom, the lights are going out.

ASHA: Because—

RAVI: Mom, the lights are out. You're supposed to stop!

Blackout. After the curtain call, RAVI addresses the audience.

Thank you, ladies and gentlemen, for letting us share our story with you and being part of our family tonight. You've been such a lovely audience. Now, we have some samosas left; please, don't be shy, come up and grab a samosa, say hi to my mom and me, tell us what you thought of the play—tell us who you thought was right *(secretly pointing to himself)*. Now before, my mom said that you were here to settle a dispute, and we're not going to take votes or anything, but I'm happy to report that the dispute did get resolved because in August 2012 I did in fact get married—to a woman of my choosing. *(referring to a photo on the TV)* That's me and my mom at our wedding in Kelowna, BC.

ASHA: I have a request now: please, help me convince Ravi to have a baby.

RAVI: No, no, show's over.

CRASH
Pamela Mala Sinha

For my mother, Rubena, and my brother Debashis

If there is beauty here, you are the reason.

To my father, Snehesh Kumar Sinha

I miss you every day. I feel you always.

ACKNOWLEDGEMENTS

To my Family

Brian Scott, Damon D'Oliveira, Maxime Desmons, Nandita Biswas, Dan Mellamphy, Sharmila Biswas, Manish Mistry, Bhavin Patel, Shaun Phillips, Catherine Fitch, Kris Bramham, Jutta Brendemeuhl, and Chloe and John Mighton.

You are the Grace in my life.

I am deeply grateful for the dramaturgical guidance of Iris Turcott and Daniel Brooks on the first and second drafts of *CRASH*. Also to Alan Dilworth for his help in polishing and realizing the play. To Andy McKim at Theatre Passe Muraille for giving the play a home, and to Matt White at Necessary Angel for making it happen again. I would also like to thank Kelly Thornton, Nina Lee Aquino, Brian Quirt, and Jovanni Sy for their encouragement and belief in a play that was not yet written.

"Open your eyes and see what the heavy thing was" is one of the first lines of Pamela Mala Sinha's masterpiece of dramatic writing, *CRASH*.

Plays are written primarily to be performed, and this play is written not only with the performer in mind but with all aspects of production detailed with brilliant precision; the lighting, the sound, and the projections all were an exciting and integral part of Sinha's extraordinary performance of her riveting play, which I saw in its second production in the magical backspace at Theatre Passe Muraille.

The experience of being witness to Pamela perform *CRASH* was like white-water rafting: terrifying, primal, raw, and finally cathartic—what every theatre experience should be. However, it was only in reading this play that I fully absorbed the piece, and had time to reflect and revel in every telling and superbly rendered detail and poetic insight. *CRASH* is a piece of dramatic literature that will be read and performed for many generations. It deserves to be entrenched in the canon of world literature in English.

This breathtaking monologue play does exactly what the above line says: It opens our eyes and shows us the "heavy thing": trauma; the trauma of the protagonist, the girl, who has been tortured and raped and struggles to remember the face of her attacker; the trauma that lurks under the surface of reality of so many lives; the trauma we close our eyes to because we feel we cannot risk seeing its fullness. The play itself is the sturdy raft that keeps us safe while we navigate the powerful currents of trauma—the playwright has such compassion for her protagonist and for her audience that she offers comfort, ironically, in the shape of another trauma, the heartbreaking illness and death of her beloved father. There is comfort there because he loved powerfully and he was powerfully loved; he was surrounded by the golden light of love as he suffered, in contrast to the titanic force of hatred the girl endures during her attack. It is the extraordinary love of the girl's family, which has given her the strength she needs to survive not just the attack, but also the relentless assault of memory.

"Can't remember isn't the same as forget."

If only she could remember his face, perhaps he could be stopped and the memory would cease tormenting her. The girl can't remember the face of her attacker, but that doesn't mean it's not there, inside her somewhere. This is another line that speaks to how theatre at its best can bring to the surface what we can't remember but have not forgotten. The girl struggles to "turn around" to see his face, but she never does, and perhaps that is a mercy. The play ends in a moment of peace—a communication with her father, whose presence she feels "like the colour in gold you were in me."

Sinha and I share a bond of soul as women engaged in theatrical writing and performance. I first met her through a long and eloquent letter she wrote to me after playing the role of Isobel in my play *Lion in the Streets*, and Dee in my earlier play, *I Am Yours*. In the letter she opened up her heart and soul and I could clearly perceive that she understood those characters perhaps more deeply than I did, that she had done what I always hope an actor will do, and that is to OWN the roles, take them deeply inside. We have met many times since then and I have always been humbled by her passion for those roles. Having seen her perform in many plays in the city, I have long been in awe of Pamela as an actress, but having seen and read *CRASH*, I am in an even deeper awe—a fellow traveller, a woman who channels experience through a theatrical and literary lens and lets the words flow until they must be shaped for performance and production. It is important to Pamela that the production elements were an essential part of her writing and they were fascinating, but for me, a believer in text as the essence of theatre, her genius lies in the words she has written to be spoken, each and every one exquisite. After the white-water ride we end on the shore, in the sun. We have been through the rapids and we have survived, along with girl, along with Pamela. Survival, however, is not healing; Ms. Sinha does not assert that the love the girl gives and receives will take away the horror, only that she does continue to love, and those who continue to love cannot ever be defeated.

Thank you, Pamela.

—Judith Thompson

CRASH premiered at Theatre Passe Muraille, Toronto, on May 1, 2012, with the following cast and crew:

The Girl: Pamela Mala Sinha

Director: Alan Dilworth
Set and lighting design: Kimberly Purtell
Sound design: Debashis Sinha
Projections: Cameron Davis
Choreography: Monica Dottor and Rubena Sinha
Stage management: Kat Chin

CRASH was remounted on September 26, 2013, at Theatre Passe Muraille in a co-production with Necessary Angel Theatre Company, with the following cast and crew:

The Girl: Pamela Mala Sinha

Director: Alan Dilworth
Set and lighting design: Kimberly Purtell
Sound design: Debashis Sinha
Projections: Cameron Davis
Choreography: Monica Dottor and Rubena Sinha
Stage management: Marinda de Beer

CRASH was written with the support of a Canada Council for the Arts Creation Grant and grants from the Ontario Arts Council's Theatre Projects and Theatre Creators' Reserve programs.

CHARACTERS
The Girl

also plays:

Constable Blier
Krista
Doctor
Little Man
Therapist

We hear the muted sounds of a memorial: a piano playing, voices, and gentle laughter.

A gold light rises on the GIRL, illuminating the landing where she stands and the staircase below.

After a moment, we hear a loud crash and the stage is plunged into darkness: only the landing and stairs are sharply lit in blue.

A crowbar appears, suspended in the air. Each of the objects buried in the GIRL's memory emerges with a crash.

GIRL: A crowbar. That's what it was. The gentle hand on her arm says open them. Open your eyes and see what the heavy thing was.

A slip appears.

This bathroom is too bright. Can't see anything. Who's that? Oh. What's this? A nightie. No, it's not. It's a slip. Silk. Real silk. And lace.

A pack of cigarettes and a lighter appear.

Player's Light. Three cigarettes, the lighter tucked inside.

A mobile of test tubes.

And this. Shut UP, he tells himself—shut up. The officer who cares too much knows the girl doesn't hear him, but he keeps talking anyway. He can't stop. He can't stop.

A final crash brings up the gold lights of the memorial. The GIRL stands above the blue stairs listening. The sounds are softer now, as if heard from behind a door.

The girl's father is gone. And now, down nine green-carpet stairs where everyone gathers one year later in memory of him . . . it's like music. A back and forth of swallowed tears and deep, heart-aching laughter, riding a love so big—bigger—than anything that ever came before. There's nothing left to do.

As the soft sound of tinkling bells rises, a Door of Light appears at the bottom of the stairs. As she speaks, the light grows in intensity.

But up here—above those stairs, facing the door her father walked through a thousand times before—there is still one more thing the girl . . . One thing she can remember. One more thing—

The door reaches its full brightness as the music leads her.

—will change everything.

The blue and gold lights flash out with a crash. A red plastic milk crate appears, floating above the landing.

As the GIRL moves further into the memory, a second set of stairs emerges: one part rises above the landing stage left, the other leads down to the stage. The milk crate sits on the highest stair.

She made her temple from an old plastic milk crate. She stole it from behind the corner depanneur. She covered it with this sort of placemat thing her mother made when she was sixteen. Her father said it didn't matter they weren't there or that it didn't look like much—

She picks up the milk crate.

God was there if she believed He was.

They weren't religious, her parents. Not the kind of religious where you drum all the things that make you Hindu into your kids' heads in case they forgot where they "came from"—they were never like that. They did Sundays at temple, but it was more about family and community than religion with them; Sikhs, Muslims, Christians—it didn't matter—they celebrated everything together.

She descends another set of stairs stage left, stopping just before the bottom.

She knew some prayers; she knew some songs; but what she really knew was that God was God whatever you called Him—or Her—and there was no right way or wrong way to believe—or not believe—as long as it made you a better person.

A rectangle of light, with the dimensions of a single bed, appears on the floor stage right.

The GIRL steps down and walks towards the bed, placing the milk crate near the downstage corner.

They meditated though; her mother once in the morning, and her father twice every day—no matter what—first thing when he got up and once more at sundown. Whatever else might change for the girl, that never did.

She lies down so that her feet point towards the milk crate.

Almost immediately, she picks the milk crate up again.

You're not supposed to sleep with your feet pointing towards your temple . . .

She begins to sing a Sanskrit prayer ("Sarasvati Vandana" can be sung or simply recited) and looks for a better spot. She sees it, downstage left.

Yaa kundendu tushaara haara—dhavalaa Yaa shubhra—vastraa vritaa
Yaa veena—vara—danda—manditakara Yaa shweta padmaa sana

The moment the milk crate touches the floor, a warm light falls on it.

She goes back to the bed and lies down once again, positioning herself so she has a clear line of sight to the altar, and finishes the song.

Pause.

She wanted it to be the first thing she saw when she woke up in the morning—the first place her eyes would go. She couldn't tell you why, she just did.

Suddenly a cardboard box lands in front of her. She sits up on the bed and flips open the lid.

This is the box she had with her and *this—*

She pulls out an embroidered mat.

—is the real mat her mother made when she was sixteen.

She pulls a framed picture out of the box.

The parents of the girl followed the teachings of Sri Ramakrishna and his wife, Sarada Devi—

She holds up their pictures.

This is them: *you can enter the same house many different ways; no one way is better than another* . . . she loved that. She took it out of her parents' temple at home. Stole it, really.

She places the pictures back inside and pulls out another framed picture.

Sai Baba said the same thing: *one God, many names* . . . something like that.

She puts it back—then sees something else.

Omigod.

She closes the lid and, taking the box, moves off the bed and over to the milk crate.

The girl was feeling really homesick her first couple of days in the apartment— her FIRST apartment EVER—and this pathetic little altar that didn't even have an incense holder was making her even *more* depressed—

She kneels down in front of the box. As she speaks, she lays out the contents on the floor: the mat, the pictures, and a bowl of yellow marigolds.

So she called home; both of them on different extensions so they could all talk at the same time. Her father told her that when he was a student in England he didn't have an incense holder either—and now here she was, in Montreal and away from home for the first time with the exact same problem! They laughed about that . . . and that's when he told her about—

She pulls out an old potato.

—the potato. Her mother said she didn't need beautiful things to make it real.

She takes a stick of incense out of the box.

She just had to believe God was there and He would be.

She sticks the incense into the potato.

The girl never really understood the equation of her family. Her father was a scientist—a statistician.

We hear the sound of a stone as it falls into water; a concentric circle of blue water ripples outwards.

In his work he collected, analyzed, and interpreted data. The girl's mother was a dancer.

Another stone drops; blue water ripples.

Collection: One statistician. One dancer. One girl. One boy.

As the last stone drops, the GIRL *puts the potato down with the rest of the objects laid out on the floor. A memory hits her.*

The first time the girl's father saw her mother she was dancing. He told the girl he thought her mother was the most beautiful dancer he had ever seen. He came back the next night and the night after that—always leaving right after she was finished because she was the only one he wanted to see. When the girl was eight her mother was dancing again and no one—*not even Mummy*—was letting her see.

It's a grown-up story, they said. They were fighting all the time but they agreed about that. That made her mad. *It will frighten you . . .* But the girl knew it wouldn't.

We hear the music that accompanies the dance fade up: muted gongs and soft drumming as a circle of white light appears centre stage.

The GIRL *sees it.*

Mummy was dancing Mahadevi.

She gets up.

Mahadevi loved God so much she wanted to marry Him. *That was funny, not scary.* It was the olden days.

She walks towards the spot—

One day the king saw Mahadevi just walking down the street and wanted to marry her.

—and steps into it, remaining inside through the following.

She said, *Okay—as long as God comes first.*

She takes on the part of Mahadevi as she remembers it, dancing the way her mother did.

"Husband inside, lover outside. I can't manage them both.
This world and the other,
I cannot manage them both. O lord white as jasmine,
I cannot hold in one hand
Both the round nut and the long bow."[1]

But one day the king got jealous of God and broke his promise so she left. But she didn't care because now she could look for God wherever she wanted. She looked and looked for a really really long time but she couldn't find Him anywhere. That made her sad. She got dirty and smelly and tore all her clothes off. When the bad men saw her naked—

Pushed, she falls.

—they hurt Mahadevi.

The music grows in intensity.

"Would a circling vulture know such depths of sky
As the moon would know?
Would a weed on the riverbank know such depths of water
As the lotus would know?
O lord white as jasmine only you would know the ways of your devotees;
How would these, these mosquitoes on a buffalo's hide?"

The dance music fades.

She died at the end—but it wasn't scary or sad because you could tell Mahadevi *did see God*:

We hear the magical tinkling bells once again . . .

I saw you in me without showing a limb in the bees and the trees, and she was probably dancing because she was so happy *like the colour in gold you were in me*, and the girl was happy too because that was the day she got to see her beautiful mummy, dancing with God.

---

1   Poetry of Akka Mahadevi, twelfth century Hindu saint.

As the memory ends, the spot and music fade out; she remains centre stage, back in the room.

The girl believed in God too. I mean, really believed. When they were little they were taught to say "Jai Bhagavan"—Glory to God—three times before eating: *(putting her hands together in prayer)* "Jai Bhagavan. Jai Bhagavan. Jai Bhagavan." It usually came out *joybhagavanjoybhagavanjoybhagavan.*

She laughs.

She moves to the milk crate. As she speaks, she begins to set up the milk crate with the objects laid out on the floor: first the placemat, then each of the pictures, the bowl of marigolds . . . transforming it into an altar.

It became so ingrained in the girl that whenever she got up to get water, salt, whatever—every time she sat down—she'd say it again. One night it got to be ridiculous—she got up five times in three minutes and said it every single time she sat down: *joybhagavanjoybhagavanjoybhagavan . . . joybhagavanjoybhagavanjoybhagavan.* Finally her brother, who was six at the time, said, *Jeez, Didi, how many times are you going to say it?!* And right away—

She picks up the potato.

—right away her father said, *Let her. Let her say it a hundred times if she wants to.*

The moment she places the potato on the altar, the Door of Light at the memorial stairs fades up again, to the sound of a tape rewinding.

When the piano and memorial sounds become clear again, the GIRL *launches herself away from the altar towards the light, where a crash catapults her into the memory of* CONSTABLE BLIER.

The memorial plays softly beneath their dialogue.

CONSTABLE BLIER *speaks in a French-Canadian accent.*

CONSTABLE BLIER: You're sure you don't see him here?

She adopts a gesture specific to the GIRL.

GIRL: *I told you—I didn't see his face.*

With a different gesture, she becomes BLIER; *the* GIRL *flows easily and quickly between these two gestures throughout their conversation.*

CONSTABLE BLIER: And you didn't know anyone in Montreal?

GIRL: Again she tells him, *No, I came to visit a friend; he left, and then I found a place of my own /*

CONSTABLE BLIER: / And you lived there a week?

GIRL: *No—three days—I already /*

CONSTABLE BLIER: / Because it seems he knew you.

The sound of the memorial ends.

He gained access to your building and targeted your apartment from inside the courtyard.

GIRL: *But how would he know which one was mine? I never went out there . . . Okay, once when I moved in to let in some air but that was the only time I ever opened that door /*

CONSTABLE BLIER: / The exact same door he knew to break down.

Pause.

GIRL: Everything and nothing. Fingerprints, a rare blood type, but no face she can remember. The guys in the garage next door used to whistle at her, but they wouldn't know her apartment number. The only person she knew in Montreal was a boy from Winnipeg, but he was her friend.

Can't remember isn't the same as forget. That's the problem. Forget is—don't want to remember. Can't remember is—don't want to forget.

Slowly, through the following, the Door of Light fades as the image of blue shimmering water appears on the face of the GIRL.

Water on fire . . . everything you know to be real, unreal; life and death walk hand in hand here at the beginning and end of the world. Kids everywhere . . . happy . . . laughing, even as everyone else around them is crying the same tears for the same reasons as hundreds of years before now. Everything the same but for each one—each time—as if no one else before had ever felt such sorrow.

Pause.

She turns sharply to look back at a door standing upstage centre. Almost immediately we hear disco music playing behind it (intro to "The Hustle") as a red glow flickers beneath it.

Sometimes during a Black, the girl would go to bars to find men. She'd carry a large knife in her knapsack.

She approaches the door. When she opens it, music blares and she is enveloped in a red light. She walks through the door, closing it behind her. The music is muted again.

She emerges behind the stage left stairs, as if inside the club. She carries a bag slung over her shoulder.

Within five minutes some guy would always come up and start talking. She'd talk back, but it was like she wasn't even there . . . just watching it all happen from the other side of the room. Watching him try to pick her up, try to impress her—the whole time thinking, is he big enough? Strong enough?

Pause.

Mean enough?

Because last call would be in about half an hour of getting there, the girl would suggest they go someplace else . . . Someplace else was always the lakeshore.

The song and club sounds become louder as she dances towards the lake-shore, downstage.

No one was ever down there at two or three in the morning—at least not the part where the girl wanted them to go: the far end, where there's nothing. No ice-cream stands, no boardwalks, nothing. You could do anything to a person down there and no one would ever see you.

As she spins into a seated position, the music fades—still present but distorted.

She leans back slightly, leaving one hand free near the open bag beside her.

The stage grows darker, with only a spot of light on her.

He would have to start. If he didn't start, it wouldn't count. The girl would give the man every reason to believe she was really into it and then—then, when there was no reason to stop—NO. She'd say no; he'd beg, *C'mon, baby* . . . she'd say no again; he'd get angry, *Are you fucking KIDDING me?!* He'd be really angry by now because she'd led him on all this time and because he was so turned on and frustrated and *PISSED OFF* all at once he'd—force her. He'd—force her to do it even though she said no—

And then—only then—or it wouldn't count—

Her hand reaches towards her bag.

The song lyric "Do it . . . just do it" plays, distorted and louder each time.

Force her or it wouldn't count—

Her body tenses as she waits for it, hand inside her bag.

The music stops abruptly.

But none of them ever did. They were all nice men. All they wanted was her number.

Pause.

She removes her hand from the bag.

It never mattered to the girl that they hadn't caught him.

She looks towards the memorial staircase.

Nothing mattered then.

When she moves towards the stairs, light falls upon them. She sits on a stair mid-way up.

Every morning and every night—all her life—the girl's father prayed.

One morning, he didn't.

Very slowly, lights over the altar fade up.

The girl's mother asked him, *Why, Babul—why are you just sitting there?* She could hear them from her room upstairs, could hear her father's broken voice, *How can I pray to a God who abandoned her, Ruba? A child who says "Jai Bhagavan" a thousand times every time she gets up from the table? That God is dead to me.* He wasn't going to pray. He wasn't going to pray ever again—and the girl didn't care. As she got up to close the door to prove how much she didn't care, she heard her mother—so quietly—*You have to, Babul; you have to. Because if you don't, you'll take away the only ground left under her feet.*

A door closes.

The girl's parents could only find one hospital where women like her could stay to get help. It was in LA.

Fluorescent lights and electricity buzz as the outline of a bed appears downstage right.

She steps down towards it.

Stupidstupidstupid girl.

*A black blanket drops from the ceiling and onto the bed with a crash—
triggering the* GIRL'S *memory of* KRISTA.

Picking up the blanket she lays it on the bed.

KRISTA: Hi, I'm Krista! I'll help you unpack—

The GIRL'S *arms are half crossed.*

GIRL: Wow, thought the girl, *they help you unpack here.* Krista picks up a gigantic bottle of Chanel No.5.

My father gave me that for Christmas.

KRISTA *adopts a gesture.*

KRISTA: Ohhh, that's so sweet. I'll have to take it for now though—

GIRL: *Why?*

KRISTA: Just—how we like to do things around here . . .

GIRL: Oh, the girl gets it—she might try to kill herself again so take away anything that's glass. There go the scissors, razor—Okay, she gets that—sewing kit—*blow dryer?*

KRISTA: Okay, you're all set—I'll see you in a bit!

GIRL: *This is so stupid* . . . the girl walks over to the window she can't jump out of and waits for something to happen.

Pause.

Her period. *Shit.*

She finds a black tampon in her pocket.

Thank god . . . When Krista sticks her head back in—

KRISTA: Just wanted to let you know that dinner's—oh. I should've taken that /

GIRL: / *What? This?*

KRISTA: Just go on over to the nurse's station; George'll give you a pad /

GIRL: / *The two-hundred-pound bald man who's picking his nose right now—I have to ask* HIM *for a pad?* Krista moves towards her—

Okay, could you just—I mean I don't get it—you think . . . what—? I mean, really—what would I do with it, like, stuff it down my throat or—? Krista takes the tampon and leaves . . .

> *The* GIRL *follows her out.*

Well you know what, Krista? Hey—Krista! Know what? If I did want to stuff it down my throat—all you'd have to do is PULL THE GODDAMN STRING!

> *The lights switch off and then, with the buzz of the fluorescents, switch on again, revealing the* DOCTOR.

The doctor knew without looking the girl would be there: at the far end of the couch, legs curled under a blanket. She had to be there—drama therapy was mandatory. She tried to get out of it at first.

Banging the shit out of something with a big foam bat isn't going to do anything for me—it's called "substitution," and I do it for a LIVING.

He thought that was pretty clever. He agreed to let her come as an observer. That was over a month ago. Now she comes willingly to support her friends . . . broken women determined to die helping each other live. Only this one didn't want to die—she wanted to kill herself. Because she pulled the covers over her head. Because that's all she did.

> *She sits down on a stair.*

> *The* DOCTOR *puts his hands on his knees, looking downstage at the* GIRL.

DOCTOR: What's the sin?

> *The* GIRL's *hands drop between her knees.*

GIRL: *Huh?*

DOCTOR: The sin.

Pause.

If I told you there was a girl—just there—

The DOCTOR gestures downstage.

She's sleeping—when all of a sudden there's a crash—a really big one. She doesn't know what's happening because she's sleeping—but then all of a sudden she realizes it's inside—it's *inside* her house—she doesn't know what to do, there's no time, so she /

GIRL: / *There's time.*

DOCTOR: What? Okay . . . okay, there's time . . . for what?

GIRL: *Jump.*

DOCTOR: Jump—?

GIRL: *Out the fucking window.*

DOCTOR: The third-floor window.

GIRL: *There's hangers in the closet—why doesn't she scratch his ugly eyes out? Why doesn't she fight him no matter how big or armed or crazy he was because then at least she'd be dead from FIGHTING rather than lying there like an idiot with the covers over her head thinking he wouldn't see you—he'd see an empty, unmade bed because you were so thin and small and still you STUPIDSTUPIDSTUP—*

The GIRL is cut off by a blackout and the sudden crash of a heavy steel door slammed shut.

She speaks from the dark.

The doctor knows as he slams the door shut this unforgiving girl, seven years away from that night and safe as she is here in this room—

A spot lights up on the GIRL, *the blanket from the bed now over her head.*

—will do it again.

She pulls the blanket down. A quiet, almost subliminal bass tone ebbs and flows.

Peek-a-boo . . . a baby's first believing. A terror so big . . . if I can't see you, you can't see me.

The light fades out.

The outline of the bed emerges in the darkness as the GIRL *lies down.*

As the girl falls asleep that night, something moves inside her.

A long pause. The droning sound rises.

The upstage door opens slightly, and a shaft of light spills out towards the bed.

Pause.

She jolts awake; the blue reflection of a rear-view mirror suddenly appears across her eyes.

A car in motion. The sound is from inside the car.

Driving from her friend's house on de Bienville to her new apartment on St. Denis. Two big suitcases in the trunk and a box beside her in the back. It's only three blocks away but he's not mad—

It's not too far . . . The next right. Just here, on the corner—

The car speeds up.

Uh—right here is fine . . .

The car keeps moving.

This is great, thanks.

The car comes to a complete stop. The blue reflection remains on her eyes.

He offers to carry her suitcases up but to be safe she tells him to leave them on the landing—*I can manage from there*—because she doesn't want him to see which door is hers.

Pause.

He saw.

Music fades up as the light on her eyes fades out and she moves stage left, entering the courtyard. As she speaks, light spills out once again from the half-open door.

Instead of leaving her building, he lets himself into the inner courtyard—

Three red doors appear above her, stage right.

—and counts out the corresponding back door on the fire escape. He looks for another way out.

She looks at the upstage door.

He sees it: the steel door off the courtyard. The boiler room. Going in, he sees it has another door that leads directly onto an alley.

The door slams shut; lights out.

A spot appears sharply on her. A cyclical loop of sound builds and builds with each new memory.

She wants to tell—she wants to scream what she wants to tell because for the first time she has something to tell—she couldn't remember the name of the company but it was only one of three in the book and she remembers the number she called from, the time of the order, the date of the order, the point of pickup, and the address of her destination. She remembers all of it and all of it would be on record because she didn't flag the cab, she ORDERED IT.

With a crash the crowbar appears, ending the looping sound. Each image appears as she names them.

Crowbar, cigarettes, lighter, fingerprints, blood type, dirty taste, dirty smell, his laugh—

Huge, oversized images of 8" x 10" negatives of men's faces appear in rapid motion, playing over the other images suspended above her.

—still no face . . .

But what she knows now, will change *everything.*

Blackout and a short burst of drumming.

A cold, stark light comes up on the GIRL, centre stage.

You have to train to be a Rudaali. Literally translated Rudaali means "weeping woman." There are specific movements, and when the crying starts, it can't be how you would naturally cry—you have to *wail.* It's really hard to keep up for days on end. But you have to. Because that's what the family hired you to do. It's not about your grief. Ever.

The drums start up again—passionate, dynamic. She begins to dance an exact, technically sharp dance of the Rudaali, building to a climax of spins; faster and faster until—

We hear the sounds of a sitar playing an alap (a solo with no rhythm) cutting through the drums; gentle but insistent, the sitar stops her, and carries on under her words, fading towards the end.

The girl's father wanted *all* his children there: her brother, her cousins, her best friends—tied to him not by blood but by love.

She does a gesture of containment from the dance.

The girl's mother sat next to him on the sofa. They waited for him to speak. Waited for him to tell them there was nothing to worry about. That it was treatable.

Gesture.

That it would be hard, but that it would be okay. But when he did finally speak, he only said, "*Take care of my Ruba . . . please just take care of my Roop.*"

Gesture.

Pause.

Suddenly, we hear the chimes of a subway door as the lights rise on the second set of stairs stage left.

She climbs them, and sits at the highest point. As she speaks we hear the moving train.

The girl and her brother took the subway to the police station because she couldn't get into a cab.

The image of the windows of a passing train play across her continuously; she is focused on someone seated in front of her.

He was away when it happened. When she finally told him, it was in a café—a *café*. Even after she understood it was her denial that made her do that, she never forgave herself. When he was born, she called him her "baby." They made bows and arrows out of vines and twigs in India, and ran barefoot in dust storms in Africa. They battled wild demons and evil gods and their forts were deep pits dug into hot red earth . . . allies in foreign lands. When weeks turned into months of seeing the sister he knew disappear, he cried into her lap one night; he felt helpless and he wanted his sister back. She couldn't hear him then but now, armed with new memory and the power to make things right, she was ready. She arrived home from the hospital with her ticket to Montreal already booked; the police were reopening her case but she didn't want her parents to go. That's when the front door opened and her brother—who was supposed to be in *India*—walked in . . . *I was in the neighbourhood, so . . . The girl's ally in foreign lands, hearing of the demon she remembered, flies over an ocean to do battle together again.*

The subway comes to a stop. As she steps off the train, she sees CONSTA-BLE BLIER *on the steps of the station below.*

She recognized him right away—the officer who cares too much. Even though they're half an hour early she can tell he's been sitting there a long time. When he puts out his hand she knows she will hug him instead . . . hug him and say, *I remember you*—

She descends the stairs and sits down as BLIER. *We hear his thoughts (with no accent) as he waits for the* GIRL.

Constable Blier remembered the girl—how could he forget her. It was supposed to be a routine check on a disturbance—he and the rookie took the call. When they walked in she said, *Who is it*, and like an idiot the rookie said *Who do you think it is? . . .* He panicked. A routine check is not a naked girl with her legs in the air—SHIT. Twenty years on the force and even he didn't get it right away. Then he saw the crowbar on the pillow on her face and he couldn't move fast enough. He helped her put on some clothes—he remembers a blue dress—cops were everywhere. She wouldn't go though . . . just kept wandering around counting CDs and cutlery, looking for something—anything—he might have stolen . . . like it had to be more than just her. He stayed with her at the hospital. She won't say a word and he can't stop talking. She isn't letting go of his hand. Or maybe he isn't letting go of hers.

A crash and blackout.

A naked light bulb flashes on and suddenly descends; a circle of blue light falls on a stool, stage left—the evidence room. There is the hum of a light bulb.

The GIRL *steps into the light and sits down on the stool.*

She waits for BLIER *to speak.*

Her hands are between her knees.

What happens now?

Pause.

He isn't saying anything. She knows the file in his hands is hers.

Leaning forward, elbows on his knees, CONSTABLE BLIER *speaks through his thick accent.*

CONSTABLE BLIER: Can I get either of you some coffee—anything to drink?

Sitting upright again.

GIRL: *This is a list of everything I remembered—dates, times . . . addresses—everything.*

CONSTABLE BLIER: Great—that's just great . . . but before we go on, I want you to know how much I admire you for being here today.

Beat.

GIRL: The girl notices he isn't looking at her list.

CONSTABLE BLIER: We have a lot of good evidence—a rare blood type, fingerprints—if we had a suspect we could identify him very easily . . .

Beat.

GIRL: *If.*

CONSTABLE BLIER: There seems to be a statute of limitations on records kept by taxi companies in the province of Quebec . . .

GIRL: He's talking too much; she hates that he talks so much /

CONSTABLE BLIER: / And every . . . few years . . . they delete them.

GIRL: *Delete.*

Beat.

CONSTABLE BLIER: The records. The . . . records.

Beat.

The taxi-company records.

Pause.

GIRL: *When?*

He speaks with great difficulty.

CONSTABLE BLIER: They deleted them . . . four years ago.

Blackout and a quick, enormous crash, cut off by a spotlight sharply illuminating her face.

The high-pitched tone and rumbling loop rise throughout the following.

GIRL: He made her eat his shit. He sat on her face and suffocated her with his ass until she did.

Pause.

She did it.

Lights flash blindingly bright with the sound of electrical static as she struggles to remember what followed—then flash out almost immediately, back to the spot on her face.

He orders the girl to hold the position. On her back, naked, pillow on her face, crowbar on the pillow, arms extended, legs in the air, he's got her by the ankles and he's jerking her legs around—she doesn't understand what position he wants her to hold. He's yelling at her and laughing at her because she looks so *stupid* and finally he jerks one leg straight up HIGH and the other one bent at the knee.

Pause.

I'M GOING NOW. I'M GOING. DON'T LOOK. DON'T MOVE. OR I'LL FUCKING KILL YOU.

Pause.

If she doesn't move—she doesn't move—he will be gone and she will be okay. She won't move.

Pause.

She hears the bedroom door—

A door slams, slightly dreamlike.

She hears him walk away—

Heavy boots step across a floor . . .

She's not moving. She's sweating with the effort. Her legs are shaking on the inside because she can't let them shake on the outside or it won't be okay.

Sound out.

She's not even breathing. She is still she is superman she can do it she will do it right and it will be okay.

Long pause.

YOU FUCKING MOVED.

Pause.

He never left—he just pretended. Slammed the door from the *inside*. Walked on the spot . . . just stood there quietly, watching her, watching. She did NOT move. He knows it. She knows it. They both know she did it right—she did it right—what he said. But it's not okay. She did it right and it's not okay. He punishes her for doing it right.

The spot on the GIRL goes out; a short burst of the Rudaali drums invades the darkness.

An outline of the bed in light appears on the upstage door. A path of light leads downstage from it, marking a hallway.

The GIRL *steps out of the black into the hallway as the* LITTLE MAN.

His arms are crossed and locked in front of him.

LITTLE MAN: There was a crash . . . a pretty big one—

GIRL: When he catches sight of the shattered door on the girl's kitchen floor.

LITTLE MAN: That must have been it, eh?

GIRL: The officer guides him back to his own door—

She walks upstage to the door, then turns and faces out.

—and asks him what happened next.

LITTLE MAN: Some running—some banging—then I called 911.

GIRL: The officer reminds him that he'd reported three crashes over several hours, not two.

LITTLE MAN: Well yes—there was the big one at first, another one kind of the same after that, and then yes . . . the last one—

GIRL: Suddenly the little man is feeling very stressed—what does it matter how *many* there were; he called, didn't he? He tells himself there's no reason to get defensive when the officer asks why it took him so damn long to pick up the phone.

Pause.

LITTLE MAN: Well I had to be sure that—

GIRL: When he spots the girl: slip hanging in two parts under a dress he'd seen on her before. She looks at him, eyes huge, then turns away.

The 8" x 10" negatives crash against the door like shards of broken glass, rapidly and continuously chiming under her words.

She doesn't want to look at them but she can't help it.

The shutter of a camera clicks as each colour photo of the crime scene appears.

As she speaks, the photos flash against the full length of the door as if she were standing inside each one of them: a mattress half off the box spring, a rumpled pink cotton daisy sheet, linoleum floor covered in wood pieces and broken glass.

Who said—who SAID—they could take those pictures; it was her room— her *room.*

Beat.

He took no care to be quiet because he knew—he KNEW—no one would call would care would risk being wrong looking stupid to save a life.

The photos freeze on one of a bashed in oak door.

All sound fades after this last image.

She's not there as she looks at those pictures of her life in a file on a desk; she's watching a movie, a film of someone who looks like her looking at pictures of another girl's life . . .

The photo goes black and tiny blue writing appears above her on the top of the door, each word (within brackets) appearing, then disappearing as she speaks.

But then the *(And he)* tiny printing *(tore my),* tiny, tiny baby printing . . . *(nightie)* writing that looks nothing like her own *(then he . . . when he . . .)*

As she struggles to remember, the writing stops, then repeats.

(. . . he . . .)

The words go black as the bulb in the evidence room fades up slightly.

She comes back. She comes back because no matter how brave or strong he is still her little brother and seeing her hell immortalized she feels him quietly dying beside her.

She moves towards the stool.

Collection: Mother. Father. Sister. Brother.

Analysis: Data set of four in love who don't fit.

Interpretation: If the data set is carefully studied, observations usually indicate a tendency to centre around some specific *point.*

A full blue spot immediately flashes over the now-seated GIRL, *as we hear and see a stone drop into the water. The light bulb hums.*

CONSTABLE BLIER *leans forward.*

CONSTABLE BLIER: There is something.

Beat.

That period during the assault you still don't remember—we believe that in that time, you *did* see his face. And like everything here—

He refers to the list in front of her.

—it is *inside* you. Even his face.

Pause.

She sits upright.

GIRL: *Then why can't I remember?*

CONSTABLE BLIER: Because he said he would kill you.

Beat.

He said . . . he would kill you if you looked.

Pause.

The sounds of the evidence room fade.

He had done this before, the officer told them—he was definitely a *repeat* offender. If she could remember his face they could save other women. It would finally matter what happened to her—what happened to her family.

Pause.

They believed it was in there. They told her they would pay for a doctor to help her remember.

Lights fade down to black.

The GIRL *appears downstage, brightly lit but surrounded by darkness.*

Back home, they found a blue-eyed doctor who specialized in memory recovery. The very first day she asked the girl what her nightgown looked like.

The GIRL *and her* THERAPIST *are differentiated only by the tone of their voices and their facial expressions.*

GIRL: *It wasn't a nightgown. It was a slip.*

Pause.

It was white.

THERAPIST: White, white? Or off-white?

GIRL: *Ivory white.*

THERAPIST: Was it cotton?

GIRL: *No.*

Beat.

THERAPIST: Can you draw it for me?

The GIRL looks at the door upstage. A slip appears, one stroke at a time, as if someone was drawing it.

GIRL: *It was silk. Real silk.*

Pause.

And lace.

THERAPIST: Very delicate, then.

A line appears lengthwise down the slip, cutting it in half.

GIRL: *Yes.*

The drawing dissolves.

Twice a week for over a year the girl did hypnotherapy with the blue-eyed doctor, trying to find the face inside her. She looked and looked for a really, really long time but couldn't find it anywhere—

A low hum creeps in slowly under the following, building.

THERAPIST: Draw the bed.

GIRL: *I don't want to draw the bed.*

THERAPIST: Draw the bed.

GIRL: *I REMEMBER THE BED—*

THERAPIST: Where was the bed?

GIRL: *I told you—in the corner.*

THERAPIST: You said the altar was in the corner—

GIRL: *LOOK.*

She storms over to the door and begins to draw. As she moves her hand, lines of light appear, drawing a bed.

THE BED WAS IN THE CORNER.

THERAPIST: And the altar?

She takes a step towards it; it lights up.

GIRL: *Here—*

THERAPIST: And where are you?

She gestures back to the door.

GIRL: THERE.

THERAPIST: Draw it.

As she draws, a life-size stick figure appears inside the outline of the bed.

Where is he?

Immediately a current of electricity is added to the hum; it runs throughout the GIRL*'s altered state of consciousness.*

GIRL: *On top of me.*

She suddenly goes still.

THERAPIST: What's happening?

GIRL: *He—he—I don't know.*

THERAPIST: Don't think about him; what are *you* doing?

GIRL: *I—I—got up . . .*

She turns her body towards the altar, and takes a few steps.

Walking . . .

She stops and raises her arm slightly.

A miniature version of the stick figure appears on the floor, as if it were standing in front of the altar.

THERAPIST: Good. Now think—you're at the altar—where is *he*; where is he RIGHT NOW?

She moves sharply to the door and violently scribbles across the entire image of the stick figure all the way to the bottom of the door.

GIRL: *RIGHT HERE RIGHT HERE RIGHT HERE ON TOP OF ME—*

THERAPIST: On top of you?

GIRL: *YESSSSSS.*

Referring to the small stick figure on the floor.

THERAPIST: Who is that at the altar—?

GIRL: *ME IT'S ME—*

THERAPIST: *(very gently)* Then who is that on the bed?

She steps back from the door.

GIRL: *Hiding.*

Pause.

The charged state ends.

Hiding. The part of herself she had left behind, there in that bed. Hiding lived through what the girl had blocked from her memory. If Hiding saw his face, then so did she.

The light bed on the floor once again appears, glowing intensely.

But the girl was afraid to know what *else* Hiding saw.

A short tone as the music fades up and the GIRL takes a step towards the bed.

It fades again. As the GIRL speaks, the outline of another light door appears, as if floating on the landing above.

At first it was small. Like not being able to walk very far, or not sitting in the low chair she knew he loved to read in. Then it got big like his cane becoming a walker—so he could be more independent—but he still needed help getting it into the bathroom, because he never used to need it in there and now he does.

The glow from the upstairs door intensifies.

One day she hears him calling out for more than just that. And even though she's not his son or his wife it doesn't matter anymore, he just needs someone, and when he smiles at her . . . they both know they've crossed a line that is beyond any she's ever wished for him as a father or he for her as a daughter, but she's grateful—so grateful that finally she could give him, show him, assure him that all that he is and all that he isn't doesn't matter anymore because that day, in that bathroom, she never loved him more.

The door fades, as the light bed on the floor appears again, but this time it is a brilliant electric blue.

As the GIRL speaks the bed rotates, gradually floating past her and up the memorial staircase.

The girl's father could never be alone anymore. Even if they were beside him, on the bed next to his own special one, he would want to get out—*I have to go.* The girl's brother was his shadow—under every step, around every turn, catching every trip. And no one could talk to the girl's mother; she couldn't hear you because no matter where she was in the house or what she was doing, she was upstairs with the girl's father.

The blue bed arrives at the top of the stairs, illuminating the landing.

One day the girl and her mother had a fight—

She runs halfway up the stairs.

In the middle of it, she got upset because her father could hear, and her mother said, *So what—so* WHAT *he* SHOULD *know what goes on in his house—he needs to see life—all of it—to fight.* And he fought. Cane to walker, walker to wheelchair: at every marker he found something to be proud of.

She follows the bed as it floats across the landing.

I walked all the way down the hall without any help . . . and later when it took two to turn him in his bed, *Your mummy and me did it alone!*

Finally the bed rests at the far end of the landing, nestled against the highest stair.

The girl finally got it. Why they were together.

She runs back towards the top of the landing and, suspending her body above the stairs, falls forward, catching herself again . . . and again.

Because now, if she let go, her brother was there as their mother fell back— catching her son as he let go . . . this is how it was for them—how it always had been.

She goes back to the top of the stairs, to the place where we first saw her. But now she is looking back at her father's blue bed, reaching for the memory of their love.

We hear a version of her father's magic music.

Even though the girl knew she had brought pain to their house, in this moment of her mother's head on her father's shoulder—as they lie laughing at the amazed faces of their children in the doorway, the girl knows their love together is bigger and braver than anything that could ever happen to them.

The magic music fades away with the bed.

Pause.

Still looking in the direction of the blue bed.

He got away. He got away . . . you stupidstupidstupid girl.

The sounds of the memorial rise once again, but are no longer muted. We hear voices, the gentle laughter, clearly now . . . and the piano playing the same piece as before—continuing on from where we last heard it.

We are back at the exact moment when we first saw the GIRL, as she stood listening at the top of the stairs.

The girl listens even harder to the voices downstairs: her best friends—those men she loves—saying to help care for him was to give love as he had given it to them for so many years. *Go to them—go down the stairs and go to them—* but she can't. She can't because something inside her swells louder than his granddaughter playing for him louder than the magic of his niece reading his letter out loud—*go down to them—*

The lights go out and we hear a crash that is louder than the others—colossal, extended—driving her across the landing and down the second set of stairs.

louder even than the feeling that she is the reason her brother laughs less—

Another crash: a shattering of even more wood and glass than the one before.

and her mother cries more; that she will *always* be the reason—

unless—

The crash is sucked out as the lights come sharply up on the door upstage centre, outlined in white light with the image of pink flowers scattered across its surface.

The GIRL stands against it—still and terrified.

The image of a pillow covers her face, a crowbar lies across the pillow, and a cigarette pack lies off to the side.

A single note vibrates under her memory.

She couldn't see with the pillow over her face but she could think and she didn't stop thinking. Obeying. Pleading. But when he—

He—

Her body turns sharply—as if being turned onto her stomach—but only very briefly before she steps out from the physical memory.

oh no.

She steps away from the door, with only her hand touching it.

The image of the stick figure from before emerges on the door; head covered by the image of the pillow, we see only its body.

That's when she left.

Beat.

Me.

Pause.

She left *me* here, and walked over—with her nightie *on*—

She looks over to her altar; light falls upon it. She steps downstage towards it.

to her little altar in the corner and asked God to come out of the picture and burn him . . .

She arrives at the spot where the miniature stick figure first appeared on the floor.

She just stood there, in front of God, repeating *burn him* over and over, demanding what was happening in that bed end in flames *now*—

The chalk scribble—now black—emerges on top of the stick figure on the bed and spreads out to cover the full surface of the door as the vibration builds.

Turn around. Turn around and look. LOOK AT HIS FACE—TURN AROUND—

The images are plunged into darkness as the Rudaali drums blast through.

The GIRL launches herself into the Rudaali dance from before, climaxing in a mad, violent spinning. The lights go out and a single, long wail erupts from deep inside her.

Almost immediately another female wail from the music intertwines with the girl's, eclipsing it with its power and grief.

It ends, and in the black, stillness.

Pause.

The reflection of blue water emerges on the floor, revealing the GIRL, spent, centre stage.

We hear the sound of a river, and funeral rites on the Ganges.

Everything floats here . . . flowers, kites, boats—even sarees float. And incense so thick it could be fog but fog doesn't smell like this. The girl's house in Winnipeg smelled like this. It looked like this too, after her father's evening prayers . . . it made a blanket of smoke that floated just above their waists; the girl and her brother used to crawl around under it like it was a roof.

A bell rings, slowly and quietly, echoing gently.

The blue water shimmers, gradually spreading over the stage around her.

The priest tells the girl's brother to wrap the ashes in red cloth and place it on his right shoulder—son carrying father, they follow.

The GIRL rises.

As she speaks, the image of the blue water rises over her very, very slowly.

A tiny wooden boat; white on top, a red border, and black on the bottom. The oarsman, old and wrapped in a forest-green shawl, waits to pull them away. The girl's mother is crying too hard—the priest tells her to stop, or his soul won't be able to do what it needs to. She tries—tries as she did so many times before when there was too much hurt, too many differences to ever want to try again—but still—

The river sounds fade out, but the bells continue to ring.

—she tries for him as he tried for her, and as her mother's voice calls out to him in the fog . . . the girl sees love so clear.

Pause.

The blue water continues to rise as she speaks: over the door, up past it, above the landing, through to the highest stair . . . as if finally, she is immersed and floating within it.

She takes a step towards the boat in front of her. The bells continue—intermittent, clear.

The girl sits next to her brother: the best of her parents in one person. As she reaches to help him pour the ashes into this water of green glass; even as they hear their mother say, *You are with us, in us; we are never without you;* even as her brother lays his head on the edge of their small boat and a sob breaks from him; even as their fingers wet touch the last of him for the last time—

She reaches her hand forward and the bell sounds gently.

The girl, floating past dancing ash and petals and prayer, sees her father's soul . . . happy.

Pause.

The smoke is getting thicker now . . . her eyes are burning but she doesn't care because marigold garlands floating on smoke on water is not something she ever wants to close her eyes to.

The water evaporates and she turns her outstretched hand and her body to face the altar as it lights up again. The last bell crescendoes into the sound of falling glass.

Behind her, the outline of the bed appears on the door.

Turn around.

Once again, the black scribble appears over the image of the stick girl on the bed, her head still covered by the pillow.

Turn around and look—

The black scribble grows, and with it the pink flowers.

LOOK AT HIS FACE—

The images spill over the edges of the door and beyond it. The sound of shattering glass grows . . .

TURN AROUND—

The sound crescendoes as the images on the bed overtake the space.

Turn around.

Pause.

As the sound, images, and altar light fade out . . . Blackout.

Pause.

Gradually the lights come up, in blue, over the two sets of stairs and the landing between them.

The GIRL remains where she was, now standing in a small pool of bright light.

The girl was crying. She was five and supposed to be sleeping. Her daddy came in and asked her what was wrong. *I forgot my horse at school.* "You have a horse?" he said. *Yes. And she's pink and her name is Lavender and I left her tied to the bike rack and now she's crying.* The girl's father went to get her a glass of water but came back with her parka and boots. "Let's go." It was only nine but it felt like midnight to her. It was midnight to her and with her nightie *on*, holding her daddy's hand she walked to school to save a horse he couldn't see. Because not seeing her horse never mattered to him. It was there because he loved her.

The lights hold on the GIRL . . . then transform slowly, into the naked light of the actual space—the stairs, the landing, the altar—stripped of illusion.

Only the spot on the GIRL remains.

That was the last time the girl saw God. The last time her feet would walk towards Him, believing He was there. She didn't look behind because she was looking ahead.

At a girl who remembered too late but would never forget.

A girl who says *I love you* a hundred times but still has no faith she is heard. A girl who lives in constant fear that love, like faith, will be taken.

A girl who never turned around.

Pause.

She turns to look at the stage left stairs and walks towards them. Blue light falls over them again as everything but the faint glow of the altar fades to black.

She climbs the stairs, the final reprise of her father's magic music leading her back to her place at the top.

The blue light evaporates; only the warm light of the memorial lights the
GIRL and the staircase below her, as in the very first moment . . .

Down the stairs, the voices she loves best.

Pause.

Like the colour in gold, you are in me.

As she takes the first steps down the stairs to join the memorial, the altar
glow fades to black.

Tiny golden lights fall from above.

The end.

ABOUT THE CONTRIBUTORS

Nicolas Billon's work has been produced in Toronto, Stratford, New York, and Paris. His triptych *Fault Lines* garnered the 2013 Governor General's Literary Award for Drama. He recently adapted his first play, *The Elephant Song*, into a feature film starring Bruce Greenwood, Xavier Dolan, and Catherine Keener, for which he won the 2015 Canadian Screen Award for Best Adapted Screenplay.

Anosh Irani was born and brought up in Bombay, and moved to Vancouver in 1998. He is the author of the novels *The Cripple and His Talismans*; *Dahanu Road*, which was longlisted for the 2010 Man Asian Literary Prize; and *The Song of Kahunsha*, which was a finalist for CBC Radio's Canada Reads and the Ethel Wilson Fiction Prize, was published in thirteen countries, and was a bestseller in Canada, China, and Italy. His play *Bombay Black* won four Dora Mavor Moore Awards, including Outstanding New Play and was included in his Governor General's Literary Award–nominated anthology *The Bombay Plays: The Matka King & Bombay Black*. His non-fiction has appeared in *The Globe and Mail* and *The New York Times* and he has written a feature-length film for director Irena Salina (*Flow*) and producer Leslie Holleran (*The Cider House Rules*).

Asha Jain grew up in New Delhi, India. Upon completion of her master's degree in 1973, she married and immigrated to Canada. While supporting her husband, Ramesh, in founding his own business, she raised two boys, Anurag and Ravi. She is a wonderful mother, wife, and now a very funny actor. She is excited to be sharing the story told in A *Brimful of Asha* with the world to finally prove her son wrong.

Ravi Jain is an award-winning actor, director, producer, and educator, and the artistic director of Why Not Theatre. He is engaged in many different arts organizations and creations across Toronto and the globe, including the programming committee for the Regent Park Arts and Culture Centre and the artist advisory committee for ArtReach Toronto. For more information visit www.theatrewhynot.org.

Anita Majumdar is an award-winning playwright and actor raised in Port Moody, British Columbia. She is an acting graduate of the National Theatre School of Canada and has trained in Kathak and other Indian dances for over fifteen years. In 2013 Anita was awarded the Governor General's Performing Arts Prize for her playwriting and was mentored under John Murrell. Her Bollywood-inspired musical, *Same Same But Different*, premiered at Theatre Passe Muraille and Alberta Theatre Projects and was nominated for the Betty Mitchell Award for Outstanding New Play. Anita is currently the playwright-in-residence with Nightswimming Theatre in Toronto.

Andy McKim spends his professional life developing, dramaturging, and directing new Canadian plays, and since 2007 has been Artistic Director of Theatre Passe Muraille, Canada's oldest theatre for developing new work. From 1986 to 2007 he enhanced Tarragon Theatre's growth as one of Canada's foremost theatres for new play development as Associate Artistic Director. Andy has directed more than fifty different productions, garnering Best Director nominations at the Dora Mavor Moore Awards. He has been recognized with the Harold Award, the Playwrights Guild of Canada Bra D'or Award, and the George Luscombe Mentorship Award.

Yvette Nolan is a playwright, director, and dramaturg. Her plays include *BLADE, Job's Wife, Annie Mae's Movement, Scattering Jake, Alaska,* and *The Unplugging.* Directing credits include *Salt Baby* by Falen Johnson (Globe Theatre), *Café Daughter* by Kenneth T. Williams, *Justice* by Leonard Linklater (Gwaandak Theatre), Marie Clements's *Tombs of the Vanishing Indian* and *The Unnatural and Accidental Women, A Very Polite Genocide* by Melanie J. Murray, *Death of a Chief,* Darrell Dennis's *Tales of an Urban Indian, Annie Mae's Movement* (Native Earth), and *The Ecstasy of Rita Joe* by George Ryga (Western Canada Theatre/National Arts Centre), as well as *The Only Good Indian . . .* and *The Triple Truth* from the Turtle Gals Performance Ensemble. As a dramaturg, she has worked across Canada on projects including *A Soldier's Tale* by Tara Beagan, *Ultrasound* by Adam Pottle, *A History of Breathing* by Daniel Macdonald, and *Ashes on the Water* by Raven Spirit Dance. She is an artistic associate of Signal Theatre.

Brian Quirt is Artistic Director of Nightswimming, which has commissioned and developed more than 30 new plays, dance works, and musical pieces since 1995, and Director of the Banff Playwrights Colony. He recently directed national tours of Carmen Aguirre's *Blue Box* and Anita Majumdar's *Fish Eyes Trilogy* and *Same Same But Different.* He has created and directed seven of his own plays, including his choral piece *Why We Are Here!* (with Martin Julien), presented at venues across Toronto. He has been Interim Artistic Director of the Great Canadian Theatre Company, Company Dramaturg at Factory Theatre, Dramaturg at the Theatre Centre, and Dramaturgical Associate at the Canadian Stage Company. He is Board Chair and Past President of the the Literary Managers and Dramaturgs of the Americas and a two-time recipient of the LMDA's Elliott Hayes Award for Outstanding Achievement in Dramaturgy.

Anusree Roy is a Governor General's Literary Award–nominated writer and actor whose work has toured nationally. Her plays include *Sultans of the Street,*

Brothel #9, *Roshni*, *Letters to my Grandma*, and *Pyaasa*. Her Opera librettos include *The Golden Boy*, *Noor over Afghan*, and *Phoolan Devi*. She can been seen on television as Nurse Patel on Global TV's medical drama *Remedy*; she was also Executive Story Editor for the show's first season. She holds a B.A. from York University and an M.A. from the University to Toronto. Her plays and performances have won her four Dora Mavor Moore Awards along with multiple nominations. She is the recipient of the K.M. Hunter Award, the RBC Emerging Artist Award, the Carol Bolt Award, and the Siminovitch Protégé Prize.

Pamela Mala Sinha is an award-winning actress and playwright working in theatre, film, and television. Her first solo play, *CRASH*, which she also performed, garnered six 2012 Dora Mavor Moore Award nominations and four wins, including Outstanding Performance by a Lead Actress and Outstanding New Play. Pamela's short story "Hiding" was published in the best-selling anthology *Dropped Threads Vol. II* (edited by Carol Shields and Marjorie Anderson) for Random House Canada, and was the inspiration for *CRASH*. Her second play, *Happy Place*, premiered at Soulpepper Theatre, Toronto, in September 2015. Pamela is currently adapting *Happy Place* as a film for Sienna Films.

Judith Thompson is a playwright, director, screenwriter, actor, and teacher of theatre, and is a two-time winner of the Governor General's Literary Award for *White Biting Dog* and *The Other Side of the Dark*. She has been invested as an Officer in the Order of Canada, was awarded the prestigious Susan Smith Blackburn Prize for her play *Palace of the End* in 2008, and won the 2009 Amnesty International Freedom of Expression Award for the same play. Judith is a professor of drama at the University of Guelph and lives with her husband and five children in Toronto.

Rahul Varma is a playwright, artistic director of Teesri Duniya Theatre, and co-founder of *alt.theatre: cultural diversity and the stage*. He writes both in Hindi and English, a language he acquired as an adult. Some of his other plays include *Land Where the Trees Talk*, *No Man's Land*, *Trading Injuries* (a radio drama), *Counter Offence*, *State of Denial*, and *Truth and Treason*. His plays have been translated into French, Italian, Hindi, and Punjabi. Rahul is the recipient of a special Juror's Award from the Quebec Drama Federation, a Montréal English Critics Circle Award for promoting Interculturalism, and the South Asian Theatre Festival Award.

Guillermo Verdecchia is a writer, translator, dramaturg, director, happy collaborator, and reluctant actor. He has received numerous awards for his theatre work. He reads much of the night and goes south in the winter.

Dalbir Singh is the associate editor of *alt.theatre: cultural diversity and the stage magazine*. He's also the editor of *World Without Walls: Being Human, Being Tamil* and, from Playwrights Canada Press, *Performing Back: Post-Colonial Canadian Plays* and a forthcoming anthology of critical essays on Canadian Theatre. He is a PhD candidate at the University of Toronto and has taught at the University of Waterloo, the University of Guelph, and the University of Toronto.

First edition: August 2015

Printed and bound in Canada by Marquis Book Printing, Montreal

Jacket design by Kisscut Design

**PLAYWRIGHTS
CANADA PRESS**

202-269 Richmond St. W.

Toronto, ON

M5V 1X1

416.703.0013

info@playwrigh

www.playwrigh

Imp

traité s

100%   ENERGIE